A·HARD
ACT·TO·FOLLOW

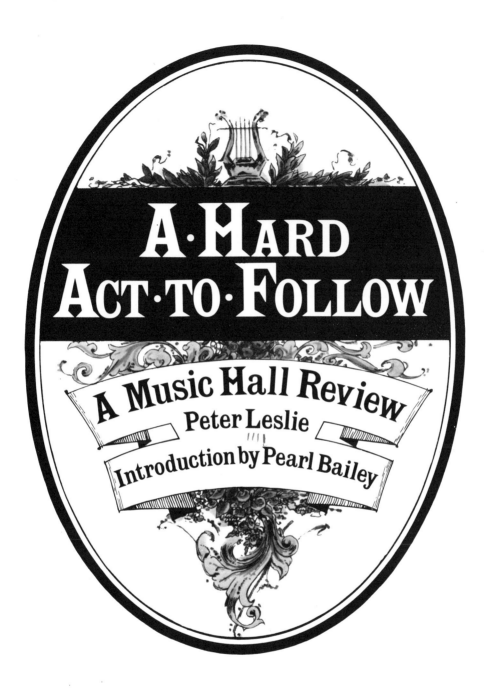

A·HARD ACT·TO·FOLLOW

A Music Hall Review

Peter Leslie

Introduction by Pearl Bailey

PADDINGTON
PRESS LTD

NEW YORK & LONDON

Library of Congress Cataloging in Publication Data

Leslie, Peter.
  A hard act to follow.

  Includes bibliographical references and index.
   1. Musical revue, comedy, etc. 2. Music-halls (Variety-theaters, cabarets, etc.)
I. Title
ML1950.L4   792.7'09   78–6157
ISBN 0 7092 0466 3
ISBN 0 448 22618 9 (U.S. and Canada only)

Filmset in England by Servis Filmsetting Limited, Manchester.
Printed and bound in the United States.

Designed by Patricia Pillay

IN THE UNITED STATES
PADDINGTON PRESS
Distributed by
GROSSET & DUNLAP

IN THE UNITED KINGDOM
PADDINGTON PRESS

IN CANADA
Distributed by
RANDOM HOUSE OF CANADA LTD.

IN SOUTHERN AFRICA
Distributed by
ERNEST STANTON (PUBLISHERS) (PTY.) LT5.

792. 709
L

Contents

AUTHOR'S NOTE   7

INTRODUCTION   A Note from Pearl Bailey   8

PROLOGUE   Black Cinderella   10

CHAPTER ONE   From Boiled Beef to Burleycue   15

CHAPTER TWO   A Little of What You Fancy   36

CHAPTER THREE   Getting In on the Act   54

CHAPTER FOUR   Artists of Influence   72

CHAPTER FIVE   Music and Marvels in the Air   96

INTERMISSION   A Glance at the Program   112

CHAPTER SIX   Chorines and Courtesans   133

CHAPTER SEVEN   Something Sweet, Something Sour   158

CHAPTER EIGHT   The Age of Superlatives   180

EPILOGUE   A Question of Numbers   233

MUSIC HALL'S TOP 100S   241

     The Characters   242

     The Supporting Cast   243

     In the Great Tradition   243

     Where They Played   244

     What They Sang   246

FOOTNOTES   248

SELECTED BIBLIOGRAPHY   249

INDEX   249

To Nicolette
who is an actress
this tribute to – and from – 'the other half'
is lovingly offered

Author's Note

This book is not a definitive history of the music hall. It is a survey, a review – a celebration, if you like – of those acts and artists whose genius led to the evolution of a particular kind of spectacle reaching its greatest glory between the turn of the century and the Depression. Such a choice of people and period must of necessity be personal and selective; the assertion that 1929 saw the end of music hall at its most glamorous is itself controversial. There will be omissions, therefore, in the view of some enthusiasts. To those who wish to pursue the subject in historical detail, I can do no better than recommend some of the books which provided background material and widened my own appreciation of the music hall scene. Among these I should like especially to single out Songs of the British Music Hall by Peter Davison, Douglas Gilbert's American Vaudeville, the French Histoire du Music Hall by Jacques Feschotte, and Raymond Rudorff's invaluable study, Belle Epoque. To the publishers of these and other works cited in the source notes, I extend my thanks for their kind permission to quote extracts.

So far as my own researches are concerned, my thanks are due also to M. Jean Devoisins, curator of the Musée d'Albi, to the staff in charge of the Rondel Collection at the Bibliothèque de l'Arsenal in Paris, to Mmes. Favresse and Grivel and M. Marbot of the Service des Estampes at the Bibliothèque Nationale, to Mme. Hélène Adhemar, curator-in-chief of the Jeu de Paume gallery in the Tuileries, to M. Pierre Quoniam, director of the Musée du Louvre, and to the personnel operating the Roger-Viollet photo archives in the Rue de Seine.

Among the many people who have been good enough to contribute personal memoirs, recall anecdotes, lend photographs and documents or help in other ways, I am especially grateful to the late André Belaval, better known as the chansonnier Braval, and to Ms. Christine Bernard, Ms. Maeve Black of the British Council library in Paris, the Comtesse Alice Hartung de la Roer, M. Henry Kahn, doyen of British journalists in France, Peter Launder, Esq., M. Jean Nugéron-Reutlinger, Mme. Maguy Renard, Mme. Arlette Sauvage, and Charles Spencer, Esq.

Finally, no acknowledgments would be complete without a special tribute to Kati Boland and Enid Moore, whose tireless researches in New York and London produced such verbal and visual treasures, and to my editor, Catherine Carpenter, to whose patience, intelligence and understanding the book owes so much.

PETER LESLIE

Tourrettes-sur-Loup, 1978

A Note from Pearl Bailey

Dear Peter,

Many years ago I met a young man at Heathrow airport in London.

Not only was he a reporter, but as it happened he was also a critic – the one who would be writing about me on stage.

As it turned out, it became a long and dear friendship.

Louis (Bellson) and I were married in London (1952) and Peter shared those moments with us too.

After years of losing each other, a letter appeared. "Pearl, I'm writing a book about people of the theater, your world, would you be my critic?"

Aha! Peter, time turns it around. Manuscript arrived thick – I knew he had said book; but wow! You would have to be a hundred years old to know or even research all of this.

Then came the reading – it touched me from the start, held me tightly in the middle, and totally filled me at the end.

I who have spent forty years (so far) in the theater was a child again, having all the wonderful things revealed to me about my world, my art; living moments so rich, feeling the pains, yes, even the jealousies; emerging into greatness, sinking into oblivion.

This is a book surely for show business folk, drama students should digest it as the best meal they could have. And those who know nothing of the theater should enter into this book, as if walking into an open theatrical door – ah! and buying no ticket.

Yes Peter, you are either a hundred years old or you're a genius.

How else could you have written it so well – and so thoroughly?

I have (as a so-called critic) a complaint. There should have been more. However, I shall have patience.

Certainly you'll write a sequel including more of the artists you have met along your path, people you have touched and obviously loved.

Thank you Peter, for having done it all – so brilliantly. Your critic – aha! – who deeply respects you, for knowing "Us."

Love,
Pearl

Pearl Bailey and her husband Louis Bellson, a member of Duke Ellington's band, in London shortly before their marriage in 1952.

Black Cinderella

During the night of April 12, 1975, a small Creole woman aged sixty-nine died of heart failure aggravated by overwork at the Salpétrière hospital in Paris. Three days later, twelve thousand people hoping to gate-crash her memorial service jammed the streets around the classical façade of the Madeleine. Two weeks earlier she had received a fifteen-minute standing ovation from the world's most critical audience at a gala celebrating her fifty years as undisputed mistress of her métier.

The woman's name was Josephine Baker. Her métier was music hall.

The Cinderella story of her life and death is as characteristic of the myths and magic, the extravagance and absurdity, the splendor and ruin and romance of music hall as the true music hall itself was of the age in which it flourished. Josephine Baker was born a pauper and she died a pauper, but she was mourned by a whole nation which had adopted her – and in between she made and lost millions. Charles Trenet wrote poems to her when he was fifteen. Simenon, the creator of Maigret, was her constant companion when he was a young newspaperman. Movie star Michel Simon fell in love with her at first sight and remained a faithful admirer all his life. She made three marriages, none of them an outstanding success. Her second husband, an Italian with a fake title, persuaded her to give him power of attorney and then decamped with her fortune while she was on tour. She was painted by Foujita and Marie Laurencin and Jean-Gabriel Domergue. She was the darling of Hemingway's Paris, and Picasso's and Nancy Cunard's. During World War II, she delivered combat aircraft to the fighting zones and was decorated by General de Gaulle for espionage work in North Africa. Even in her seventieth year, she had lost neither the zest nor the vitality nor the consummate professionalism of her youth: the revue starring her was booked solid for three months when she died.

Appositely enough for a Cinderella, her eyes were closed at the end by a real-life princess – who subsequently paid for her funeral. Grace of Monaco had become a close friend in Josephine Baker's later years, and it was she and her husband Rainier who came to the rescue when the star, hounded by creditors, was forced to sell the dream château in the Dordogne where she had brought up twelve orphan children of different races. It was Prince Rainier and Princess Grace who persuaded the Monegasque Red Cross to lease the destitute family a villa at Roquebrune for a nominal rent, they who arranged the Monte Carlo gala which launched the music hall queen on her last triumphal tour, and – according to some newspaper reports – it was they who financed the revue *Joséphine* at Bobino which was to prove such a glorious swan song for the slum child from St. Louis, Missouri, who first dazzled Paris in 1925.

Bobino's director, André Levasseur, and the movie actor, Jean-Claude Brialy, between them took care of the Madeleine memorial service and the oustanding rent of Josephine's Paris apartment. She attracted generosity of this kind because of her own generous nature. One evening not long before the war, she was singing in a plush cabaret in Paris when she saw the once-great Mistinguett, now long past her prime, arrive alone at the entrance. Trailing her handmike, Josephine threaded her way between the diners, took over the guest from the head waiter, personally ushered her to the best table in the place, and then went back to the stage – without missing a beat of the song. It was the kind of throat-catching gesture of which show business myths are made.

And the Josephine Baker story was as colorful as any of the myths of music hall. Standing bareheaded at her funeral with Line Renaud and Sophia Loren, Carlo Ponti was heard to murmur to his wife: "Take a good look, Sophia, at something you've never seen before and will never see again: the burial of a star who was also a queen."

Queen of the music hall Josephine certainly was – the last of a sovereign succession stretching back for more than a century, trump card in a pack vibrant with personality, latest in a line of ladies whose enchantments transcended the tinsel in which they were wrapped. Now the queen is dead. But this time no one shouts: "Long live the queen!" Because there is no one to take her place – and music hall itself has died.

Before the chorus of disagreement grows too loud –
to spare the breath of those about to cry, "What about
Line Renaud?... What about the Casino de Paris, the
London Palladium, the Olympia?... Have you never
heard of the Lido or Las Vegas?" – an attempt must be
made here to define terms. We are talking about music
hall. Not vaudeville, not variety, not revue, however
intimate or spectacular, and certainly not burlesque.
Music hall.

So what, as the man said, is the difference? What was
music hall, and how did it die?

Definitions are always difficult and often misleading.
This one is more difficult than most because the term
has been widely misused, loosely to cover many types
of popular entertainment – and also because the
genuine article is itself abstract rather than concrete, an
atmosphere rather than an event. Perhaps there is a
parallel to be found in the script of a wartime Jack
Benny radio show. Says Benny, playing the anxious
host, to his major-domo, the great American comic
Eddie Anderson: "What's in that soup, Rochester?"

"What ain't, boss!" replies Rochester.

Thus the French show business historian Legrand-
Chabrier, asked for a nutshell description of music hall,
replied with the definition *a contrario*: "A coalition of
every kind of spectacle that is not theater."

The phrase's first official entry in a dictionary
(*Quillet*, published just before World War I) read:
"Concert hall or theater, with orchestra, where varied
spectacles are presented; fragments of music and song,
dramatic sketches and living tableaux; spectacular
revue making great use of lighting effects and mechanical devices, dancers, acrobats, etc." A *Pocket Oxford*
published between the wars said curtly: "Hall for
mixed entertainment, including songs." The current
Random House Dictionary gives: "A hall for musical
entertainments . . . a variety theater"; and the *Penguin
English Dictionary* says: "Comic variety show; theater
for this."

Already we see that the term is used in two senses:
to describe both the show itself and the showplace. The
earliest posters and playbills advertising such mixtures
of talent as those specified by *Quillet* – "varieties" in
England, "vaudeville" in the United States, "*attractions*" in France – used the phrase "music hall" to
describe the premises where the performance was
given. It is likely that the term therefore attached itself
subsequently to what went on there as well: the chicken
came before the egg.

Such a glib explanation nevertheless carries a built-in

paradox. No single component of what came to be labeled as "music hall" (minstrels, parodists, reciters, satirists, singers, dancers, jugglers, acrobats, musicians, comics, etc.) was new or original; most of them had been common throughout Europe and North Africa for centuries, and in America for over one hundred and fifty years. The particular mixture, too, was "as

Making as many farewell tours as an opera queen, Josephine Baker was starring in a revue that was booked solid for three months when she died in 1975. This particular goodbye – at the Olympia in 1959 – was said when she was fifty-three.

13

before." Yet there *was* a phenomenon known as music hall; it did exist and it was immediately recognizable as such.

In fact it was *the manner in which it was presented and experienced by its audience* that acted as catalyst to produce something new and original out of these well-known but disparate elements.

The most significant feature of the early halls was the interaction between artists and audience which was peculiar to them and their time. It was this more than the stars or their material – brilliant though these may have been – that gave the medium its vigor and its strength and its unique flavor during its heyday in France; it was the lack of this particular empathy which led to a different type of development in the United States and certain other European countries.

Divorced from its ethos, early music hall could be described mechanically as a variety or vaudeville show, with or without a unifying theme or décor, produced in a place where the audience could eat, drink, comment and exchange badinage with a master of ceremonies while they watched. Yet this form changed: the showplace, with its boisterous linkman and its rowdy spectators, went out of favor; but the show itself, in trouper tradition, went on – transferred to the theater proper. It was still unique, identifiable, recognizable as music hall. It was just that, like any vital organism, it had developed.

That development happened to reach its apogee in France between the end of World War I and the Depression. But the internationally famed "Frenchness" of music hall in that country again lay less in what was actually performed than in the framework supporting it. So that although the last queen to reign over that sparkling territory happened to be black, American and basically a dancer, the succession had been eclectic enough to accommodate previous monarchs with talents as varied as those of Mistinguett and Chevalier, Gaby Deslys and Fernandel, Yvette Guilbert and La Goulue, Louise Balthy and Emilienne d'Alençon and Polaire, Dranem and Polin and the Dolly Sisters and Thérésa – who was perhaps the first and the longest-lived of all. They charmed and delighted, excited laughter and tears and admiration and enthusiasm, in an unbroken and magical line stretching back over the glittering years to the middle of the nineteenth century.

But to trace the dynasty to its origins, it is necessary to cross the English Channel and investigate the social life of Londoners before the time of Charles Dickens.

CHAPTER ONE

From Boiled Beef to Burleycue

"HELL," BERNARD SHAW REMARKED in the third act of *Man and Superman*, "is full of musical amateurs; music is the brandy of the damned."

Either the Shavian aphorism is shallower than usual, or the kingdom of Lucifer must be awash with alcoholics – for men have sung or chanted in groups, to celebrate or to lament, since the cave dwellers first organized themselves into tribes. They have also grouped together to marvel at the skill and dexterity of those stronger or more agile than themselves. Both forms of entertainment have remained distinct from the drama and, when the early Christian church suppressed the theater in the sixth century, each flourished throughout Europe at fairs and festivals, spread by the companies of itinerant minstrels, jugglers and acrobats who roved the continent in those days.

In the Dark Ages, tumblers and musicians diverted the war lords in their strongholds, while minstrels and skalds brought the common people news of epic victories, natural catastrophes and legendary exploits when they sang. Medieval nobles welcomed entertainers in their households. And here too there was someone – the resident fool – to comment and inform, to poke sly fun at the events of the time. When the church relented so far as to permit the public performance of "improving" mystery, miracle and morality plays (which could be said to fulfill a similar function in allegory), these often incorporated music and the dance. The court masques so popular in the Tudor era, which allowed blue-blooded spectators to take part in the same way as the crude audiences at taverns and inns, also relied a great deal on dancers and musicians.

The Elizabethans were entertainment-minded; their toughness and enterprise was tempered by a love of wit and beauty. It is no coincidence that the age of Drake and Hawkins and Raleigh was also the age of

Entertainment in a medieval household.

Bacon and Donne and Webster and Marlowe – or that the public, stimulated, thanks to Burbage and Shakespeare, by the development of the indoor theater, should have warmed, too, to the displays given in alehouses and tavern yards by the troupes of singers, dancers and acrobats who were enjoying such an upsurge of popularity. The queen herself was known to relish these performances.

Public interest in such quasi-professional activities was matched throughout the country by an equal delight in what would now be called "do-it-yourself" entertainment – a direct result of the new, post-Renaissance freedoms, allied to improved education through the invention of printing, which permitted the Elizabethans to indulge their intoxication with words. The situation was paralleled in most European countries. What was peculiar to Britain was a tremendous popular enthusiasm for sports, until then the preserve of the nobility and gentry. This originated in the fifteenth-century supremacy of the English archer, who had proved himself the master of mailed knights on horseback. The pride and self-sufficiency resulting from this particular excellence led to a new sense of awareness and individuality among the people. Even after gunpowder had begun to supersede the bow and arrow, archery remained the national pastime; there was a revival of quarterstaff and wrestling; prizes were

Elizabethan mummers performing in a tavern yard – thanks to Burbage and Shakespeare, the public warmed to such alehouse displays.

offered for public contests with the singlestick or swords and bucklers.

Several separate, though related, traditions therefore lay behind a common interest in informal, non-theatrical entertainment, both private and professional, which ranged from simple glee singing to the more skillful crafts of the gymnast and juggler. Actors retained by noblemen, who were permitted at certain times to take on work outside the baronial hall, were quick to notice this interest, and they started to introduce acrobatic "interludes" to separate the acts of their plays. The tradition was to be revived and broadened after Cromwell's puritanical suppression of playhouses. For when the Restoration theaters-royal★ obtained their charter in 1663, the king's patents expressly prohibited "wholly spoken theatrical activity for gain" anywhere else in London. To avoid breaking the law, proprietors of other theaters were therefore obliged to add elements from the circus, the fair or the world of music to the dramatic entertainment they supplied. They could thus maintain the fiction that they were charging admission to what was in effect a variety show – with the drama thrown in free as an added attraction.

Such a "composite" tradition soon spread beyond the confines of the theater. In the seventeenth century, Sir Thomas Browne found in "that vulgar tavern

★ The theaters-royal were Drury Lane and Covent Garden. When the royal court moved to Bath, and the companies of these theaters followed it there, the charter was extended until their return to the Theater Royal, Haymarket. The patents were not revoked until 1843.

17

Drury Lane orange girls among the audience in the time of Charles II. They had other things to sell besides fruit. (Period note: the candle lighting, an improvised fan to clear the stifling atmosphere, spikes preventing the riffraff from climbing into the more expensive seats.)

music, which makes one man merry, another mad" something of "a divinity more than the ear can discover." Samuel Pepys, too, wrote of the conviviality of coffee houses and taverns, the variety of entertainment to be found there. So, perhaps more frankly, did Boswell in his *London Journal* a hundred years later. By the beginning of the nineteenth century, a pattern was established. In Shakespeare's time, sellers of cakes and nuts had mingled with the audience, crying their wares. In the reign of Charles II, "orange girls" sold fruit (among other, more personal, delicacies) at Drury

Lane. Now eating and entertainment still went to-gether – but the latter was supplied free with the food and drink sold at cellars and supper rooms, public houses and taverns, song clubs and pleasure gardens all over the country.

The most famous pleasure gardens – there were more than two hundred in and around Greater London alone – were the Vauxhall, the Cremorne, and the Surrey Zoological Gardens, founded in 1831 by Edward Cross. The Cremorne, which opened in 1837, boasted a sports ground, flower-bordered lawns, mock temples, lovers' bowers under the trees, and pavilions for public dancing. It was licensed for indoor and out-door concerts and ballets, and there were acrobats, conjurers and wirewalkers to defy the credulity, as well as a selection of sideshows in stalls. Sited near the Royal Hospital on the Chelsea Embankment, the Cremorne – like the Vauxhall Gardens across the river – was a favorite pick-up area for the mashers, swells and blades of the time. It was also a popular rendezvous for Chelsea painters and their models. The French writer Hippolyte Taine described it in his *Notes on England*[1] as "a sort of *bal Mabille* where the day's mad-ness was carried far into the night.... All the men [were] well or at least neatly dressed, the women were prostitutes, but of a higher rank than those in the Strand.... I have never seen such overflowing animal spirits."★

To these delights the Surrey added a lake, the menagerie which gave it its name, and the celebrated "panorama" against which the climax of a nightly fire-work display simulated the eruption of Vesuvius. Later the wild beasts were to be sold and a huge concert hall built, opening with a gala performance of Handel's *Messiah*.

By this time a publican named William Rhodes, licensee since 1820 of a Strand tavern named the Coal Hole, had taken over the disreputable Cyder Cellars in nearby Maiden Lane and developed the role of "president" or "chairman" during the entertainment. In both places he acted as master of ceremonies to introduce the performers, heckled and was heckled by the noisier customers, and added, to the succession of singers he offered, sketches, conjuring acts, and a seemly precursor of striptease entitled "plastic poses." This last attraction, a forerunner of the "tights" craze, was similar to the "tableaux" which enlivened museum shows in the United States some years later.

Women had always been – and still were – barred from such rowdy stag haunts, even as performers. It

Cruikshank's drawing of Joseph Grimaldi, the first man to earn star billing for the Clown. In the late eighteenth century, Grimaldi also popularized the English-style pantomime, which was developed from the Harle-quinade and the commedia dell'arte. He is pictured here in "Harlequin And Friar Bacon."

★ So-called "animal spirits" were to cause a public scandal and lead to the forced closing of the Cremorne in 1877.

AUTHOR'S COLLECTION

The pocket-size Sans Souci theater was built in 1793 by Charles Dibdin – mainly as a showcase for his own talents as songwriter, dramatist and solo performer. Composer of more than one thousand songs, Dibdin passed on the tradition to his son Tom, who wrote special material for Grimaldi.

was not until 1860 that the first professional female singer, a Miss Caulfield, appeared at the more respectable Evans's Song and Supper Rooms, in Covent Garden. Maiden Lane lies between the Strand and "the Garden"; scarcely a hundred yards separates the three of them. It seems likely, therefore, that Thackeray used Evans's, the Cyder Cellars, and perhaps the Coal Hole too, as models for his fictional "Cave of Harmony" when *The Newcomes* was first published in serial form in 1853. According to the narrator:

> Going to the play then, and to the pit, as was the fashion in those merry days . . . we became naturally hungry at twelve o'clock at night, and a desire for Welsh-Rabbits and good old glee singing led us to the "Cave of Harmony," then kept by the celebrated Hoskins, among whose friends we were proud to count. . . . We enjoyed such intimacy with Mr. Hoskins that he never failed to greet us with a kind nod; and John the waiter made room for us near the President of the convivial meeting. We knew the three admirable glee singers, and many a time they partook of brandy and water at our expense.

Most of the artists in these "saloon theaters" or "tavern concerts" were amateurs, although the more

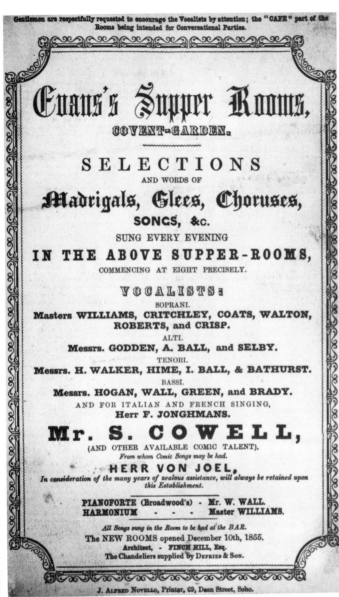

Cover of a song book given to customers in 1850 by the management of Evans's Supper Rooms. Sam Cowell, originator of "Villikins And His Dinah," was among the regulars. Evans's may have been the inspiration for Thackeray's fictitious "Cave of Harmony."

popular ones were frequently rewarded with free food and drink, and publicans with an eye to increased business would sometimes pay the occasional professional soloist as an extra draw. But it was left to a larger establishment to install a properly equipped stage and thus separate the bar from the performers. This was a thousand-seater hall called the Winchester, which opened in 1840 in the Blackfriars Road, just south of the river. Once an indoor circus, then the home of exaggerated melodrama, the refurbished premises were the first to be described on playbills as a "Music Hall."[2]

One of the showmen most impressed by the innovation was Charles Morton, owner of the St. George's

Specialty acts were as popular as singers in the mid-nineteenth century. This artist's impression shows Professor Risley and his two sons performing at Drury Lane in February, 1846. The critic of the London Times *noted an "absence of all painful contortions or tottering over-tasking of the ligaments," adding that even the most nervous could be under no apprehension for the safety of the children, "who are flung about in the air as though they could support themselves on it, were it necessary."*

Tavern, which he had made into one of the most popular meeting places in the city for those who liked to sing with their supper. Morton was a hustler, a slum boy who had worked his way up through bartender to publican, and he had a genius for guessing what the public was going to want tomorrow. By 1848, when he was only twenty-nine, he had saved enough money to buy a barracklike building in Lambeth named the Canterbury Hall. In opposition to the Winchester, he transformed the premises into an elegant and spacious showplace, richly decorated, with rows of marble-topped tables below the high stage, a wide entrance foyer and graceful stairways curving up to the loggias. The capacity was no less than fifteen hundred.

Opening in 1854 with a scintillating bill of "varie-

ties," the New Canterbury was an immediate success. Theater historians have always considered it to be the first true music hall, largely because, although food, drink and entertainment were still provided under the same roof, now there was a small supplementary charge at the entrance – and this, being specifically for the performance, "formalized the shift from saloon and supper room entertainment to the music hall proper."[3]

Morton had plenty of imitators. And, as so often happens when there arises a social need, others seem to have arrived at the same solution independently: the Alhambra in Leicester Square, which was to become the model for the world-famous Folies-Bergère in Paris, opened as a music hall within weeks of the New Canterbury. Many more were to follow it.

In 1861 Morton himself built the Oxford (from whose auditorium the tables were before long to disappear), and then effected his third transformation by turning the decrepit Old Mogul theater in Cambridge Circus into the Palace, most stylish of metropolitan music halls.★

These two houses epitomized a division which led to the emergence of two distinct types of music hall – a dichotomy later to be reflected in two separate program concepts. On the one hand was the intimate, classic hall derived from the saloon concert, as repre-

The first true music hall – Charles Morton's New Canterbury, which opened in Lambeth, London, in 1854. Fifteen hundred enthusiasts could eat, drink and make merry beneath the enormous gaslit chandeliers while the "heavy swells" and their ladies sang and cavorted on stage. An extra charge was made for the performance, but the artists still lacked footlights and a proscenium arch.

★ **Later in his career, Morton, known as "the father of British music hall," took over the Philharmonic Hall, where he presented with notable success a long series of operettas, many of them imported from France. He remained a veritable emperor of show business – but especially of the true music hall – right up to the day of his death in 1904 at the age of eighty-five.**

A contemporary print of Weston's Music Hall (later to become the Holborn Empire) in London. Drinkers and diners still throng the tables crowding the orchestra, the music comes from a piano and a harmonium on stage, and despite the triumphal arch in back, there is still no proscenium separating the singers from their audience.

sented by the Oxford, the Grecian, the Olympic, the Metropolitan in Edgware Road, Collins' in Islington, founded by the music hall singer Sam Collins in 1863, and many others in the London suburbs and throughout the country. On the other hand were the larger, more "theatrical" places, florid and grandiose, typified by the huge Empire in Leicester Square (first a theater, later a music hall, now a movie theater), Weston's (later the Holborn Empire, cradle of British band comedy, destroyed by enemy action in 1941), the Royal Standard (now the Victoria Palace), which opened the same year as Collins', the Hippodrome, founded in 1900 by Edward Moss, and, latest of all, the London Palladium, which dates only from 1910.

This second category, replete with cupids and red plush and gilt, often equipped with vast promenades where the love god's arrows might profitably be shot, gave birth to the extravaganza and the spectacular revue to be developed so successfully in Paris. The 2,200-seat Coliseum in St. Martin's Lane, perhaps the largest and "smartest" of all, drew a crowd more fashionable than the usual music hall regulars to the vast auditorium beneath its glittering dome by adding stars of opera and the drama to its sumptuous programs. And there is still evidence of former glories to be found at the Hippodrome – which by an ironic twist of fate has turned back the clock, evolving from a theater to a late-night eatery with imported stars to entertain the diners. Beneath the immense stage, there are iron rings to which in bygone days they tethered horses used for turning machinery operating the fantastic fountains and cascades featured in the aquashows which were the specialty there.

On the whole, these grander halls catered for a transient, "once only" clientele. Star salaries and high production costs meant that the producers were unable to amortize these expenses and make a profit in a single week like the owners of the small "classic" halls. The latter, on the contrary, relied on regular neighborhood patrons – men and women whose tastes were in any case more parochial and perhaps less refined than those of the swells in the fashionable West End. As a rule, the bills were therefore changed every week instead of running for a short "season" as some of the more pretentious productions did. Even these "intimate" halls could nevertheless draw on a tradition of composite entertainment dating back to the days of the Restoration. Managers forced, in those earlier times, to surround their plays with singers and specialty acts to avoid infringing the patents granted to the theaters-royal soon found that the mixture of music and melodrama, spectacle and song, comedy and illusion and excitement, was as big a draw as the grand tragedies offered by the legitimate theater. And the formula had survived. Thus, from the earliest music hall era, the singers shared the limelight with other forms of popular entertainment. The links between halls and taverns gradually loosened; the similarity to the theater proper strengthened – especially in the outward, visual sense; the rows of tables were dispensed with, floors became raked, stage lighting and curtains were used. The chairman remained, nonetheless, as master of ceremonies, introducing the performers in traditionally long-winded style, suppressing the noisier elements in the audience, whose involvement in the show could also be traced back to the seventeenth century and beyond. There remained as well, right to the end,★ the wide bar spanning the rear of the auditorium through whose open windows the drinkers could still watch and listen to the show.

By the late 1860s and early 1870s, the halls enjoyed so great a popularity throughout the country that they had practically ousted the theater in public esteem. But despite similarities in the kind of acts presented – despite, indeed, a constant transatlantic interchange of such acts after the end of the Civil War – the music hall formula as such never caught on in the United States. Early vaudeville and burlesque, stemming in part from the American minstrel show, shared a number of components with English music hall; but

★ The last true music halls in London were the Alhambra, Collins', and the Metropolitan. The Alhambra was pulled down in 1936 to make way for a movie theater. The other two survived – no longer as "halls of music" but as variety or vaudeville houses – until well after World War II. Then the "Met," through a crass example of official planning, was demolished despite public outcry as part of a clearance scheme for a highway (which in fact bypassed the site several hundred yards to the south). And Collins' in Islington rang down its final curtain comparatively recently.

Forerunner of the smaller, more "intimate" hall, the Oxford was Morton's second venture, opened in 1861. The premises were later acquired by J. Lyons and transformed into the Oxford Street Corner House.

the similarities were superficial and misleading, inasmuch as they masked profound differences in taste, both public and professional.

Vaudeville,* at its best, was quite simply a variety show, with the accent on professionalism rather than sumptuous décor or lush settings. Douglas Gilbert described it as "America in motley, the national relaxation . . . the theater of the people, its brassy assurance a dig in the nation's ribs, its simplicity as naive as a circus."[4] The twice-nightly performance, he wrote, was "a complete characterization of a pleasantly gullible, clowning America, physically bestirring itself, sunnily unsophisticated. Its social implications, reflected in the response of its audiences, are pronounced because its entertainment was largely topical fun. The trend of its humor was the march of those times. . . . Its life was incredibly brief – some fifty or sixty years. For many of us the end came with the folding of the New York Palace as a two-a-day in 1932. No precise date can be fixed for its beginning."

For burlesque on the other hand – although it is often regarded as vaudeville's illegitimate sister – an exact birthdate can be defined. The year was 1869. There were two midwives: a beefy English actress named Lydia Thompson, and a fictitious Madame Rentz whose name graced the first troupe of "female minstrels."

The American public had been alternately thrilled, scandalized, fascinated and outraged since the early 1850s by a phenomenon known as "tights plays." These had their origin, first, in a "deliciously infamous" episode in which the notorious Adah Isaacs Mencken was cast as the Mazeppa of Byron's poem and appeared on stage lashed "nude" to the back of a horse; and secondly in the equally notorious 1866 melodrama, *The Black Crook*, which featured more than four score heavily built dancers equipped with flesh-colored tights which clung provocatively to their limbs. In fact Miss Mencken's "nudity" incorporated opaque tights, a wide sash, a flesh-tinted leotard and trunks reaching almost to the knee. But in days when, as Cole Porter was to point out, even "a glimpse of stocking" was considered to be something shocking, the sight of three-fifths of a female leg was enough to set the reformers shrieking. Worse, *The Black Crook* beauties had nothing whatever to do with the plot – a feeble dramatization of obscure German folk tales. They were in truth the members of a stranded ballet company, interpolated between the acts for no better reason than that they happened to be in town. It was a pioneer

* The term vaudeville is thought to be a corruption of voix de ville (literally "voices of the town," thus songs of the people or tales of the city streets). Rozières left the Comédie Italienne to open a Théatre de Vaudeville in Paris in 1792; topical comic dialogues used as interludes between the acts of an opera were known as piéces en vaudeville in the early nineteenth century. The first recorded use of the word in the United States was in 1871, when "Sargent's Great Vaudeville Co.," billed as from the National Theater in Cincinnati, opened at Weisiger's Hall in Louisville, Kentucky.

decision which was to have far-reaching effects: for the first time in show business history female bodies had been, as it were, exhibited on an American stage for the sole reason that they were agreeable to look at.

The public outcry was loud and prolonged. Tights plays became synonymous with sin. *The Black Crook*, forerunner of the modern leg show, ran for sixteen consecutive months at Niblo's Garden in New York City.

Two of the showmen who cashed in on the scandal were Mike Leavitt and the great P. T. Barnum. It was Barnum who compounded salaciousness with exotica by signing up Lydia Thompson and her Imported English Blondes, Leavitt who borrowed another circus name and invented Mme. Rentz's Female Minstrels.

Lydia Thompson, a child pantomime star, had subsequently won fame as a dancer by out-stamping a celebrated Argentinian on the London stage, and then toured most of the countries of Europe in musical comedy. Had the genius who wrote her advance publicity been born later, he would surely have been hired by Goldwyn or de Mille. "At Helsingfors," the handout read, "her pathway was strewn with flowers and the streets illuminated with torches carried by her ardent admirers. At Cologne, the students insisted on sending the horses about their business and drawing the carriage that contained the object of their devotion themselves. At Riga and other Russian towns on the Baltic, it became an almost universal custom to exhibit her portrait on one side of the stove to correspond with that of the Czar on the other side. At Lember, a Captain Ludoc Baumbarten of the Russian dragoons, took some flowers and a glove belonging to Miss Thompson, placed them on his breast; then shot himself through the heart, leaving on his table a note stating that his love for her brought on the fatal act."[5]

Even if its punctuation and syntax might be held to be equivocal, the message of this bulletin was not: Miss Thompson, it was evident, was a personality to be reckoned with. She opened, with the celebrated blondes, at Woods' Museum and Menagerie (later Daly's Theater) on New York's 30th Street. The show was a sensational success. In fact, Lydia Thompson and her troupe continued touring the United States for almost twenty years. But the initial Barnum production was itself no innovation: it was a pseudoclassical extravaganza called *Ixion*, a heavily facetious comedy of the type then fashionable in Britain, America and Italy under the general name of burlesque. The word was used in its literal sense, such pieces being travesties

Lydia Thompson – importer of foreign blondes (and of vice, according to the Grundies). Inaugurator of the "tights play," she spent twenty well-paid years displaying her legs to American audiences, was so popular in the Baltic that her portrait was said to be given equal prominence with the Czar's – one on either side of the stove, in every house in Riga.

or parodies of the classics and current successes.

The foreign blondes and their tights were therefore the only factors raising *Ixion* above the normal level of such shows. It was left to Mike Leavitt to take the definitive step that would ultimately give the word burlesque a new meaning and establish the leg show as an American institution. It didn't seem an outsized pace at the time. Instead of having his ladies in tights perform roles in a play, he borrowed the format of the minstrel shows which had blossomed during the Civil War, substituting the girls for the straw-hatted comedians on stage in blackface. Mme. Rentz's Female Minstrels were thus the forerunners of the chorus line, the strippers, and *Les Girls*. Led by the formidable Mabel Santley, America's first home-grown burlesque queen, they were there, like the ballet in *The Black Crook*, to be looked at for their own sakes. The Rentz-Santley productions in fact set a pattern that was to act as a burlesque model for many years. Customarily, the shows, like Caesar's Gaul, were divided into three parts. In the opening, the girls would be seated minstrel-style in a half circle, complete with "straight man" and "interlocutor" (who would of course be transvestite "boy-girls" in male attire). The "girl-girls," in slit skirts and tights, would vary the comedy patter with songs and dances, also appearing in the final portion, called the "after-piece," which was usually a standard-type skit or travesty. In between came a selection of variety and specialty acts collectively referred to as "the olio" (from a Spanish word meaning mixture or mélange). The girls rarely appeared in the olio, although the male specialties were expected to double roles in the finale, which would probably be cursed with some dreadful punning title such as *The Swan and Edgar, Bohea Man's Girl* (a parody of *The Bohemian Girl*), *'Twill Be (Trilby), Much Ado about a Merchant of Venice* or *The Mick Hair-Do* (after W. S. Gilbert).⋆

This formula was not confined to early burlesque: it was also common in less salubrious forms of entertainment. To a greater or lesser degree, it was adopted by beer halls, turkey shows, dime museums, behind-the-tent productions and honky-tonks all over the United States.

Most typical of these "illegitimate" stage entertainments were the museums and the honky-tonks, respectively concentrated in the East and the West. The museums – seemingly a phenomenon that was purely American – presented an uneasy mixture of freak show and vaudeville. Developed from P. T. Barnum's

OPPOSITE:
Mabel Santley, America's first home-grown burlesque queen. Instead of finding an excuse to show their legs in a play, her troupe of girls toured the country in a transvestite performance of the traditional minstrel show.

⋆ "It was the English development of burlesque which affected the American stage directly. Thus the most distant offshoots of the first English burlesque, The Most Lamentable Comedy and Most Cruel Death of Pyramus and Thisbe, produced in 1600, were the New York presentations of John Gay's The Beggar's Opera and Sheridan's The Critic . . . witnessed by President Washington at the John Street Theater, New York, 1788. Not long after – in 1811 – John Poole produced a travesty called Hamlet, thereby originating what was to be called legitimate burlesque."[6]

pioneer establishment on Ann Street in New York, they were usually housed on two separate floors, one being a "curio hall," the other a diminutive theater. Customers were shepherded around the exhibits by a lecturer, usually styled "the professor," who "with a grand manner and an ornate vocabulary manipulated a long pointer, schoolmaster-style, to emphasize his discourses on the various 'one-of-a-kind acts' and unique freaks. . . . The goggle-eyed paying customers strolled about, casting a furtive glance at the dog-faced boy, with his blotched black and white skin, or standing enthralled before the intrepid sword swallower as he satisfied his peculiar appetite for sharp knives and jagged blades, or regarding, with mute horror, the baby embryos pickled in bottles. From the freaks they would proceed to the waxworks, an edifying collection of uncanny life-sized figures of wife killers, suicides, martyred presidents, poisoners and child wonders, all neatly clad, with waxy, too-pink skins and luxurious false hair, staring sightlessly out at the world."[7]

The curio hall lecturer, with his long-winded comments on giants, three-legged men and armless wonders, was the nearest transatlantic equivalent of Britain's music hall chairman. But the parallel did not extend to the theatrical performance. As soon as the band struck up to start the show, he went back to the entrance to collect the next batch of clients.

The shows ran thirty or forty minutes, roughly once every hour, from ten o'clock in the morning onward. They were limited to comics, song and dance acts, jugglers, illusionists, marionettes, etc. The stages were too small to accommodate aerialists, tumblers, or any kind of pageant, and the schedules were too exhausting for animal acts. An old-timer who once played in the one-act dramas customarily closing museum shows confessed: "When we played a war piece, everybody had to be a private: there wasn't room to get a general's epaulettes through the stage entrance!"

Museum work, according to Douglas Gilbert, paid from $20 to $30 more a week than the standard vaudeville minimum. "But the performers earned it. With a strong attraction in the curio hall like Laloo, Bertha Mills, or Jo-Jo, the variety performers were forced to race their acts, crowding show upon show to disgorge one audience and cram in another. Performers have been known to play as many as seventeen shows a day in museums when the curio freaks were as big a draw as the three aforementioned. And these three were terrific. Laloo was a young chap with a twin brother growing out of the top of his stomach; the growth had legs and arms but no head. Bertha Mills exploited her feet which were nineteen inches long and a big guffaw to gaping hicks. Jo-Jo was the celebrated dog-faced boy."[8]

Continuous performances were a feature of many honky-tonks too – especially those in the far West. Basically, the honky-tonk was a development of the western saloon familiar to movie buffs. In the seventies and eighties, seeing that the buskers who played and sang for "throw money" were popular with drinkers, saloonkeepers established a pattern of entertainment not unlike that of contemporary burlesque. As with the early English music halls, this was subsidiary to the food and drink sold – but the comparison ended there. Comics and specialties played the honky-tonks, but the main attraction was girls – both those in the show and the house girls, who were usually prostitutes. There were also "wine room girls" who were obliged to display themselves on stage during the opening, though they took no part in the actual performance; their job was to persuade the customers to buy them drinks, and to drink more themselves. In the old come-on tradition, they got a percentage on every drink they talked the suckers into buying – and their own "liquor" of course was colored water, cold tea, or some other innocuous fluid that only cost a tenth of what the client was charged. If the john was wise to that and insisted that real liquor was served, there were ways of dealing with this problem too. At one honky-tonk in Texas, the girls adroitly tipped their drinks into a concealed trough, where it flowed back to the bar, was rebottled, and then sold again to the same customers watching the show.

If the house girls were expected to go on stage at the beginning of the show – an "actress" was more desirable than a "hostess" – the genuine female performers in turn were expected to "work" the wine rooms and the boxes. "In fact," says Douglas Gilbert, "it was obligatory for them to do so when not appearing on the stage or changing costumes. Often this plagued a performance, as when an actress entertaining a couple of good spenders was needed on stage. In such instances it was the policy of all variety houses never to mess up a party. If a girl performer overheard her cue while she was arching up to a cowhand (in from the range with six months' pay), she just forgot it, and the actors ad-libbed themselves out as best they could. If the girl was a single, that is, if she appeared in a specialty of her own, a substitution was made.

"The 'boxes' were interesting hideaways and rather quaint. They were small compartments fitted into both sides of the balcony and draped with lace curtains caught up at the sides – more like a boudoir than a rendezvous. To these the boys with big money and extensive thirsts were escorted and the curtains drawn so that they could cuddle the girls and see the show in privacy. Although the nature of [this] work made for looseness, few of the actresses and wine room maidens were promiscuous. Ladies of the evening had their own racket, picking up where the wine room girls left off."[9] Sex in the honky-tonks, in fact, was as much a promise-all-give-nothing racket in those days as it was to become in the nude shows and strip clubs that killed music hall half a century later.

There were, however, positive aspects to the entertainment provided at museums and honky-tonks. In a country already accustomed to medicine shows (where the entertainment served simply to collect a crowd together so that the quack doctor could "push" his remedies), there was a ready-made audience for the politer forms of vaudeville and burlesque once they became acceptable to a "double" (i.e., mixed) clientele and proliferated from coast to coast. Secondly, by adopting the minstrel format allied to the tights routine, they laid the foundation for what was later to have such a profound effect on European music hall – the American chorus line. Thirdly, they acted as a talent nursery for the future stars and specialties of the big variety circuits. "There were lots of chances in those days to sneak into show biz," Joe Laurie, Jr., wrote.[10] "There were free-and-easies, store shows, museums, showboats, burly shows, dramatic shows, medicine shows, wagon shows and minstrel shows . . . the field was large and there was room for nearly everybody with or without talent. The managers had nothing to lose. They paid a small wage (you furnished costume and music) and could cancel you any time they pleased, so there was nothing to lose in giving an amateur a chance."★

The transition from stag audiences to doubles was inaugurated by Tony Pastor, who played in the United States a role similar to Morton's in Britain. In October 1881, he opened a house on New York's 14th Street with a bill, as one wag put it, so clean that any child could take its parents there. Later he took over other theaters, and when Benjamin F. Keith followed suit in Boston with the first house of what was to be vaudeville's most famous circuit, the division between "family" variety and stag burlesque seemed ratified.

★ Joe Laurie, Jr. also tells a story concerning Joe Jefferson, the man who made Rip Van Winkle famous. Walking along Broadway with his son one day, Jefferson raised a hand in greeting as they passed an elderly gentleman. "Who was that?" the son asked curiously. "That," said Jefferson, "is an old amateur who has been in the theater for many years."

This is not to say that "burleycue" (as the locals often pronounced it) had no rules. Olio performers were frequently forbidden to use risqué dialogue, suggestive situations or double entendre – but this was simply to avoid reducing the impact of the afterpiece, which was usually as blue as the performers could make it without actually being arrested.

Today, a century later, these "daring" sketches would seem pretty tame. (Among the words denied the olio performers were "damn," "hell," "slob" and "sucker.") Nevertheless, they succeeded in killing off the original parodies, skits and travesties which had given burlesque its name, leaving in their place only the crudest of comedy, the minimum of spectacle, and the most blatant sexual provocation offered by performers whose talents decreased as their vulgarity became more pronounced. Leaving, in fact, the blueprint (if the term may be permitted) for the American burlesque show for years to come.

There was crudity too in the English music hall, but it was a rumbustious crudity characteristic of the period, an overt vulgarity that could be shared by both sexes★ – yet, paradoxically, it was less direct, and therefore less honest, than the puritan, holier-than-thou attitude which separated variety entertainment in the United States into "clean" vaudeville and "dirty" burlesque. Hypocrisy typified the Victorian persona, especially in the queen's own country: instead of boldly declaring "*this* is permissible, *that* is not," the arbiters of public taste therefore adopted the Nelsonian strategy: almost *anything* was permissible – so long as it was neither admitted nor referred to directly.

It was this difference in attitude which explained the stylistic divergences between British and American variety in that era. And it was this which explained the tremendous importance of innuendo in early English music hall.

★ History is silent on precisely which hall in England was the first to play to a "double" audience, but Morton's New Canterbury must certainly have been among the trailblazers.

CHAPTER TWO

A Little of What You Fancy

IT WAS THE UNFORGETTABLE Dan Leno who is said to have described London as "a large village on the Thames where the principle industries carried on are music halls and the confidence trick." The line refers to one of the most enduring of the stock characters to appear on the halls: the greenhorn provincial taken for a ride by city slickers (but who often proves smarter in the end than his tormentors). There were many other stereotypes, each given a flavor of individuality by the performer who used it as his or her stage persona.

The henpecked husband, the lecherous yokel, the roistering dandy who takes what he wants, the working girl who gives the rich swells their comeuppance, the coward who wins by cunning – they caper and cavort, wheedle and strut, bluster and brag and joke behind the footlights along with the bumbling officials and wronged maidens and man-eating mamas who make up the larger-than life reflections of the society that produced them throughout the history of music hall.

Most original, and most typical of the late nineteenth century, was the *lion comique* exemplified by George Leybourne and The Great Vance. The term, which was used to denote the "heavy swell," the hard-drinking Victorian equivalent of a modern playboy, complete with waxed mustaches, cane, and silk hat or boater, derived from Leybourne himself. When he introduced the song "Champagne Charlie" at the New Canterbury in 1867, the manager of the hall, J. J. Poole, said of his performance that he was "a regular lion of a comic" – and the phrase, for some reason Frenchified, remained in use to describe all those well-dressed, slightly raffish figures who played the part of the spend-thrift man-about-town, often in real life as well as on the stage.

The song, with its echoes of reckless extravagance and generosity ("Whoever drinks at my expense, I

COMPANION SONG TO "CHAMPAGNE CHARLIE."
SUNG BY
GEORGE LEYBOURNE.
Price 3/-
"BURGUNDY BENJAMIN COOLEST OF MEN,
ALWAYS KEEP COOL, THAT IS MY RULE,
BURGUNDY BENJAMIN COOLEST OF MEN,
BY ALL I'M CALLED COOL BURGUNDY BEN !"
WRITTEN BY
W. GREEN ESQ.
MUSIC BY
ALFRED LEE.
LONDON:
C. SHEARD 192 HIGH HOLBORN.

SUNG NIGHTLY, WITH THE GREATEST SUCCESS
WRITTEN BY
F. CAUGHAN ESQRE
BY
VANCE.
COMPOSED BY
JOHN COOKE JU
Price 4/-
LONDON. CHARLES SHEARD, 192 HIGH HOLBORN, W.C.

treat 'em all the same: from Dukes and Lords to cab-men down, I make 'em drink Champagne"), crystal-lized a dream world for the working-class audience – a world of gay dogs and no responsibility and night life in the remote and unattainable West End. Its catchy one-step rhythm, as well as the tune and content, recalls such later hits as "The Man Who Broke the Bank at Monte Carlo" and "Gilbert the Filbert." The latter, older readers may just remember, was the self-styled Colonel of the Knuts – "The knut with a 'K'; the pride of Piccadilly, the blasé roué." Leybourne's song was rivaled in its day by "Clicquot," introduced by his own great rival, Vance, who had made his name with "Act on the Square" at the Oxford in 1886.

Equally popular, and equally typical of the times, were those more truly comic artists, the self-deflating who possessed "the capacity for extracting wonder-ment and surprise out of the obvious." Among them were such hallowed music hall names as Leno, Albert

George Leybourne (left), the original "lion comique," and his show business rival, The Great Vance. The song sheets reproduced here, successors to "Champagne Charlie" and "Act On The Square," were published in the late 1860s. Despite the rivalry, the two heavy swells shared the same music publisher. Another interesting point emerging from a study of contemporary music hall ballads is that – so impor-tant were the words in those days – the man who "wrote" the song, i.e., the lyricist, was distinguished by an "Esquire" after his name, whereas the composer of the music was not.

37

Vesta Tilley – following in father's footsteps. Male impersonation was considered neither "bent" nor sexually perverse by the Victorians, and Vesta Tilley's entire act was based on a series of "drag" impressions. Writers of a later era dubbed her "the pocket Astaire."

Chevalier, George Formby, Sr., Gus Elen, Harry Champion, George Robey and Sam Cowell, who topped Morton's opening bill at the Canterbury.

Elen's "If It Wasn't for the 'Ouses in Between" and "'Arf a Pint of H'ale"; Formby's "The Man Was a Stranger to Me" (which naively recounts the filching of the singer's watch by one of Leno's con men); Chevalier's "The Future Mrs. 'Awkins" and "My Old Dutch" (written as a tribute to his wife, who was George Leybourne's daughter); and Leno's own "Young Men Taken In and Done For" (with its ambiguous double innuendo woven around the perennial joke of the lodger and the landlady's daughter) – these were all songs springing from the social context of their audience. With these artists the audience could identify.

No metropolitan music hall initiate could fail to appreciate the rueful acceptance of life-as-it-is, the ironic description of Gus Elen's East End slum backyard, dressed up to look like a nursery garden with the leftovers from tradesmen's barrows, from which "'Endon to the westward could be seen, and by climbin' to the chimbley you could see acrost to Wembley . . . if it wasn't for the 'ouses in between!" Few of the regulars, in London or the provinces, would be unfamiliar with such problems as those outlined in Harry Champion's "Have You Paid the Rent?," the temperance-ridiculing "Don't Go Out Tonight, Dear Father," or Chevalier's cockney requiem for the donkey that had drawn his barrow, "Jerusalem's Dead."

In the same way, music hall audiences delighted in the overblown characterizations of such indomitable ladies as Nellie Wallace, Florrie Ford, Marie Lloyd, Vesta Victoria and Bessie Bellwood. They loved to hear of poor girls putting one over on the swells; they relished the information that virtue was not always impregnable, because life was full of do-gooders who preached that it was; they laughed at the panache of the dominant virago, because there would be paler examples of her across the street and in every public bar. And they warmed, of course, to the hints of clandestine sexuality that never lay far below the surface of straight-laced Victorian decorum. Such female equivalents of the *lion comique* could be permitted, too, to carry this stage persona out of the theater and into real life – although such lives could never really be called "private." It gave the paying customer a sense of intimacy with the artist to share in this way a "naughty" reputation. And in the theater there was, of course, that other kind of complicity: the special in-

TOP:
Marie Lloyd – the too-blue Englishwoman. She knocked 'em in the Old Kent Road, but her mastery of innuendo baffled American audiences and proved too much for provincials in Britain. This picture shows her (next to driver) with her three sisters on her way to a charity concert at the London Coliseum in 1908.

LEFT:
Bessie Bellwood. One of the first great female "characters" produced by the early halls, she knew how to put a rowdy audience in its place.

39

group satisfaction of sharing with the performer the forbidden implications of innuendo.

This, together with the healthy practice of debunking the pretentious, was one of music hall's main contributions to the entertainment scene. There were two favorite techniques: the artfully placed pause which allowed the audience's minds to leap ahead of the artist's words and draw the (ostensibly) wrong conclusion; and the facial expression, body movement or intonation that added a scabrous dimension to words that seemed perfectly innocent on paper.

The tradition has persisted, recent masters of the art being the late Max Miller and the British comedian Frankie Howerd, although of course many comics (notably the great Jack Benny) have used the device without becoming in the least suggestive. But, if contemporary evidence is to be believed, the implied sexual undertones and overtones extracted by Marie Lloyd from such simple songs as "I've Never Lost My Last Train Yet" and "A Little of What You Fancy Does You Good" were "blue" in the extreme. (Vesta Tilley must have run her close – besides bringing a new slant to the term Gay Nineties – when she sang "Following in Father's Footsteps" in full male drag – and subsequently based her entire act on a number of male impersonations.) The allusions did have to be implicit, however. If the sexual content transgressed some indefinable borderline so as to become explicit, the audience became embarrassed.

This was especially true of the working-class audiences which made up the clientele of the smaller, "classic" halls. Two of Marie Lloyd's West End triumphs – "I'm One of the Ruins Cromwell Knocked Abaht" and a celebration of the female form entitled "Every Little Movement" – were hissed off the stage when she sang them at the Paragon music hall in Whitechapel. What was acceptable at Daly's, the Gaiety, or (perhaps with a warning from the manager) at the London Pavilion, got the bird in the poorer East End. Oddly enough, Marie Lloyd died the death, too, in the United States – although Vesta Victoria, with a similar, though less suggestive, act was a riot.

In the early days of the halls, Bessie Bellwood, one of the first great female characters produced by the medium, was able to overcome and subdue a rowdy or hostile audience by the force of her superb repartee. Paradoxically, her most famous song, "What Cheer, 'Ria!," tells the story of a girl who comes to grief at a hall with just such an audience – because she pays extra to sit downstairs with the nobs instead of going up to the gallery where she belongs. Her mates in the cheap seats above catch sight of her and start barracking. And then . . .

> Of course I chaffed 'em back again, but it weren't
>   a bit of use.
> The poor old Chairman's baldie head they treated
>   with abuse:
> They chucked an orange down at me; it fell into
>   a pot;
> The beer went up like a fountain and a toff copped
>   all the lot!
> It went smack into his chevvy and it made an
>   awful mess,
> But what gave me the needle was, it spoilt me
>   bloomin' dress!
> I thought it's gettin' warm in here, so I goes
>   toward the door . . .
> When a man shoves out his gammy leg and I fall
>   smack on the floor!

Between the verses of this song there were sections of patter which carried the story further and made ironic comments on what had happened before. Dan Leno, George Robey, and many others used the same technique, which led eventually to the establishment of two distinct types of act: the straight singer of songs and the stand-up comic. Such a division had come earlier in the United States, because of the minstrel show tradition opposing the two "straight men" and the interlocutor – effectively a precocious example of the stand-up double act.

A transitional stage – most readers will have seen examples even today – was that of the performer who came on stage *threatening* to sing or play (Jack Benny, Jimmy Durante, Vic Oliver, Jimmy Wheeler, Arthur Haynes), only to interrupt himself continually with a flood of stories and anecdotes until he had time for nothing but one short number before his exit.

This kind of music hall comedy shares with other forms of "illegitimate" drama the one thing abhorred by tailors of "the well-made play": the audience is spoken to directly; it is not pretending to eavesdrop outside a room from which the fourth wall has been removed. For a moment the actor, as in much modern drama today, relinquishes his stage personality (usually, in music hall comedy, to complain in some way at the perversity of life) and speaks *as himself*. In one way, the spell is broken. Yet this kind of "alienation," unlike Bertold Brecht's *Verfremdungseffekt*, in no way leads to the loss of that empathy he deprecated. "In the music hall, the aim of breaking continuity is simple – to raise a laugh – but the effect is more complex. Involvement is broken in the act . . . and a different kind of relationship is developed between the person of the performer and the audience rather than with his persona. But the detachment from the persona (the breaking of empathy) is not at the expense of final, overall involvement; for the audience though momentarily detached and alienated, becomes thereafter more deeply involved."[11] This seems as good a way as any of describing an aside.

The manner in which this continuity break was employed varied greatly from artist to artist. Dan Leno used it to paint simple but vivid word pictures setting the scene for his songs. Others sided with the audience to scoff at the melodrama of numbers with unhand-me-sir! lyrics. Sam Cowell, in the famous "Villikins and His Dinah,"[*] actually gave a running commentary on the song as he sang it, preceding each verse with a confidential explanation of *why* it had to be sung (e.g., before the wronged daughter's suicide, through swallowing "poison" labeled *British Brandy* – that one was always good for a laugh – "Now this is the most melancholy part of it, and shows what the progeny was druv to in conskivence of the mangled obstropolousness and ferocity of the inconsiderable parient").

In every case the aim was to heighten the pathos-comedy-bathos relationship peculiar to music hall, the effect relying on skillful use of timing, change of tone, and variations in the types of word play (allusions, malapropisms, puns, etc.). But there was one other element that exercised enormous influence on the emergence of the music hall comic, and that was the tradition of the clown proper. Cowan's pleonastic nonsense asides – themselves a burlesque of the style of speech adopted by music hall chairmen – are in a direct line with the exaggerations of circus Joeys.

Ever since the Englishman Astley founded the modern circus in 1770 by conceiving the idea of the ring and putting a roof or a tent over it, there had been a continuing cross-fertilization between theater and circus. Astley's Amphitheater, built on the site of the Royal Grove, just south of Westminster Bridge, featured melodrama mingled with circus acts – chief among the latter being breathtaking feats of horsemanship by Astley himself. Nearby in Blackfriars Road, Charles Dibdin and Charles Hughes built another amphitheater which they called the Royal Circus, home of many spectacular productions featuring trained animals.[†]

* "Villikins and His Dinah" was introduced at London's Grecian saloon, adjoining the Eagle tavern (immortalized in the words of "Pop Goes the Weasel"), by Frederick Robson in 1844. Robson, described by Henry Irving as "great enough to know that he could only be great for three minutes," was considered to be a master of the abrupt change from broad comedy to heart-rending pathos.

·

† Burned down in 1803, the Royal Circus was rebuilt and then turned into a theater by R. W. Elliston of the Haymarket Theater. Subsequently it was taken over by Dibdin's son Tom and became famous for exaggerated melodrama. This was in fact the building which in 1840 became the Winchester Music Hall (see page 21). Later renamed the Surrey, it was to enjoy a certain vogue. It was demolished fairly recently after a gradual decline as variety house and then movie theater.

·

On the other side of the city, Sadler's Wells had been producing spine-chilling dramas mixed with dazzling water shows on the adjacent New River ever since 1765. In the winter, this North London theater was one of the capital's most successful homes of pantomime – and it was here that Joseph Grimaldi, said to have been the greatest clown ever, started his brilliant career. Three and a half miles away, in the centrally situated Leicester Place, Charles Dibdin built a tiny theater called the Sans Souci. Opening in 1793, it was devoted mainly to one-man shows given by Dibdin himself, playing and singing a selection of the one thousand songs and musical compositions he had written. Occasionally he would vary the program with other acts (one of them was a boy acrobat named Edmund Kean). Both these facts were to have a profound, if indirect, influence on English music hall more than half a century later.

Grimaldi, by his single genius, altered the concept of English pantomime. Most theater enthusiasts know that the form derived from the *commedia dell'arte*, brought to the country by Arlecchino in the reign of James I, with traditions dating back to the Roman Saturnalia.★ By the beginning of the eighteenth century, the "Harlequinade" – as it was now called – was well established. Then a dancing master named Webster wrote a Christmas fantasy titled *The Tavern Bilkers*, using the stock characters from the Harlequin-

An early Victorian pantomime – perhaps, from the evidence on stage, Grimaldi's "Mother Goose." There are echoes of the card game "Happy Families" in Mr. Doughey the Baker; and the outsized carving knife and fork wielded by the Clown are typical of the Harlequinade.

★ Not many people know that the "perverseness" of pantomime traditions also dates back to the Roman Saturnalia. During that pagan Christmastime festival, men dressed as women, women dressed as men, slaves sat at table and were waited on by their masters and mistresses; every normal action was turned upside down. This is why, in pantomime, the "Dame" is always played by a man, the "Principal Boy" is a girl, and the kings and nobles are always "stony broke" and waiting for the debt collectors to move in.

ade but adding a great deal of slapstick humor, disguises and burlesque dancing. It was produced at Drury Lane in 1702, and it set the pattern for pantomime until Grimaldi's time.

The formula established was to have an "opening" or first part, which could be a farce, an operetta or even a straight play – the kind of performance, in fact, which was later to *close* museum shows, burlesque and honky-tonk performances in America. This was interrupted after about half an hour, when Harlequin sprang up through the trap, danced with Columbine, the symbol of womanhood, and then waved his wand to "transform" the members of the company into the characters of the Harlequinade, which was still the main part of the entertainment. This would involve singing, dancing, topical jokes, and plenty of knockabout comedy – but the keynote would be romance. Harlequin, the man of magic, the man who always got the girl in the end, moving lightly as thistledown around the stage as he mimed his part, would cast his spell over the whole performance. He was in fact the star (Garrick played him in his youth, and so did Kean, though Irving contented himself with the Demon King).

Grimaldi changed all that. Son of a clown and grandson of a clown, he began his stage career when he was only three. An English theatrical historian wrote:

> So great was his genius that he put the Clown on top of the world. . . . He could sing, he could dance and he was a splendid actor; he could play in dramas, anything at all. Above all, he could make people laugh. He made the Clown the arch-figure of mischief. He stole the sausages, the geese, the oysters; he cheated all and sundry, including his old father (in the play), who had now become the Pantaloon. . . . Grimaldi was a great acrobat and tumbler as well and would perform amazing feats in that way, leaping through windows, over people's heads, in and out of trap doors, through what seemed to be solid walls which had cleverly hidden slits in them called "vamps." . . . He always won, except against Harlequin.[12]

Apart from orienting the pantomime away from romance and toward comedy, Joseph Grimaldi was also responsible for the appearance of fairy tales and nursery rhymes in that form. With Tom Dibdin, he wrote *Mother Goose*, the forerunner of England's classic nineteenth-century Christmas pantomime. After that, the Harlequinade grew shorter and shorter, the "opening" longer and more important, until the Harlequinade vanished altogether, leaving only the legendary "transformation scene" as a reminder of its existence. It was almost as though, to avenge his perennial defeats over the girl, the Clown had turned Harlequin's magic somehow against its master.

At the height of his fame, Grimaldi would do three or four shows a night – each at a different theater. Starting at Sadler's Wells, he would run three miles downhill to perform at Drury Lane, hurry across to Covent Garden for a third appearance, and then toil back up to the Wells for the finale. Like so many great artists before and after him, Grimaldi died almost penniless, in 1837, seventeen years before the New Canterbury opened its doors. But like Tarlton and Kemp, whose "jigges" gave such pleasure to the Elizabethans, he left a legacy of comedy that was to have a profound effect on the character of the music hall.

The heritage of Grimaldi's genius, added to the impact of those one-man shows given at the Sans Souci by Dibdin's father, was to lead eventually to the evolution of the all-spoken stand-up comic act which would outlast music hall itself and form the foundation of variety and vaudeville.

Like the pantomime clowns, the stars of music hall had to be topical. There were plenty of stirring events going on in the world outside the theater in those days. In 1819, the year before William Rhodes took over the Coal Hole, England was rocked by the Peterloo outrage, when a parliamentary reform meeting was broken up by armed soldiers; Lord John Russell's first Reform Bill was passed in 1831, as Cross opened the Surrey Zoological Gardens; the Crimean War shadowed the inauguration of the New Canterbury – Inkerman, Balaclava and Sevastopol were all fought in 1854; Morton was still building the Oxford when the American Civil War started in 1860. In the same year, Garibaldi united the whole of Italy for the first time, and England signed a "treaty of commerce" with France (which was so soon to import the music hall itself). And slavery was abolished in the United States in 1863, as the music hall singer Sam Collins rang up the curtain for the first time on his own theater in Islington.

But unlike the *Kabaretten* of Berlin, the Parisian *boîtes*, the "pop" theater of Brecht, or the modern acts of a Joan Baez or Lennie Bruce, the music hall was never "engaged" in a political sense. Its references to the front-page headlines of the day were oblique and usually ironic, predicated on the assumption that all propagandists, of every color, were either fools or knaves. So far as "the news" went, a popular success of the eighties called "Would You Be Surprised to Hear?" was typical – for the phrase was familiar to every newspaper reader in the country. It prefaced virtually every question put by the prosecuting lawyer in the interminable Tichborne inheritance case.★

Max Beerbohm had an explanation for the music hall's lack of political commitment. In 1898, soon after he replaced Bernard Shaw as dramatic critic on *The Saturday Review*, he wrote: "The mass of people, when it seeks pleasure, does not want to be elevated: it wants to laugh at something beneath its own level. Just as I used to go to music halls that I might feel my superiority to the audience, so does the audience go that it might compare itself favorably with the debased rapscallions of the songs."†

Peter Davison has a less patronizing explanation, and it is worth quoting at some length from the conclusion of his painstaking and extremely detailed analysis of popular music hall material. If the music hall did not deal with certain aspects of life, he says, this was because it did not find them particularly relevant to its own experience of life.

Sophisticated political revue must have a greater meaning and appeal for those who are involved, or feel involved, in the political struggle than it can have for those who feel resigned to be affected by political decisions but unable to influence them. By and large this was the position of the working class when the music halls were at their height. Similarly, sophisticated sexual witticisms will appeal more to those whose sexual standards are not rigidly defined. The music hall song was a product of a way of life which could do little to affect political thought and whose moral code, though not coincident with that of other classes in England, was firmly rooted, if not always followed. . . . [The songs] are able to present simultaneously the worlds of fancy and reality; they can offset involvement and detachment; often they are self-critical and have an excellent capacity for ironic self-deflation; they are often richly aware of the peculiarities and possibilities of the English tongue; but above all, at their best,

★ The Tichborne claimant, Arthur Orton, arrived in Britain from Wagga-Wagga in Australia, asserting that the fortune of Roger Tichborne, believed lost at sea, was rightfully his. After a long trial, the claim dismissed, he was convicted of perjury. When he was released from jail, he went on the halls himself as a "freak" attraction, addressing the audience on prison, trials, juries and his own experiences – but he was no more successful there than he had been in the courtroom.

— • —

† Beerbohm was not always so superior. He was a great fan of Dan Leno's, and wrote an essay extolling the genius and technique of the little man whose talents had enabled him to find such pleasure in the music hall. "No actor of our times," Beerbohm said, "deserved immortality as well as he."

— • —

they express in a way no outside observer can, however sympathetic to it he may be, the experience of that way of life from which they spring. At its best, in revealing this experience, the music hall song has wholeheartedness and warmth, independence and tolerance, ironic deflation and a fine balance between the comic and pathetic aspects of any existence.[13]

Thus "Boiled Beef and Carrots," "Any Old Iron?" and "Where Did You Get That Hat?"; thus "Heaven Will Protect an Honest Girl" and all those "uplift" songs like "A Motto for Every Man"; thus Vesta Victoria's "Waiting at the Church" and Robey's "Bang Went the Chance of a Lifetime!" And thus, too, such wry comments as the song dating from London's Great Exhibition of 1851, which was revived by Stanley Holloway in 1960. Visiting the Crystal Palace and its wonders, the singer – Leno's hick from the sticks – is delighted to meet a charming "Dark Girl Dressed in Blue." They spend the day together, marveling at the exhibits; he obliges the lady by giving her change for a £5 note (about $10). But when he offers the note in payment for a drink on his way home, it turns out to be counterfeit, leaving him to face . . . a dark man dressed in blue.

The police, the rent collector, the bailiffs, mothers-in-law, the drunken husband and the shrewish wife, the spendthrift who had gambled away his pay before he got home on Friday night – such were the dragons slain by these seedy St. Georges. Patriotism and the more chauvinistic aspects of Victoriana were pandered to and at the same time subtly ridiculed; the rednecks were kept happy and, for those with the wit to see it, the satire was there. What Fanny Burney called "the delusive seduction of martial music" was frequently accompanied by mocking words like those of Little Tich's "One of the Deathless Army." And some of the lyrics applauded by the reputedly jingoistic nineteenth-century audiences would seem audacious even today – for example "Do It No More,"[14] a cheeky comment on public concern at the population explosion, which had just promoted itself from anthropological theory to scary fact. One verse of the song describes Queen Victoria and Prince Albert (who were ultimately to have nine children) during an intimate conversation, in which "V unto A so boldly did say":

The State is bewildering about little children,
And we are increasing: you know we have four,
We kindly do treat them

George Robey. Later teamed with Violet Loraine in the famous "Bing Boys" revues, the man with the eloquent eyebrows was the first to sing "If You Were the Only Girl in the World."

RADIO TIMES HULTON PICTURE LIBRARY

And seldom do beat them,
So Albert, dear Albert, we'll do it no more.
  Do it no more!
  Do it no more!
No Albert, dear Albert, we'll do it no more!

With little alteration, the subjects that had them falling about in the Old Kent Road served also for the comics when the wholly spoken act established itself as something separate from patter between songs. An audience brought up on melodrama ("Dead, dead, dead . . . and never called me Mother!") was not going to cavil at the exaggerations, the awful puns, the intoxication with verbal hyperbole of a George Robey or a Dan Leno. In his essay on Leno, Beerbohm credited the comedian with "shifting the center of gravity" from the song to the monologue, while retaining as his subject "the sordidness of the lower middle class, seen from within." Yet, he wrote, "how gloriously it blazed, illuminating and warming! All that trite and unlovely material, how new and beautiful it became for us through Dan Leno's genius!"

An equally eminent writer paid similar tribute to Marie Lloyd. "No other comedian," said the late T. S. Eliot, "succeeded so well in giving expression to the life of the music hall audience, in raising it to a kind of art. It was, I think, this capacity for expressing the soul of the people that made Marie Lloyd unique."[15]

The great Dan Leno: one of the "seedy St. Georges . . . facing powers beyond his frail capacity." His was the genius (Max Beerbohm wrote) responsible for "shifting the center of gravity" from the song to the monologue – and ultimately the stand-up comic turn. This photo, taken at Drury Lane in 1896, shows him as "the Baroness" in a production of Cinderella *which also starred Herbert Campbell.*

It was perhaps this very quality that accounted for that artist's lack of success in the United States. For neither the soul nor the people were yet familiar to Americans. Marie Lloyd's kind of music hall, in a certain sense a *subjective* experience for an audience, was therefore foreign to them. Vaudeville and the better parts of burlesque were objective, more stylized, for ethnic reasons which were evident. Mongrel though they are, the British do not separate into enclaves or ghettos – the crossbreeding is too distant for that. But immigration in nineteenth-century America was on such a scale, and the country so vast, that no subjectively experienced common denominator could be found among such widely differing audiences.

49

Comics, therefore, tended to compartmentalize, to base their stage characters on racial traits rather than psychological types. Bookers and agents listed "Dutch" acts, "Polish" acts, "Jew" acts, blackface "Darkie" acts, "Seriocomic Hottentots," "Novelty Italian Tramps" and so on. Even the types of dancing were nationally cataloged. Doubtless this explains why Will Fyffe, Harry Lauder, Albert Chevalier and Yvette Guilbert went over big while Marie Lloyd flopped. The paying customers knew where they were with Scotsmen, Cockneys and French girls; the soul of all womanhood was a mystery yet to be unveiled.

There was an old Scottish joke that told of a pastor in a remote area introducing amateur artists at a village hall concert. "An' noo, folks," he announces, "Morag McLennan will sing 'Banks an' Braes'."

A voice from the back: "Morag McLennan's naethin' but an' ould hoor!"

The pastor's eyebrows raise; his lids droop. "*Ne-vair-the-less*," he says firmly, "Morag McLennan will now sing 'Banks an' Braes'. . . ."

Nevertheless . . . Marie Lloyd was the direct fore-runner of the Pearl Baileys, Sophie Tuckers, Judy Garlands and Ethel Waters of later days, just as Leno's "sense that he is facing powers beyond his frail capacity" was the precursor of that bafflement at the complexity of life exhibited by Buster Keaton, W. C. Fields, Tony Hancock, Jacques Tati and the immortal Sid Field. In the same way, Field's double act with Jerry Desmonde, Stan Laurel's with Oliver Hardy, Eric Morecambe's with Ernie Wise, Leon Errol's with the tempestuous Lupe Velez, even the anarchic antics of the brothers Marx, can be traced back to the original pantomime partnership between a sad-eyed and diminutive Leno and the gigantic, stentorian-voiced Herbert Campbell.

There is, however, a lesson to be learned from the Lloyd fiasco. It could be summarized in the English phrase, "horses for courses" – in other words, don't enter a sprinter for a steeplechase. Three theaters in the

Inside, Koster & Bial's was "built on the lines of an English music hall – a square balcony, all boxes, with chairs and tables on the orchestra floor." The resemblance to Morton's New Canterbury, including the arched promenade, is evident.

⸺⸺

* By a curious coincidence, one other American phenomenon reproducing a facet of the English music hall was centered on the name Morton. James J. Morton was a tall deadpan comic specializing in pointless jokes, songs that were repeatedly interrupted by their singer, and stories ruined by the blundering incompetence of the narrator. In the 1890s he varied this act with comments on the performer preceding him and confidential information on those to follow. This was so successful, and so amusing, that he was hired to introduce and comment on entire touring bills – the first master of ceremonies and vaudeville's nearest approach to an English chairman. A second coincidence: Morton's first MC appearance was at the American Music Hall, at 42nd Street and Eighth Avenue. Unlike its Chicago namesake, and despite its name, this house was in fact a straight variety theater.

⸺⸺ • ⸺⸺

United States attempted to import the British music hall formula complete. These were Koster and Bial's in New York, the American Music Hall in Chicago, and San Francisco's Orpheum. Each was publicized and exploited as "continental," each offered bills featuring foreign artists, none was a success.

Various factors contributed to this failure. The imported acts seldom played other variety houses: they were too expensive for the "continuous" managers, for one thing. Unless they already had Australian dates booked, when they could play New York, Chicago, the West Coast, and then sail to the Antipodes from California, European acts found it uneconomic to cross the Atlantic for three such widely separated bookings. The three music halls thus found it necessary to pay more than they could logically afford to sustain the "foreign" reputation they had created. Yet they had little control over the takings. Admission charges were nonexistent or derisory; to remain competitive with home-grown burlesque and vaudeville, the managers were forced to rely on sales of food and drink. Add a built-in resistance to an idiom unfamiliar to the audiences, and you have a blueprint for bankruptcy.

Koster and Bial's was typical. "A seat stub from any other theater was good for admission there, for the accent, and the money, was on spirits and wine. It was a ramshackle place with a stage entrance in West 24th Street and built on the lines of an English music hall – a square balcony, all boxes, with chairs and tables on the orchestra floor."[16] According to contemporary engravings, the place, with rococo domed ceiling, colonnaded promenade, and marble-topped tables was indeed very similar to Morton's New Canterbury, although more than thirty years separated their openings.*

The original was on 23rd Street, just west of Sixth Avenue. Later, Koster and Bial moved to a more exotic setting on 34th. Here straw-hatted and derbied stags sat at make-believe sidewalk café tables under a canopy of artificial palms, watching increasingly indecent acts on the huge stage. In a $500,000 partnership with Oscar Hammerstein, "K & B" tried to boost their flagging receipts with an injection of smut. But New Yorkers had yet to be "educated" to sophisticated late-night erotics, and anyway the city's show biz center was moving steadily northward: 23rd and even 34th were now downtown as theater districts. Police court appearances increased as the number of clients dwindled, and Koster and Bial's finally closed in July, 1901, condemned by the Broadway columnist of the

Morning Telegraph as "a den of sin and a sink of iniquity." (How surprised he would have been to hear the same phrases used as part of a smash-hit song by Carol Bruce fifty years later – in the Rodgers and Hart musical, *Pal Joey*.)

Long before the turn of the century, however, there had been changes made in the English music hall itself. In many houses the chairman was dispensed with. Food had disappeared altogether. They stopped serving drinks in the auditorium. But the interaction of audience and performer unique to the medium – the sense of *complicity*, of finding a partner to share the pain of those wounds inflicted by the slings and arrows of outrageous fortune – these persisted even though the formula had changed. Music hall for many people had become as much a way of life as television today. Like Mr. Lovell in Fanny Burney's *Evelina*, they came as a matter of course. ("I have no time to read playbills," said that gentleman. "One merely comes to meet one's friends and show that one's alive.")

It was this more than anything else that impressed foreign showmen visiting London – and it was the audience-actor rapport that the French, in particular, had been striving to recreate in Paris since the late 1860s and early 1870s.

Acceptance of a stage personality transported from the theater and into real life certainly extended to the United States. The reputations of Lydia Thompson and Pauline Markham (above), loveliest of her Imported English Blondes, were in no way tarnished in public eyes when the two ladies, incensed by a suggestion that the blondes were lacking in maidenly virtue, horsewhipped Wilbur F. Story, dramatic critic of the Chicago Times, *in the street. A similar incident added to the popularity of May Howard (opposite), the burlesque queen of the 1890s. And nobody stopped paying to see Miss Markham when she brazenly admitted to being the mistress of a southern state governor.*

CHAPTER THREE

Getting In on the Act

OUTSIDERS CAN OFTEN gauge something of the mystique of a profession or an in-group by examining the jokes its members tell about themselves. Scotsmen, for example. Doctors. Jewish people. Black Americans. Psychiatrists. But in every case the stories originating from *within* the group are very different from those about the members told by outsiders. Sassenach jokes featuring the canny folk north of the Tweed customarily center around meanness and thrift, whereas in their own jokes the Scots favor astuteness and enterprise. If a black man has a role in a joke told by a WASP, it will usually be because of his supposed physical endowment. Black humor from Harlem or St. Louis is subtler and *much* more sophisticated. The main difference in Jewish stories, as told by Jews and by Gentiles, is that the former are shorter and funnier.

So it is with music hall people. Two representative "outside" jokes are the one about the variety act calling itself the Four Sophisticates (unfortunately unprintable, even today), and the one about the booker turning down an orchestra of trained mice, complete with miniature instruments which they actually play, "because the leader looks too Jewish." Neither story tells us anything at all about the profession or the attitudes and mores of those following it.

Two favorite greenroom stories do (and remember these are for private consumption, not for performance on stage). The first concerns an aging conjuror and illusionist of the old school whose act has been by-passed by whizz-bang youngsters. He has been out of work for months when he reads in *Variety* that a man he once did a favor has been appointed manager of a moribund vaudeville theater in a drab provincial town. He writes and reminds the man of the obligation, asking for one more chance to make it. The manager agrees, and books him for the following week.

The old conjuror misses band call on the Monday morning because he doesn't have enough money to pay his train fare and has to rely on hitching. He goes on cold in the first house, and the act is a disaster. The orchestra cues are all wrong; his props are worn out; the rabbit falls through the crown of the hat; he louses up the vanishing-glass-of-water routine. Finally he is trembling too much to balance the billiard cue and plate on his chin. The audience boos and they have to bring the curtain down on him.

Between houses the manager storms into the old man's cramped dressing room. "I'm sorry," the has-been quavers. "Guess I must be a little rusty. But it'll be okay second house, I promise."

"Second house?" shouts the manager. "There'll be no second house for you, tonight or any other night! I gave you your chance and you bitched it. I got eight girls sharing a six-by-six upstairs and I could use this room for four of them. I want you out of this theater in fifteen minutes! Out!"

Despairingly, the old man repacks his props in a heavy tin trunk, hefts it on to his shoulder, and trudges away from the stage door. Nobody tells him goodby. His last chance – and he fouled it up. Without money, without hope, he stumbles wearily toward the outskirts of town and the long wait for a hitch back home. It starts to rain. The trunk he is humping is biting into the flesh of his shoulder. His threadbare topcoat is drenched; his trousers cling wetly to his legs; his hat brim collapses and cascades water inside his collar. Then the soles of his shoes part company with the tops.

As he squelches past a doorway, a slatternly whore leans out into the downpour and simpers: "'Ullo . . . *saucy!*"

The second story concerns a child actor, a ten-year-old boy employed in a seaside concert party. As required by English law, he has spent the morning doing his school lessons. Now, after lunch, he is sitting at a table in his room, writing (also as required by law) his once weekly letter home. As the pen moves hesitantly across the paper, he mouths the words of the letter aloud:

"Sea View – Saturday . . . Dear Mum and Dad, I hope you are well. I am having quite a nice time here. . . . We had Shepherd's Pie again for lunch . . . Um. . . . The digs are all right, though it is quite a long walk to the pier . . . Um . . . Oh, yes! . . . It is fun being on stage, specially when I have to dance with Miss Brockway, who is Columbine.

The Company are very nice to me. One old gentleman who is the Clown is always buying me candy . . . Um . . . We do two shows a night, one at six and the other at eight, with matinees on Wednesday and Satur – *Holy Suffering Christ!*"

And he flings down the pen and dashes frenziedly from the room.

Attitudes similar to those implicit in these stories, chief among them a kind of ironic despair at the perversity of life, informed the artists who created the early English music hall and their contemporaries in Paris – although in the French capital the *material* was slanted more at a political angle. In England the seventeenth-century practice of hiring special rooms in taverns for drinking and singing had led to the formation of those glee clubs for which Purcell wrote some of his wittiest and most risqué rounds. Later – along with the public house "discussion groups" which paralleled them – these clubs were used as a means of spreading such dangerous and seditious dogmas as freedom and self-determination. But with the coming of the music hall, the subjects of the songs became politically "respectable" – even if at times they remained risqué morally.

The spread of the music hall habit naturally stimulated a huge demand for new songs – and for new singers to perform them. This demand, writes Charles Chilton, was "so great that men of talent as composers and singers were able to supplement their meager livings by rushing from one tavern in the town to another to perform. Chimney sweeps, engineers, street traders, scavengers, coalmen, dustmen, plied their trade all day and sang their way to fame at night."[17] Those lacking a voice or personality themselves could always find a market for their compositions. "Some singers," Chilton adds, "bought their material ready-made from balladmongers who displayed their ballad sheets on long poles and sold their songs by the yard." One that reached the Victorian equivalent of the hit parade was "Poor Old Horse," originally bought from such a vendor in London's Seven Dials in the 1850s.

In France there was also a tradition of songs, broadsheets, tracts and lampoons dating from the eighteenth century, most of them as scurrilous and bitter as their English counterparts. But whereas satire in the song saloons of London lost much of its political content as their audience broadened at the beginning of the nineteenth century, the situation in Paris was different. The *café chantant* – France's equivalent both in word and deed – remained politically "engaged" to a certain

CHARLES GODFREY'S GREATEST SUCCESS.

THE MASHER KING

WRITTEN BY
HARRY ADAMS.

COMPOSED BY
E. JONGHMANS.

The spread of the music hall habit in the last few decades of the nineteenth century stimulated a huge demand for new songs. Here is another example, featuring one of the lesser known "lion comique" stars, Charles Godfrey. The artist portraying him, interestingly enough, is the one responsible for the likeness of The Great Vance on page 37.

extent, siphoning off only the more extreme expression of protest into a separate establishment: the cabaret of the *chansonnier*.

A modern English–French dictionary translates the word as "balladmaker," but the *chansonniers* were more than that. By the turn of the century, they were an institution, peculiarly French, specifically Parisian. More than any other kind of performer, they typified that smart and yet democratic, sophisticated yet iconoclastic chic in which even today the metropolitan French take such a delight. The formula they used was simple enough – a kind of one-man satire show, much of it improvised in rhyme or song – but it was so topical, so up-to-the-minute, replete with scabrous allusions, "in" jokes and the latest argot, that the content was incomprehensible to many provincials, let alone foreigners.

Many of these entertainers – writers, composers and

PHOTO: HARLINGUE-VIOLLET

Montmartre in 1900. Although this picture of a holiday crowd at the Moulin de la Galette is obviously posed, it does give an idea of the "country" atmosphere around the guingette immortalized by Renoir.

rebels, as well as satiric commentators on the day-to-day scene – started their careers in Montmartre, although there were "boulevard" examples as well. There was a reason for this, and it derived from the very special position of Montmartre vis-à-vis the city of Paris.

The area had been outside the administrative confines of Paris until 1790, when Lower Montmartre – what is now the Pigalle-Clichy quarter – had been annexed by the capital. The *Butte* itself, the five-hundred-foot hill crowned by the domes of the Sacré-Coeur, remained outside until 1860. There were two important social developments resulting from these facts. In the first place, wine merchants taking their produce through the barriers at the city gates before the annexations had been obliged to pay high tolls on their wares. There were in consequence a large number of taverns, wine shops and other drinking establishments just outside the city limits in Montmartre, where the citizens could slake their thirst more cheaply than they could in the center. The taverns attracted a floating population of prostitutes, confidence tricksters, liquor smugglers, gypsies, dancers and other entertainers. Lower Montmartre was therefore a raffish night-life district before the beginning of the nineteenth century.

Secondly, the *Butte* became a symbol for the rebellious Commune in 1871, when insurrectionists hiding there murdered two generals before the abortive left-wing coup was smashed by the army, leaving fifteen thousand working people dead in the streets. Montmartre as a whole was therefore identified not only with wine, women and song, but also with disaffection and protest; the song would most likely be rebellious and anti-establishment, if not downright revolutionary. It was hardly surprising, therefore, that before the florid neo-Byzantine foundations of the Sacré-Coeur were laid in 1875,[18] the quarter had also been adopted by painters, poets and other "bohemians."

It was a picturesque, still rural area in mid-Victorian times. The narrow, crooked streets housing the artists' colony were surrounded by market gardens, a vineyard, and a stretch of open heath on whose upper slopes windmills still turned. High up near the summit was the Moulin de la Galette, a mill transformed into a dance hall to be immortalized by Renoir in 1876. Like the other taverns and *café chantants* grouped at the foot of the hill, the Moulin catered largely for a working-class clientele, seasoned with a sprinkling of underworld characters and garnished at weekends with "respectable" couples who had come slumming from the fashionable quarters below. Such customers did not always want to be regaled with sentimental trivialities, patriotic jingles or the frilly effervescence of music by Offenbach and his kind. Often, like the music hall audiences in England, they wanted to hear about a life not so far removed from their own – or even about those less fortunate than themselves. Paris, after all, was something more than high-class vice, "naughty" magazines, and the popping of champagne corks along the *grands boulevards*. That was the picture presenting the city to foreigners as the pleasure capital of the world, "but whereas such accoutrements of sin helped to create the legend of a wicked *fin de siècle* Paris, the more humdrum vice and degradation of the meaner streets and districts provided material for a new form of popular art that often became a poetical evocation of the poorer life of the city as it moved toward the twentieth century."[19]

The new form was the so-called *chanson réaliste*. It derived from the "realist," antiromantic tendency in French literature which, from Balzac through Flaubert to Zola, had occupied itself with the life of "ordinary" everyday people. In song form, it concentrated on the more picturesque examples of the deprived – the workless, the hobos, the girls forced through poverty to sell themselves, the apaches who lived off them. Most importantly, it was what the patrons of the Moulin de la Galette and the *café chantants* wanted to hear. And through them it led to a more specialized audience and therefore a more specialized establishment – the "artistic" cabaret which bred the *chansonnier*.

This darker side of the glittering *Belle Époque* coin inspired ballads, laments and political satires which often reached a high artistic level – a genuine "poetry of the pavement" (or *voix de ville*) which founded a tradition in popular entertainment more recently represented by such moviemakers as Marcel Carné, Jacques Becker and Jean Renoir, the singers Edith Piaf, Georges Brassens and Juliette Greco, and poets like Jacques Prévert, Georges Ribément-Dessaignes and Britain's Adrian Mitchell.

The first showcase for the new *chansonniers* was a small Montmartre cabaret named the Chat Noir (the Black Cat) after a stray tom discovered on the premises and adopted while the place was being decorated. It opened not far from the Place Blanche in 1881, under the ownership of Rudolphe Salis, a provincial "bohemian" and failed art student. Salis reckoned that a quarter already popular with tourists and drinkers, and becoming increasingly esteemed by artists and intellectuals, should prove a gold mine for anyone who opened the right kind of *boîte*, where writers, poets, painters and fellow bohemians could meet. Based on the existing Nouvelle Athènes and Grand' Pinte, the Chat Noir was decked out in a style known as Louis XIII – something not unlike "Olde Englyshe," overflowing with copper pans and pewter and ancient weapons against a background of dark oak. Thanks to a providential meeting with a group of symbolist writers whose favorite café on the Left Bank had just closed down, Salis was blessed with instant success. At the Chat Noir such satirists as Jules Jouy and Xavier Privas found an audience ready to appreciate their songs; here too intellectual pacemakers like the illustrator Willette and the poet Jean Richepin could be sure of finding congenial company. Almost overnight, the place became *the* fashionable night spot for literary and artistic Parisians. It was so popular that Salis was forced to move to larger premises nearby in the Rue Victor Massé.

Here, in a decor now medieval in homage to the beggar poet François Villon (whose spirit the Chat Noir claimed to revive), talented entertainers were imported to amuse a public broader than Salis had imagined. Here, rather after the style of the Coal Hole and the early English music halls, Salis acted as a kind of chairman, encouraging his regular customers to address "each other and distinguished visitors with courtly reverences and long-winded, fantastic titles." According to Raymond Rudorff, the atmosphere was nevertheless "resolutely antibourgeois and anticonventional."[20]

Actors and singers kept up a stream of mockery and invective aimed at society, politicians, the rich and the *demi-monde*, often to the great delight of the same classes they were attacking.[21] It was there that the new type of mocking, seditious and rebellious song was encouraged . . . songs of everyday life and social protest were also becoming frequent. Society ladies, foreign tourists, bankers, playwrights and journalists found themselves attentively listening to songs of a world of which they knew little except, perhaps, through the books of Zola.

"Mr. President" also played a part in the popularization of the Chat Noir's other great attraction – the famous "shadow theater" which was a precursor of the cinema. The basic idea was Jules Jouy's. To dramatize some of his songs, he used puppets and cut-out silhouettes whose shadows were projected onto a screen while he performed. Later, as the puppet manipulators became more adept, the concept was widened until the shadow show became a whole act on its own – something not unlike a modern animated cartoon, complete with music and a running commentary intoned by the chairman. One of the most ambitious of these productions, which grew into an immense tourist attraction, was an entire Napoleonic saga designed by the famous caricaturist Caran d'Ache (whose name still graces a brand of pencils, pastels and crayons sold in France today).

MUSÉE D'ALBI

The Chat Noir's most important contribution to popular entertainment was nevertheless made before Salis moved to the Rue Victor Massé, for it was in the original premises that he first presented to his clients Aristide Bruant, who was to become the greatest *chansonnier* of all.

Bruant was born one hundred miles south of Paris in the year of Britain's Great Exhibition. He fought as a guerilla in the Franco-Prussian war, enlisted in the regular army for a spell, and then came to Paris to work on the rapidly proliferating railway system. The French capital was at this time one of the most heavily fortified cities in Europe. After the revolutions of 1789, 1848 and 1871, strongholds had been rebuilt to protect the center with an inner ring of walled sections each a quarter of a mile long and over thirty feet high. Outside this central nucleus, two concentric circles of forts defended the approaches, one two miles away from the inner fortifications, the other on the heights overlooking the Seine Valley. Inside the twenty mile perimeter of the inner ring, Paris looked much as it does today; the Second Empire *Préfet*, Haussmann, had already cut his broad boulevards through the maze of medieval streets. But it was not here that Aristide Bruant gained the experience that he turned into art. The inner ring was pierced by sixty-five gates or entrances, ten of them for railway lines – and it was there, working in the "sad wasteland" between the outer boulevards and the fortifications, that he grew to know the tramps and rag-pickers, the petty thieves and down-and-outs who were to be the subjects of so many of his songs. In that muddied no man's land of lean-tos and shanties known as "the zone," he ate and drank and worked with the homeless and the hopeless, noting the richness of their slang, the ferocity and impact of their observations. He had always been a singer, but he had progressed no further than military songs, comic numbers and sentimental ballads. Now he incorporated his new-found knowledge in a different type of work – a series of "proletarian" ballads, often titled with the names of the districts inspiring them, which provided a bitter social commentary on the lives of the common people and the underworld. Salis allowed him to sing them at the Chat Noir – and to sell his own words and music to the patrons in lieu of payment.

Soon Bruant's songs about "the other half," and the searing patter he interpolated between such successes as "*A Batignolles*" and "*A La Villette*," were the talk of Paris. When Salis moved to the Rue Victor Massé, the one-time railway worker raised a loan, acquired the Chat Noir's old premises for himself, and opened his own cabaret, which he called the Mirliton.

Bruant spent no money on décor. The Mirliton boasted simply a piano, a scrubbed bar counter, and crude wooden furniture. But it was here that he created a new folklore lionizing the urban outlaw and the inhabitant of the poorer faubourgs. Detesting cant, hating hypocrisy and pretentiousness, Bruant sang for a working-class audience. If the swells wanted to come and listen, he would not stop them. But he wasn't going to pretend he admired them or was impressed by their wealth. In fact, one of the first show business gimmicks he learned was that the more you insulted the customers, the more they liked it. It was just that his contempt for the greater part of his audience happened to be genuine. Striding up and down as he sang, he would hurl out the words, according to Jules Lemaître, the contemporary critic, in "the most cutting voice, the most metallic voice I have ever heard." It was, Lemaître added, "a voice of rioting and the barricades which could dominate the roaring in the streets on a day of revolution; an arrogant and brutal voice which penetrated into your soul like the stab of a flick knife into a straw dummy."

Bruant's success story began in the second half of the 1880s. Ten years later his habitual black corduroy suit, broad-brimmed hat and scarlet scarf formed perhaps the best-known brand image in the whole of Paris. To natives and tourists alike, he must have been something close to a cross between Lennie Bruce and a latter-day François Villon. For the music hall, however, his importance lay less in his personality than in his material. His best compositions, says Raymond Rudorff, "were distinguished by simplicity, poignancy and truthfulness. There was no glossing over the sad facts of life and none of the sentimentality that delighted English music hall audiences when they went to hear 'Cockney' songs."[22]

But before this salutary influence – and that of contemporaries such as Eugénie Buffet and Jehan Rictus – affected the French music hall, many changes had taken place in that medium itself.

Thirty years before, when there was no French music hall at all, Parisians seeking informal entertainment were offered a choice falling into several distinct categories. There was the pre-"artistic" cabaret or *boîte*, small, intimate, usually crowded with regulars who would drink and shout their approval of the *patron* or *patronne's* art in the smoky gaslight far into the night. There was the Second Empire *bal musette*, where the less intellectual could enjoy themselves in a simpler, more extrovert way. Here, though the owner or a gifted amateur might occasionally oblige with a song, the attraction was dancing and the small orchestra providing the music for it. Manet and Renoir were among the painters fascinated by the gaiety of the *bals musettes* in and around Paris in the latter part of the century, Manet's bar interiors and Renoir's *Bal à Bougival* recapturing perfectly the air of supercharged excitement, the hectic glare and glitter of these vanished joys.

In the spring and the summer, such indoor attractions were echoed in the open air by the *guingette*. Traditionally this was a small riverside pleasure garden,[23] but there were *guingettes* in the center of Paris too, especially in the Champs Elysées district, which at that time was a wooded area of huge mansions set in private grounds. Here and there between the properties of the rich, there would be benches and tables under the shady trees, bottles and glasses and siphons winking in the lamplight on warm evenings, perhaps an accordion blaring out the latest waltzes and polkas for the couples dancing beneath the lindens. Here, sheltered from the bustling boulevard crowds and the clip-clop and rattle of *fiacres* and drays and horse-drawn buses along the street, *midinettes* who had been slaving all day would come with their beaux to find a breath of romance among the flowered arbors.★

The Moulin de la Galette was a *guingette* which had once been a *bal musette*, but it was open all the year round. The couples who climbed the steep, winding Montmartre streets and braved the weekend brawls to dance there would find that the evening often ended with a singular attraction. Beyond the wooden barrier separating the tables from the dance floor, local girls gathered in groups to improvise their own versions of the Second Empire quadrille as the brassy orchestra blared out a final Offenbach selection. The dance, which involved a great deal of whirling around and a daring lifting of skirts to show flounced petticoats, was known as the *chahut* – and the more pitchers of the Moulin's special mulled ale the dancers had drunk, the better it went. Later, the *chahut* was to play an important role in the night life of Montmartre and indeed the whole of Paris. But at that time it was just one way of dancing at one particular place.

Elsewhere, the final category on the informal entertainment list, for those who preferred to take their amusement ready-made, was the *café chantant*. Basically, as we have seen, this French equivalent of the pre-music hall song saloon was simply a place, indoors or outdoors, where drinks and refreshments were served while singers performed. Many of these boisterous cafés established reputations which spread far beyond their own immediate neighborhoods. Among them were the Café des Aveugles, the Cadran Bleu, the Café des Sauvages, the Pavillon de Hanovre, and such garden resorts as the Tivoli and Frascati's. Perhaps the best known was Les Ambassadeurs, one of a group in the Champs Elysées. Founded in 1764 as a simple open-air bar, the premises benefited by the addition of a small pavilion in 1772, became a *café chantant* in 1840, and introduced a roofed bandstand to protect the artists eight years later (though the paying customers remained at the mercy of the weather).

Among the trees nearby was the Pavillon d'Horloge, first directed by Besselièvre and then taken over by the impresario Zidler, who added public dancing as an extra attraction between songs. Beyond this was a plot of open land which for fifteen years had been leased by a conjuror named Lacaze as a venue for his outdoor performances. It was acquired in 1850 by Ancelet, who built a small hall, opened it as a *café chantant*, and then added a restaurant, dubbing the establishment the Folies-Marigny. It was here in 1855 that Offenbach presented his first operettas (limited by law to three characters), which he christened *opéras bouffes* because the audiences dined as they watched. (In demotic French the word *bouffe* is equivalent to the American grubfest or blowout or the English nosh-up. It is derived from a verb meaning to swell up or inflate.)

The last of the Champs Elysées group was the Café Morel. Founded in 1841, it was bought in 1860 by Goubert, the proprietor of a popular *café chantant* in the Faubourg Poissonière called the Alcazar d'Hiver. Seeing the opportunity to retain his winter clients during the hot weather. Goubert renamed the old Café Morel pavilion the Alcazar d'Eté, added a restaurant, and opened in a blaze of summer glory with Thérésa, the first of the great pre-music hall stars, as top of his bill. Like Frederick Robson in England, this vibrant and volatile singer, with her powerful and stirring voice, was renowned for her ability to carry an audience from the heights of comedy to the depths of tragedy within the compass of a single song. Starting her career in the days of the Second Empire, she was the toast of Paris for over forty years, finally dying in 1893 after a distinguished "second career" as a straight actress.

Goubert was ambitious and enterprising. To support the brightest star of the day, he introduced farcical sketches and ballets into the program at his new establishment, thus becoming one of the first to transform the *café chantant* into the *café concert*. The number of musicians in the orchestra was augmented from twenty-five to thirty – and then to an astonishing seventy. The program was further strengthened by the addition of the singer Pacra, founder of the performers' union, the *Société Mutuelle des Artistes Lyriques*.

By 1867 clowns and eccentrics had also been added to the attractions at the old Alcazar d'Hiver. This composite program, which included ballet too, featured the actor-poet Glatigny, intimate of Théodor de Banville, who introduced the acts Montmartre-style in improvised rhyme. Not to be outdone by

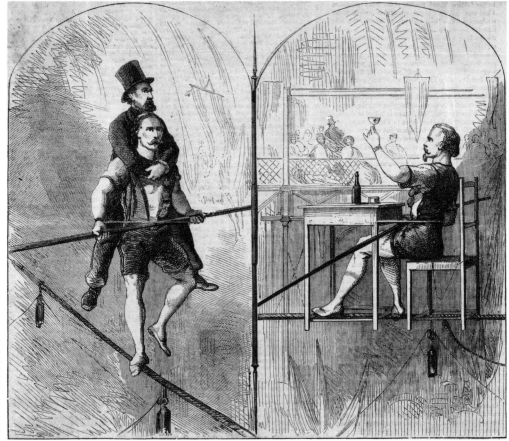

Goubert and his two Alcazars, Pierre Ducarre, the director of Les Ambassadeurs, decided to appeal to the inner rather than the outer client: he added a restaurant, hired the best chef in Paris, and transformed the place into a rendezvous for gastronomes. But it was left to a competitor named de Lorge to make the definitive move which would result in the emergence of a music hall that was truly French in its classic form.

In March of the same year, 1867, de Lorge approached the city authorities with a view to regularizing an anomaly in the law. Until that time, much as the Royal Charter had inhibited the drama in London, the *Code Napoléon*, which is the basis of all French law, had discriminated against one branch of the entertainment business – but in France it was the legitimate theater that gained and everyone else that lost. Producers of variety shows or anything other than straight plays were forbidden by this law to make use of costumes, scenery, make-up or even specialized properties. There was thus no possibility of the attractions at a *café concert* welding themselves into anything as coherent as a revue. And in any case it was forbidden

From the 1850s onward, acrobats, tumblers, dancers and other specialty acts seasoned the song content at English music halls and café concerts in Paris. One of the most impressive was Blondin – the man who walked over Niagara Falls on a tight-rope. This engraving from the Illustrated London News *shows him carrying a man on his back, and eating his dinner balanced on the rope during a performance at the Crystal Palace in 1861.*

67

The "notorious" Blanche d'Antigny – one of the first of the grandes horizontales, the courtesans who used the music hall as a shop window for their charms.

to advertise the entertainment on posters or in any way on the street.

De Lorge was not planning a revue, but he did wish to use costume, make-up and a few props. He was the owner of a *café chantant* called the Eldorado, which had been built six years previously on the site of an old circus merry-go-round in the Faubourg St. Martin. And by a piece of unusual good luck he had managed to hire the tragedienne Cornélie, who had just walked out of the Comédie Française after a quarrel with the management.

With her as top of the bill, and a few dancers and jugglers to pad out the collection of singers already contracted to him, he could turn the Eldorado into a successful *café concert* overnight – if only the actress could play some of her most famous scenes and appear in excerpts from the classics.

De Lorge pleaded his case with some vigor. It was ridiculous, he argued, that Mme. Cornélie should be permitted to appear on one Parisian stage "in character" – and be denied the same advantages on another little more than a mile away. She was, after all, the same person, playing the same roles in the same way.

Anna Judic. She starred in Offenbach's La Créole *in 1876, then reversed the usual procedure, transferring from "legitimate" theater to music hall, where she remained a headliner until after the turn of the century.*

The logic of de Lorge's argument appealed to the judges and he won his case. From then on, the law accepted the *café concert* in the same legal category as the theater proper. The Eldorado soon became one of the most popular in Paris – notable, among other successes, for Thérésa's rendering of the Zola-esque songs of Jules Jouy.

Directors were quick to profit from the relaxation. Once artifice was admitted, the doors were open to imagination and invention as well. Something very like the English music hall formula crystallized. Comedians, skaters, musical "fantasists," specialty acts added themselves to the singers and dancers appearing at the *caf'conc'*, as the Parisians affectionately called it.

The huge Palais Chinois in the Boulevard du Prince Eugène (later to become the famous Ba-ta-clan), inaugurated a series of aquashows, water ballets and

The model for the Folies-Bergère. This program from the Alhambra, in London's Leicester Square, dates from the 1880s and proves that the chorus line had arrived in Britain earlier than some people think. The theater, designed in the Moorish idiom by Hayter Lewis, opened in 1854 under the name of the Royal Panopticon of Science and Art. It was converted to a circus in 1856, changed into a music hall in 1860, and burned down in 1882. Rebuilt and reopened a year later, it remained a show place for vaudeville, comic opera and revue until it was demolished to make way for a movie theater in 1936.

productions in which special lighting effects and mechanical marvels were as important as the artists. Still more vast was what the posters described as "the biggest *café concert* in the capital" – the original Casino de Paris in the Rue de Lyon. To block this opposition, de Lorge employed Offenbach's collaborator, Hervé, as orchestra conductor in 1868. At that time the bill at the Eldorado included Pacra, Mme. Amati, Marie Lafourcade and Suzanne Lagier, later to be supplemented by Théo, who specialized in Offenbach songs, and the notorious Blanche d'Antigny. Across the street at the Concert du Cheval Blanc, the curtain went up for the first time on a young woman destined to become the great dramatic actress Agar. The premises, once an *auberge* or inn, then a *guingette*, afterwards a *café chantant*, were themselves to find fame seven years later when Vergeron effected yet another change and transformed them from a simple *caf'conc'* into the Scala music hall.

The final link with the flourishing English prototype was in fact forged in 1869. It was, for show business, an eventful year.

In Britain, on March 13, *London Echoes* revealed for posterity the origin of nudity on the professional stage. "When Mlle. Marianne de Camargo, daughter of a *soi–disant* grandee of Spain and *première danseuse* at the

Paris Opera during some twenty years of the reign of Louis the Well-Beloved, came to the conclusion that her petticoats were too long for the proper execution of those graceful pirouettes and *battes de jambe* for which she was renowned, and boldly made her appearance on the stage with a 'kirtle cut by the knee,' she incited a social revolution," announced the journal's columnist.

The playgoing world (he resumed after a pause to regain his breath) had been divided upon the point, but "after a desperate contest" the partisans of the innovation had prevailed and it had become the established custom for *figurantes* to "display" themselves. "Since then the petticoats and bodices of the fair nymphs who sport themselves for our entertainment and their own profit . . . have manifested a decided tendency to shrinkage, and this most notably since burlesque has been such a prominent feature in our dramatic literature."

In the United States, a month later, Miss Lydia Thompson, ably assisted by her troupe of 250-pound beauties, was unwittingly founding that other style of burlesque which was so inexorably to become inseparable from the naked female form.

And in Paris, on May 2, an establishment opened where "you could eat and drink and smoke while you watched a continuous performance of songs and variety similar to that provided by the early English music hall."[24]

The place – which had yet to become associated with the nude – was built on the site of a café whose freehold had belonged to the store, "The Pillars of Hercules." It was modeled on the Alhambra music hall in London. And it was called the Folies-Bergère.

CHAPTER FOUR

Artists of Influence

To say that the French music hall in its classic form resulted from an amalgamation between the native *café concert* and an entertainment formula imported from England is perhaps an oversimplification. Certainly the *form* of the production was based on cross-Channel models,★ but no social phenomenon develops in isolation and there were many other influences at work as well. Not least among these were the performers themselves, a great many of whom came from outside France. For France, read Paris – because despite the strong cultural traditions of its separate provinces, from the point of view of style and fashion the country was more centralized than any other in Europe. In England vigorous and autonomous music hall traditions flourished in Manchester and Nottingham and Leeds and the Northeast; Italy was alive to the influences of Milan, Turin and Naples as well as those of Rome; Germany could accept innovations originating in Hamburg, Stuttgart and Munich in addition to Berlin. But in France – except for a period in World War I when high society fled to Marseille – Paris was Paris and the rest simply did not count.

Through these artists, therefore, Germany, Italy and Russia all contributed to the emergence of French music hall as a distinctive form, particularly after the introduction of specialty acts into the program, for in all those countries the circus tradition producing such talents was strong. Later the United States was to make its contribution also – mainly in that special emphasis on the glorification of the female form typical of Broadway revue. But in the 1860s Lydia Thompson was still trying on her first pair of tights – and the Civil War didn't leave folks too much time to think about sex as an exportable commodity.

In Germany, throughout the whole of the nineteenth century, the circus, both in its touring form

★ There was one important exception to the rule that French music hall production followed the form of the English: the chairman never went to France. The wordy, hectoring master of ceremonies directing the way the evening went did not fit any recognized Gallic image (which may possibly explain why the revue formula blossomed so quickly in France).

73

under the Big Top and in permanent quarters, played an increasingly important role on the entertainment scene. There was also a strong concert tradition, at spas and health resorts as well as in the big cities. And of course, here, as in Central Europe as a whole, there was the *Kabarett* – first in a form similar to the French *café chantant*, later with restaurant, an orchestra for dancing, and variety acts to supplement the songs.

It was inevitable that there should be, as it were, a cross-fertilization between these three separate traditions. And from this developed the *Spezialitätentheater*, with its composite productions featuring singers, musical acts, illusionists, acrobats, sword swallowers, wire walkers and even parodists and satirists. These last, comparable in some ways to the Paris *chansonniers*, derived from the equally specialized political *Kabaretten* of Berlin. It was in the capital, too, that the Valhalla, Europe's first theater consecrated to spectacular revue, opened its doors. In the second half of the century, its example was followed all over the country, with Hamburg especially vying for the lead position. Berlin's famous Wintergarten theater opened in 1884 as a concert hall, but two years later it was transformed by Baron and Doorn into a vast music hall whose stage was large enough to serve also as a circus ring. It was here that the famed bareback rider Thérèse Renz, from the same circus family lending its name to Mme. Rentz's Female Minstrels in the United States, first presented an equestrienne act in a music hall. Later the comedian Otto Reuter opened the Palast-Theater in Berlin, which was soon to attract such glittering stars as La Belle Otéro, Cléo de Mérode, and the immortal Yvette Guilbert from France. A third hall to gain European renown was Rudolf Schier's Apollo, one of the first to feature clairvoyance and thought-transference acts on stage.

Curiously Italy, which throughout its history had fostered the *divertissement* in every form, was late in establishing a music hall formula. It was not until the end of the nineteenth century that there was a fusion between the local equivalent of the *café chantant* and other popular elements more typically Italian – in particular the Neapolitan song, sophisticated derivatives of the *commedia dell'arte*, and gymnastic routines encouraging the audience to laugh as well as to gasp and marvel. Even then the transformation was social and economic rather than "organic." The Italian *café chantants*, unlike their counterparts in Paris and the song saloons in London, had attracted only a limited clientele drawn from the bourgeoisie and the intelligentsia. It was to broaden this public that the *Teatro d'Attrazione* was created.

Here again the program comprised international variety elements seasoned with indigenous attractions, especially in the fields of comedy and popular song. The circus contributed its quota. And there was, too, a tradition peculiar to Italy: the *Macchietta*. This was a specialized comic monologue, a satiric routine in which comedians and even straight actors, costumed and made-up, improvised verses to music rather in the manner of the *chansonniers* – except that, whereas the Parisians normally worked alone in their own cabarets, the *Macchietta* took its place along with the ventriloquists and impressionists and other specialty acts on the variety stage.

In Italy[25] as elsewhere, halls specifically designed for the presentation of these entertainments sprang up in every major town. Notable among these were the Concerto delle Variete, the Salone Margherita, Jovincelli's and the Orfeo (Rome); Marisetti, San Martino, the Eden, the Eldorado, the Trianon and the Apollo (Milan); and, in Naples, Umberto's, another Eldorado, another Eden and a second Salone Margherita which was designed as a showplace for stars specializing in Neapolitan song.

Russia differed from the Western European countries in that for centuries the poorer people had been used to open-air entertainment – a tradition which (barring seasonal shut-downs due to the severe winters) derived more from the traveling fair than from the indoor cabaret. Here, naturally, jugglers, trapezists, tumblers, bear tamers and other specialty acts were in the ascendant; physical skill took precedence over the spoken word; the folk dance and the ballet eclipsed the song, which until the beginning of the nineteenth century was a supplementary rather than a principal attraction.

In one respect, however, the land of the Czars was ahead of its time: the improvising buffoon, a clownish figure who filled the roles of tension-reliever and "chairman" linking the acts together, had always played an important part in such composite spectacles. There was, too, a strangely democratic air about these summer entertainments. Before the birth of Diaghilev (1872) or Chaliapine (1873), the bourgeoisie and the aristocracy mingled unself-consciously with the workers among the audiences. Later, shopkeepers, government employees and the military frequented the shows in the pleasure gardens of Moscow and St. Petersburg, much as their counterparts in London had at the

"A theater which is not a theater, a promenade where you may sit down, a spectacle which you are not obliged to watch" – the Folies-Bergère in the Belle Epoque. It was not until this promenade in back of the auditorium was installed in 1871 that the hall found favor with the public, and then it was more "because the ladies of Lower Montmartre treated the innovation as an extension of the sidewalk than because of any attractions on stage."

Surrey and the Cremorne half a century before. Doubtless it was in deference to these more sophisticated elements that the earliest singers to find fame in this field varied their romantic ballads and popular folksongs with extracts from the opera and musical comedy. Among those whose names have survived from the era before Ivan Rujsin created Russia's pioneer variety theater were Buleschov, Lazarev and the redoubtable Elizaveta Sandurova, who was born in 1772 and died in 1826.

Rujsin himself, who died in 1850 at the age of sixty, was a composer and satiric singer whose function yet again approximated that of a Montmartre *chansonnier*, and his influence spread throughout the country as the symbiotic process already observed in England, France, Germany and Italy resulted in the proliferation of pleasure gardens, *café concerts*, and finally music halls in all the major cities. Once the entertainment was housed in an auditorium, the Slavic formula was greatly enriched by the importation of artists from other countries, notably France and Germany, but the Russian public was always particularly appreciative of these local satirists inspired by current events. Two of them, Nikitin and Moncharov, starred in Moscow's first true music hall when V. Lentovsky transformed the Hermitage pleasure garden into the Garden of Marvels – and their successors were still drawing crowds long after the Soviet régime was established.

On the whole, the French music hall influenced more than it was influenced by the Russian. But if the latter only matured after it had been fertilized by the addition of foreign talent, at least it was a two-way traffic: specialty acts from east of the Oder were to have a growing effect on programs in Western Europe, while the impact later of the Imperial Ballet was to prove incalculable.

In Paris, once the no-costumes-no-scenery law had been relaxed and the Folies-Bergère had adopted the Alhambra formula, theaters all over the city broadened their bills to embrace every conceivable kind of entertainment – although as yet the music hall directors had looked seriously neither toward scenic artists nor costume designers to enrich the settings of their productions. The indefatigable Goubert added skaters to the attractions at the Alcazar d'Eté and increased the size of the orchestra at the Alcazar d'Hiver to forty musicians under the baton of Javelot. The show there now ran from 7:30 to 11:00 P.M.

Strangely enough, although their example was followed elsewhere with satisfactory results, the first few productions at the Folies-Begère were not entirely successful. It was not until Sari took over as director in 1871 and installed the notorious *premenoir* circling the back of the auditorium that the place found favor with the public – and then it was because the ladies of Lower Montmartre treated the innovation as an extension of the sidewalk rather than because of any attractions on stage.

There were other music halls which lacked the golden touch. In 1865 Offenbach was obliged to move his *Bouffes-Parisiens* to the Passage Choiseul (an eighteenth century arcade in the Opera district, beside which the small theater still exists), leaving the Marigny to associate itself with a series of unhappy productions following a season with Charles Deburau's company of mimes.* Later managements fared no better and the hall was demolished in 1881 to make way for the Victorian equivalent of a pinball saloon and bowling alley. It was rebuilt as a bijou theater in 1893, returning to the music hall formula from time to time, especially in the presentation of summer season tourist variety. But although the auditorium was architecturally sublime,† the theater's subsequent history occupied itself more with flops than with hits.

Even the now-celebrated Bobino was among the also-rans. Founded in 1812 as a showcase for fairground attractions, the crude and draughty *Baraque à Bobino* slapped on a fresh coat of greasepaint and made a

* Jean-Baptiste Gaspard Deburau was born in Kolin, Bohemia, in 1796 – a man described by Sacheverell Sitwell as "one of the most poetical actors who ever lived."[26] Deburau's son, Jean Charles, was born in Paris in 1829, founded the celebrated mime troupe bearing their name, which is linked in French theatrical history with the creation of the archetypal stage pierrot later to be developed by Jean-Louis Barrault and Marcel Marceau.

† Movie buffs will recall the Marigny music hall in Marcel Carné's Les Enfants du Paradis, a film based on the life of Deburau – or at least on incidents occurring in his life – in which Barrault played the famous mime.

77

second entrance during the first music hall boom as the Folies–Bobino. But it never won public approval until, in 1880, it moved from its original site near the Rue de Fleurus and reopened in the busy Rue de la Gaieté in Montparnasse, where it still presents extravaganza revues today. The Folies-Bergère itself went bankrupt in 1885 after Sari, in an unsuccessful attempt to "refine" his programs, had produced a disastrous series of classical concerts there. It was taken over by M. and Mme. Allemand, then joint owners of the Scala, who tempted the great Aristide Bruant away from his own cabaret to star at the Folies in the forerunner of Paris's first *revue à grand spectacle* a year later.

The first-night audience were of course familiar with the king of the *chansonniers*. They were used to his acid commentaries, they knew the broad, sardonic features and the leonine hair, the quizzical eyes beneath their thick brows. But they had never before seen him in so splendid a setting. They reveled in his caustic humor, rocked with laughter at his quirky use of underworld slang; they gasped at the trapezists, marveled at the acrobats, cheered the dancers; and they reserved a specially warm burst of applause for the wry fatalism of Anna Judic, the star of Offenbach's *La Créole* as long ago as 1876 but singing now for the first time on a music hall stage. The show, in short, was a smash hit.

Among the first-nighters who cheered loudest was a tall, thin medical student, Gabriel Tapie de Celeyran, son of a grand family in the southwest, and his cousin – a thick-lipped, bearded cripple with abnormally short legs who bore the noble name of Henri de Toulouse-Lautrec. At that time only twenty-two years old, Lautrec had recently arrived in Paris to continue his studies as a painter. He was still dazzled by the gaiety and vigor and exuberance of life in the capital, the teeming café society, the intensity of artists' theorizing in studio and garret, the lubricious opportunities of the Montmartre bawdy houses. His eyes, normally wary behind a lorgnette, were bright that evening with excitement. He had forgotten the aggressive demeanor behind which normally he hid his self-consciousness and distress in the joy of watching these brilliant performers at work.

He was to immortalize them all. Deformed and physically restricted himself through the effect of inbreeding, he lived a vicariously energetic life by capturing the activity of others on canvas. Lautrec was fascinated by vitality: the moving model excited him more than the landscape or the studio pose. In the

last fifteen years of the nineteenth century, he recorded more vividly than any movie camera the bustle and rush, the frantic glitter and vulgarity, the heady soufflé of romance and panache that was the essence of night life in *fin-de-siècle* Paris.

And if Renoir and Manet allow us to breathe the atmosphere on the audience's side of the footlights, and Dégas illuminates the stage, Lautrec takes us behind the scenes, in among the artists as they work or rehearse. The sketch for the famous Montmartre *Quadrille de la Chaise Louis XIII* was drawn soon after that Folies first night – the dancers exploding with movement while half a dozen lines catch Bruant, hands in pockets, hat on the back of his head, watching approvingly in the background. Surpassing the camera again, the painter shows us not only the stars but also the minor performers; not just the artist on stage but

also a skater snatching a quick drink, a chorus girl
adjusting her ballet skirt, dancers among the crowd
after a show, a group of singers in the corridor leading
to the Folies dressing rooms. Thus, among the flood
of lithographs, drawings and paintings that poured
from Toulouse-Lautrec's attic studio, we can still see
with the artist's eye Bruant singing in his cabaret,
Bruant on a bicycle, Yvette Guilbert taking a curtain
call, an unknown trapezist in mid-swing, Marcelle
Lender and Mary Hamilton, May Milton and Loie
Fuller, the frail phthisic charm of Jane Avril and the
hothouse beauty of Anna Held, who was later to marry
Florenz Ziegfeld.

Like his contemporary Aubrey Beardsley in England,
Lautrec was a master of line. But whereas the decadence
in the Englishman's work came from within, Lautrec's
only reflected that of his subjects. Above all he had a
genius for capturing movement: Ida Heath high
kicking, a girl rolling a stocking up her leg, a woman
straining to lace up a corset – on the two-dimensional
page, the figures vibrate with life. In the marvelous

Mary Hamilton at the Moulin-Rouge – one of Toulouse-Lautrec's most brilliant on-the-spot portraits.

lithograph of Valentin le Désossé dancing with the voluptuous La Goulue, one can almost *feel* the sinuous reversing swoop of the waltz step – and see in the mind's eye the advance to which it was the sequel. At the same time, the few scratches on the stone that make up the profile of "the boneless one" tell us more about that dancer's personality than a whole volume of biography.

Happily the painter's talent did not stop short at recording what he saw while he saw it. The whole of the superb "circus" series was drawn entirely from memory, without a single note – to prove that he was not insane at the end of an enforced stay in a madhouse which was part of a "drying-out" cure after one of his bouts of alcoholism.

Although Lautrec's art was sneered at by traditional critics – who accused him of glorifying the grotesque and laying too much emphasis on the uglier side of life – the music hall by its very nature was less hidebound in its attitudes. The life providing so much of his subject matter was also to furnish the majority of his

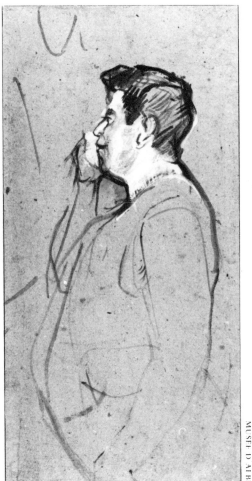

MUSÉE D'ALBI

LEFT:
"Surpassing the camera, Lautrec shows us not only the stars but also the minor performers. On the two-dimensional page, the figures vibrate with life." Here, dabbing the sweat from his face after a summer performance, is Gaudieux, an actor who was a favorite with café-concert clients.

RIGHT:
Polin at the Scala. "He was able to murmur, almost to whisper his songs in a fashion that still sounded crystal clear in the furthest corners of the theater." The drawing is by Toulouse-Lautrec.

clients. Bruant was among the first to recognize the value of the peppery little cripple's work, and he commissioned a poster advertising the Mirliton. Other managements followed suit. Soon music halls and cafés all over Paris were using Toulouse-Lautrec lithographs to decorate their playbills. With Chéret and Bonnard, Lautrec in fact originated the modern "impact" poster (another parallel with Beardsley, who played a comparable role in England). More important still, the work of these painters, and the pictures of Van Dongen, drew the attention of music hall directors toward the "legitimate" artists who were to prove so profound an influence on the development of the spectacular revue in the years to come.

Bruant's success at the Folies-Bergère did not go unchallenged. In the same year, 1886, after a two-year season at the Alcazar d'Hiver starring the aging Thérésa, Goubert opened *En Revenant de la Revue* at the Alcazar d'Eté. This, too, was an immense success, largely through the personal magnetism of its top-of-the-bill, the legendary Paulus. Tremulously intense, scorching the stage as he paced elegantly with his top hat and cane, Paulus was the *boulevardier* who provided Paris's answer to London's *lion comique*. But there was another reason for his – and the show's – success at this time and place. The title referred not to a music hall production, but to a military review. And Paulus, probably the first variety star to mix in politics, was a fervent supporter of General Boulanger, the war minister around whom a cadre of dissatisfied officers gathered in 1886 in the hope of provoking a coup d'état.* In a potentially explosive political atmosphere, a show which openly backed the cause of a right-wing dissident was bound to succeed in the Champs Elysées district, where the majority of the audience were likely to be members of an equally dissatisfied middle class and therefore "Boulangistes" to a man. The revue's title song was adopted as a battle hymn by the general's campaigners – but in the event, although he achieved a stunning personal election victory, Georges Boulanger's nerve failed at the last moment and no presidential coup was attempted.[27]

The debacle did no harm to Paulus, who had made his name four years earlier at a small hall off the Faubourg Saint-Dénis called the Concert Parisien. At that time it was simply an old *café chantant* in the center of which a performers' rostrum had been set up. Built on the site of an eighteenth-century convent, the premises were later bought by Auguste Mussleck and modernized in time for a reopening in 1889 with a revue giving Yvette Guilbert her first important role.

The year was an important one for the music hall and for Paris as a whole. It was the year in which the world-famous Bal du Moulin-Rouge was inaugurated in the Place Blanche, Pigalle – and it was the year of the third of the capital's great universal exhibitions (which was, of course, the reason why the Concert Parisien and the Moulin-Rouge chose it for their grand openings).†

Paris was flooded with sightseers and tourists from all over the world. Thirty-two million attendances were registered at the exhibition, which ran from May to November. And among these people who had come to share France's faith in the "new scientific age of progress which Jules Verne had forecast," to admire the brilliance and creativity of Europe's builders, engineers, industrialists, scientists and artists, there must be a large proportion prepared also to marvel and admire the creativity of her singers and dancers and

* Another supporter once jailed for her Boulangist sympathies was Algerian-born Eugénie Buffet, one of the few female equivalents of Bruant. Paradoxically for a right-winger, she was a singer whose material smacked always of revolution and change. Making her name at the Cigale with her "Sérénade du Pavé" in 1892, she moved later to the Gaieté-Rochechouart and then Les Ambassadeurs, still playing the part of the pierreuse or street walker which had first brought her to fame. Her voice was "not to be cataloged – unlike anything you may hear at lyric theaters or concerts, or even at café chantants." The description is that of Jean Richepin, many of whose rebel songs she sang.

———— · ————

† From 1867 onward a universal exhibition was held in Paris every eleven years until that of 1900. The 1889 edition, which was marked by the building of Gustave Eiffel's tower, had a special significance as the centenary of the French Revolution and therefore a celebration of France's republican system of government.

———— · ————

AUBREY BEARDSLEY

OPPOSITE:
"Art Nouveau in three dimensions, the original psychedelic girl" – an Aubrey Beardsley poster design inspired by the dancer Loie Fuller.

LEFT:
"Scorching the stage as he paced elegantly with his top hat and cane" – Jacobi's poster for Paulus, France's answer to the "lion comique." The star was one of the few music hall artists to make use of his position to further a political cause.

musicians. Or so thought the small consortium of impresarios responsible for the launching of the Moulin-Rouge.

At the beginning there were three of them: a one-time wholesale butcher named Zidler, and two brothers called Oller. They had already opened the Hippodrome and the Jardin de Paris (really the old Pavillon d'Horloge under a new name) in the Champs Elysées. These could be relied on to attract customers from the French middle classes and those tourists surfeited with the exhibition displays across the river in the Champ de Mars beneath Baron Eiffel's Tower. But Zidler and his colleagues, convinced that Montmartre was to be the city's future pleasure center, were looking for something to draw these crowds away from the fashionable Right Bank areas. There was already a huge clientele to be tempted from the existing cabarets and *caf'conc's* in Montmartre; all that was

needed was some special "angle," some new packaging that would bring the more respectable public up the hill to what had previously been considered rather a raffish quarter.

It was at the Moulin de la Galette that Zidler had his brilliant idea. The evening was ending with a more than usually boisterous *chahut*. As he watched the amateur dancers twirling and spinning, the impresario recalled that there was a small *caf'conc'* called the Elysée-Montmartre at the foot of the hill – and that it was the custom there too to finish the festivities with a *chahut*. The only difference was that the girls at the Elysée-Montmartre were a regular team, and therefore that much better than the freelances at the Moulin. It was Dufour, the bandleader at the Elysée, who had first had the idea of reviving this Second Empire quadrille once known as the cancan, he who had encouraged the local girls to improvise on its basic steps, and finally he who had instituted the ritual of using the dance as a finale. The idea had paid off: the Elysée was always jammed; dancers even overflowed into the adjoining garden, where drinks were served beneath artificial palm trees made from zinc; Toulouse-Lautrec sat there sketching most nights at a specially reserved table. Suppose – Zidler must have thought to himself – one could put on the same kind of show in slightly more reputable surroundings? Suppose one could present the brawling, gutsy, vulgar essence of Montmartre night life in a place that was nevertheless fit for ladies and gentlemen to enter? What was necessary, he mused, was a new kind of café dance hall – something that would combine the best elements of the *bal musette*, the *guingette* and the *caf'conc'*; a place that must be special as well as fashionable, as attractive as it was alive. The entertainers were already available at the Elysée-Montmartre; all he had to do was offer them better terms and sign them up – and then find a suitable showplace that could be transformed the way he wanted it.

The Oller brothers were enthusiastic. Together they started combing the *quartier* for an appropriate site. They found it only a stone's throw from the Elysée-Montmartre itself* – an abandoned garden facing the Place Blanche with a disused dance hall at one side. They installed a huge dance floor, a high, wide stage for orchestra, singers and specialties, and galleries surrounding three sides of the hall where nondancers could sit and drink.

Zidler commissioned Willette, the illustrator who was a customer of the nearby Chat Noir, to execute

OPPOSITE TOP:
A chahut at the original Bal du Moulin-Rouge in the 1890s. The tables were between the pillars on either side of the big dance floor. The illuminated sign in the center of the band-stand from which Yvette Guilbert first sang announces the galop final – and, judging from the picture, the beaux of the Belle Époque were not prepared to stand in line outside a cloakroom to retrieve their hats.

OPPOSITE BELOW:
Lautrec's sketch for the Quadrille de la Chaise Louis XIII. Aristide Bruant, hands in pockets, hat on the back of his head, watches approvingly as Gauzy bounces behind two of the girls executing the porte d'armes.

* **The Elysée-Montmartre still exists. Between the sex shops and pizza parlors of the Boulevard Rochechouart, a flight of wide, steep stairs leads straight to the small auditorium, where the seats are set diagonally facing a diminutive stage across one corner of the room. Nude shows compete with all-in wrestling on that stage today, but it was for a time the home of the Jean-Louis Barrault–Madeleine Renaud company, after they had been basely stripped of their state subsidy and their theater for political reasons, and before they had installed themselves in the disused railway station on the Quai d'Orsay that is now their showplace.**

the decorations. It was Willette who conceived the idea of surmounting the single-story entrance lobby with a giant mock windmill whose scarlet sails could be mechanically turned. In the garden behind, an assortment of delights continued the rustic motif and put to shame the Elysée's tin palm trees. These included an open-air extension to the main bar, reproductions of a Normandy farmhouse and a miniature Spanish palace, and loops of fairy lights strung beneath real trees, under which patrons could sit and drink or the ladies of Montmartre solicit their clients. At one end of the garden was an enormous stucco elephant which Zidler had acquired from the exhibition in the city below. A rectangular opening in the flank of this creature revealed a small stage on which a limited number of specialty acts could be performed. Appositely enough, the opening attraction was a belly dancer named Zelaska. (Later a roofed pavilion was added for the performance of more ambitious acts.)

From the moment the artificial sails of the Moulin-Rouge began to turn, the place was an instant success.★ It was perhaps no coincidence that the opening shared the limelight with another, equally scintillating, innovation: in 1889, for the first time, electric lighting brightened the streets of Paris.

Whether it was the ambience, the décor, the entertainment, or the fact that such bawdy, earthy pleasures could be sampled in comfort, it is impossible to say. But Zidler's wildest optimism was more than justified. The crowds did flock to Montmartre from the more fashionable quarters; the tourists did take to the area as the center of Paris night life; at last, as one contemporary put it, "le tout Paris[28] has been given an opportunity to enjoy the 'real Montmartre' without loss of dignity and with a delicious sensation of participation in the most democratic of Parisian pleasures."

Before long, the Place Blanche was jammed every night with carriages from the snob districts of Neuilly, Passy, the Chaussée-d'Antin and the Faubourg St.-Honoré. Local street traders, artisans and their girls, clerks, shopgirls and prostitutes lined up with the swells to pass in under the red sails. Zidler hired a fleet of three-horse omnibuses to convey clients back to the more select Jardin de Paris in the Champs Elysées once the final *chahut* was over.

The place's reputation, says Raymond Rudorff, "gave immense impetus to the diffusion of a great erotic myth – the myth of a naughty, free, uninhibited city of *frou-frou* and champagne, of the wild music of the quadrille which seemed to urge rich and poor

★ This first establishment was the <u>Bal</u> du Moulin-Rouge. It was basically a dance hall with a number of supplementary attractions, chief among them the dance later stylized as the cancan. Not until 1903 were adjoining premises acquired and a vast music hall auditorium built. From that time there were two Moulins-Rouge, side by side, under the same management. The remodeled <u>bal,</u> with its steeply raked tiers of dining tables and its hydraulically rising dance floor, still presents revue; the site of the old music hall is occupied by a movie theater with the same name.

alike to forget their cares and live for love and laughter only."[29] There was of course hypocrisy in the Third Republic as there was in Victorian Britain and America. But a surviving tradition of the public enjoyment of physical pleasures left the French less prudish and more inclined to indulge in the belly laugh. Perhaps this was why, as Rudorff says, "the age was one that was highly receptive to sexual suggestions. The fetish of the female leg, ankle and bosom which was so pronounced in the late nineteenth century, the frankness of well-known writers, and the florid, flowing lines of interior design and furnishings which were to reach a paroxysm in the art nouveau style all played a part in giving the French nineties an aura of intense eroticism." This was nowhere more evident than in the world of music hall. Even publicity pictures of artists as "respectable" as Gaby Deslys could show a kneeling dresser lifting the star's skirt to fix a frill over a black stocking reaching halfway up the thigh. But despite the "bohemian" image, replete with its poets and painters, its gay ladies beneath the flaring gas jets and the new electric signs, the reality, Rudorff adds, was more down to earth. "There was little in common between the lavish imitation of the cancan offered by the modern Folies-Bergère and the cinema and the real Moulin-Rouge with its not so glamorous ladies who danced with

A rare photo of the celebrated Moulin-Rouge quadrille stars in action. Authorities disagree over which girl is which – particularly since the picture has suffered a great deal of retouching – but the most reliable concensus establishes the quartet in the foreground as (left to right) Grille d'Egout, La Sauterelle, La Goulue and Rayon d'Or. In the background are Cadudja, La Môme Fromage, Serpolette (doing splits) and Nini Patte-en-l'Air.

La Goulue entering the Moulin Rouge. This giant Toulouse-Lautrec painting is executed on two rectangular panels of burlap. Bought and then exhibited by the Moulin-Rouge boss, Zidler, it was later given to the dancer herself – who separated the panels and then lost one of them as her personality disintegrated. The missing portion was discovered years later in a junk-shop and miraculously reunited with its "other half." It now hangs above the entrance to the Jeu de Paume gallery in Paris.

more gusto than choreographic precision. . . . The girls who performed were not chosen for their looks but because they were strong and their appeal – or rather that of their dancing – was direct, unabashed and crude. There was no false glamor and no barrier of footlights to set them in another dimension from their audience."

Of all the girls whom Zidler had (to the management's dismay) recruited from the Elysée-Montmartre, the one with the most "direct, unabashed and crude" appeal was undoubtedly Louise Weber, a one-time washergirl and artists' model who was born in Montmartre in 1865. As danced at the Elysée, the Moulin de la Galette and the Moulin-Rouge, the revived quadrille (or *quadrille naturaliste* as it was called) was an improvisation for girls only, with a number of basic movements of which the most "daring" were the *porte d'armes* (shoulder arms), the *grand écart* (splits) and that sudden revelation of frilled petticoats over the backside which terminates the cancan that we see in night clubs today. The *quadrille naturaliste* usually ended in the splits, as the dancers plunged to the floor one after the other following a combined *porte d'armes*.★ Together with the music, it formed a spectacle – as the onlookers crowded close in the hope of glimpsing an inch of bare flesh – that was earthy, energetic, vital and exciting. In the person of Louise Weber, it became also lascivious and extremely erotic.

The journalist Georges Montorgeuil, reviewing her performance in 1890, described her as "pink and blonde, about eighteen years old [she was in fact twenty-five], with a willful, vicious and flushed baby face, a nose with quivering, impatient nostrils, a nose of one sniffing after love, nostrils dilating with the male odor of chestnut trees and the enervating bouquet of brandy glasses, a mouth gluttonous and sensual, a look shameless and provoking, the milk-white bosom freely escaping from the corsage . . . the pretty girl unaware of any modesty or constraint." The gluttony had not passed unnoticed by others, for ever since she first started dancing at the Elysée-Montmartre, Mademoiselle Weber had been known as *La Goulue* (The Greedy One). In a period when women were encased from head to foot in corsets, stays, ground-length skirts and layer upon layer of petticoats, such extrovert exhibitionism was unprecedented. Together with the innumerable drawings, paintings and lithographs she inspired from Lautrec, La Goulue's reputation did as much as anything to establish the myth of that "naughty nineties" for which Paris was to become famous.

"She converses with that desire whose progression she reads among the flaming glances lanced at her," Montorgeuil said later in his review. "She provokes by the display of bare flesh, or at least that which may be divined amid the turbulent swirl of her underclothes as she deliberately permits a glimpse . . . of her naked skin between garter and the first fold of petticoat by lifting her leg." The invitation in such maneuvers, he added, was "brutal, blunt, without feminine grace, almost bestial." And as a climax to "the salacious meanderings of her sullied imagination," in which loins and midriff were used in turn, La Goulue perpetrated "a last audacity when, bending double the better to stress her lewd intention, she insolently flings back her petticoats to make a callypygean display of her behind." Reading the lines today, one wonders just what was supposed to be so sexy about the 1960s.

La Goulue's team mates at the Moulin-Rouge, some

★ The porte d'armes is the step, sketched frequently by Toulouse-Lautrec, in which the dancer performs a high kick and then, catching the ankle at the zenith of its upward travel, holds it there while spinning rapidly on the "point" of the other foot.

of whom came also from the Elysée-Montmartre, were almost as unusual as herself, if somewhat less exaggerated. Their names, nevertheless, were as bizarre as her own, numbering among them *Cri-Cri, La Sauterelle* (The Grasshopper or Locust), *Nini Patte en l'Air* (Nini Foot-in-the-air), *Le Môme Fromage* (Cheese Baby), *Cadudja, Serpolette, Mélinite, Rayon d'Or* (Golden Ray) and *Grille-d'Égout* (which means the grating placed over a drain, sump or soakaway in the street). Of these, Grille-d'Égout was the closest to La Goulue. Despite her unattractive nickname – bestowed on her by the journalist Henri Rochefort because she had two prominent front teeth which showed against the darkness of a mouth that was often open – she was in fact not an unattractive young woman. "She was better spoken and behaved than La Goulue whose coarse boisterousness she seemed to condemn, and her style of dancing was correspondingly different. Where La Goulue was frantic and seemed to go into an orgasmic ecstasy at the climax of the *chahut*, Grille-d'Égout was precise, dignified and almost intellectual. Together they were a sensation."[30]

Nini Patte-en-l'Air was one of the original group lured away from the Elysée by Zidler. Short, wiry and haggard-faced, she was older than the others, dancing with a controlled, electric tension that was almost painful to watch. Nini looked after some of the younger girls, acting as a kind of matron at the hostel where they lived – and where she gave dancing lessons to aspiring teenagers wishing to learn the *chahut* for themselves. Grille-d'Égout gave lessons too, but she taught a "respectable" version of the dance, as befitted a young woman who lived at home with her family. It was she who instructed the tragedienne Réjane in the basics of the *quadrille naturaliste*, Moulin-Rouge style – and the great actress herself who introduced a watered-down version of this at private performances in high society.

Mélinite was a nickname for Jane Avril (*Jeanne la Folle* was another), whom Toulouse-Lautrec made almost as famous as La Goulue through his posters and drawings. A treasure to a present-day psychiatrist, Jane Avril was in every way an opposite – and therefore a complement – to La Goulue. She was a genteel girl, half-French and half-Italian, said to be the daughter, "on the wrong side of the blanket," of a Roman playboy. A pale, thin, languid child with large eyes and red hair, she had run away from home at the age of fifteen to haunt the *bals musettes* of Paris. By the time the Moulin-Rouge opened, she was known in every

Lautrec's Jane Avril – "There is less pleasure in it if you get paid."

caf'conc' and dance hall from the Left Bank's Bal Bullier to the Jardin de Paris in the Champs Elysées. She had also been a part of the original team at the Elysée-Montmartre – but unlike the others, she had always steadfastly refused payment for her performances, "because there is less pleasure in it if you get paid."

For Jane Avril, dancing was a personal and private obsession. She was never happy at the Elysée, which she considered "vulgar and indecent" because "women with a shameless air danced there . . . arm in arm with bookmakers who looked like butchers or worse."

The Moulin-Rouge was much better, she thought – especially when Zidler allowed the orchestra to play on for an extra half hour when the customers had gone, so that the quadrille stars could rehearse and Lautrec could sketch without interruption. The *chahut* itself was nevertheless a trifle indelicate for Jane. She preferred to give improvised solo performances, swaying sinuously to the music of romantic songs in a way that one critic described as "foreshadowing the intricate, curvilinear rhythms of art nouveau." Later, Zidler had the sense to produce her at the Jardin de Paris, where the English poet Arthur Symons, that critic of *The Yellow Book* and authority on *fin-de-siècle* decadence, wrote that "she had about her an air of depraved virginity . . . the more provocative because she played as a prude, with an assumed modesty, décolleté nearly to the waist." She was, Symons enthused, "a creature of cruel moods, cruel passions . . . an absolute passion for her own beauty" – and she was popularly supposed to be a lesbian. It was perhaps partly because of this reputation for perversity that she was the darling not only of *The Yellow Book* aesthetes but also of such fellow "decadents" as Mallarmé, Verlaine, Paul Fort and the humorist Alphonse Allais. There was, after all, no risk of genuine emotional involvement with so remote and unattainable a mistress.

Earthier and less ethereal were some of the other unpaid stars who enlivened the dancing at the Moulin-Rouge, among them Anquetin, the elastic-limbed Gauzy and of course Valentin the Boneless. As may be seen from a number of Lautrec's works, Gauzy and Valentin sometimes joined the girls in the wildly gyrating finale of the quadrille. Like Jane Avril, Valentin was an obsessional dancer. His extraordinary profile with its lantern jaw, hooked nose and tall hat was as familiar to patrons of the Moulin de la Galette and the Elysée as it was to the crowds packing the Moulin-Rouge. To him, though, this ritual end to the evening was not so much a dance as some kind of catharsis, a physical release; the dance was something you shared with one other person. "There is," he said once in a much-quoted remark, "no other dancer than La Goulue – for the waltz, I mean: the quadrille is nothing but a *chahut*!"★

Valentin's angular, explosive figure was seldom seen at the more select halls like the Jardin de Paris – even when Zidler reserved one of his fleet of omnibuses to convey the quadrille stars to the Champs Elysées for a second show after the Moulin-Rouge closed. Valentin preferred to stay in his beloved Montmartre, where

★ It would seem from Valentin le Désossé's usage that the word chahut was a general term, implying any dance that was coarse, earthy and presumably undisciplined, the revived Montmartre quadrille being just one example of it. Although it had been coined fifty years before, and was used by Montorgueil in 1890, the term cancan did not return into general use until the stylized, choreographed version of the quadrille was adopted by the Moulin-Rouge, the Folies, and other music halls in the mid-1890s.

he was a frequent and welcome visitor at Toulouse-Lautrec's table. He was himself from an impeccably bourgeois background. His real name was Renaudin; his brother was a notary – and he was in fact the proprietor of a flourishing wine store in the center of Paris. Nothing is known of the psychological motives underlying his passion for exhibitionist dancing; little more of a short, mysterious and equivocal liaison he had with La Goulue. Had it not been for Lautrec, and *his* passion for capturing movement in line, Valentin le Désossé might have remained for posterity no more than an enigmatic reference in some contemporary newspaper columnist's diary.

It was, nevertheless, Valentin and the *quadrille naturaliste* girls who drew the crowds to Montmartre, undisciplined and amateurish though their high-spirited antics might be. At the height of their fame, however, Zidler and the Ollers signed up a stopgap performer who was to become the most professional of all music hall stars, and whose reputation, unknown to them, was to spread far beyond Montmartre, Paris, or even France.

She was born into a poor family in Paris in 1867, two years after the birth of La Goulue. She managed to acquire an elementary stage training, but her first appearances – at the Bouffes-du-Nord music hall and the Théatre des Nouveautés, when she was twenty – were not a success. Later she sang in Lyon and at the Eldorado in Paris, where she ploughed through the usual *caf' conc'* repertoire, again without arousing much enthusiasm. The year the Moulin-Rouge opened, she was performing a specialty at the Concert Parisien – a comic song called "Miss Valerie," which related the story of an English nursemaid who successfully repelled the advances of her employer's husband. The imitation British accent in which she sang this song went down well with the local audiences, and she was subsequently hired to perform sketches and sing an occasional ballad at the rather staid Eden music hall, at that time located in a warehouse belonging to the Pygmalion department store in the Boulevard Sébastopol.

It was after this contract terminated that Zidler offered her a season at the Moulin-Rouge. She was to sing on the big stage every evening before the dancing started. She made her bow in 1890, a year after the *bal* was inaugurated, and she immediately fired the imagination of Lautrec. Her name was Yvette Guilbert.

CHAPTER FIVE

Music and Marvels in the Air

WHEN FIRST SHE BEGAN singing at the Moulin-Rouge, Yvette Guilbert had not finalized the repertoire which was to make her famous. She was still searching for the kind of material that would permit her to face music hall audiences with a variety of that "realism" which Maupassant and Zola served up to their readers and Bruant to the customers at the Mirliton. It was in fact either at the Mirliton, the Chat Noir or that other *chansonniers'* haunt, the Boîte à Fursy, that she met Léon Xanrof, whose *chansons réalistes* were almost as popular as Bruant's in the 1890s. Xanrof had gained his experience in the wineshops of the faubourgs along the outer boulevards, working-class taverns where anarchists and other revolutionaries had been singing, writing and reciting anti-establishment tirades since the days of Charles X. Such songs as his *"Le Fiacre"* and *"Les Quat'z' Étudiants"* were welcomed by the theorists of the Left as a means of sowing seeds of protest and discontent among the working people in a relatively painless fashion. They were welcomed by Yvette Guilbert as a medium through which she could more fully express the talent she knew was within her. During the summer closing of the Moulin-Rouge, she compiled a program mainly of Xanrof compositions, seasoned with the better numbers from her existing repertoire and including one "realist" song she had written herself: *"La Pocharde,"* in which she mimed the part of a destitute and drunken old woman. Then she went to Belgium, where her new-style act was an immediate and tremendous success. Back in Paris, she returned to the Eden, whose management was dubious of the audience reaction to so bleak and pessimistic an approach. They need not have worried. The new Guilbert was an overnight sensation, and *"La Pocharde"* became the talk of the town. Soon she was back at the Moulin-Rouge – topping the bill.

*"Oh, so tall! Oh, so thin!" –
Toulouse-Lautrec's lithograph
of Yvette Guilbert taking a
curtain call at the Moulin-
Rouge perfectly catches the
appeal of the "very modern
singer" whose performance so
fascinated the critic Jean Lorrain.*

As her reputation blossomed, tempting offers flooded
in from music halls and *café concerts* in the more fashionable parts of Paris, especially after Réné Maizeroy, an
editor and literary critic, had written a laudatory
article on her performance in the sophisticated newspaper *Gil Blas* (whose illustrated supplement already
featured Steinlen drawings and transcriptions of
Bruant's songs). Yvette preferred to remain in Montmartre, but Zidler generously encouraged her to "go
down" to the center; it was, he said, the only way of

97

cementing an international reputation, however frequently *le tout-Paris* might toil up the hill to applaud her as a symbol of the high bohemia now. From then on, her professional life was an unbroken success story.

Her songs won her the acclaim not only of the vast music hall public, but also of that small but brilliant band of literary and artistic figures whose opinions ruled the tastes of Paris's "top people" in the Belle Epoque. Her admirers included the Comédie Française star Sylvain, who would bring students to analyze her gestures and diction, the influential journalists Jean Lorrain and Catulle Mendès, the illustrator Willette, and such eminent writers as Edmond de Goncourt, Zola, Pierre Loti, and Octave Mirbeau. Among the appreciations which have survived her are:

"A great, a very great tragic *actress*, who causes your heart to constrict with anguish" (Edmond de Goncourt); "There is not a trace of the rowdy restlessness and forced 'go' of the English music hall singer about her" (Bernard Shaw); "Intelligence and the art of expression absolutely exceptional. . . . Perhaps the supreme figure, and certainly the most original, of the music hall song" (Jacques Feschotte); "The supremacy

of her art lies in the beautifying of the terrible" (*The Yellow Book*); "Of all the singer-poets of the nineties she performed the greatest services for what must henceforth be considered an integral part of the living culture of that time" (Raymond Rudorff); "More than Bruant – as much perhaps as the Chat Noir itself – Yvette Guilbert, at the end of the nineteenth century, contributed to raise the level of the French popular song. . . . What a terrifying problem for the singers who have to interpret her material!" (Jacques-Charles).

A contemporary article by Jean Lorrain incorporates a description of Yvette Guilbert on stage which reads like a Chéret or Lautrec poster come startlingly to life.★ The "precious" style adopted by Lorrain, a literary dandy and self-confessed homosexual who romanticized the fashionable taking of drugs, explains also why the singer, like Jane Avril, appealed as much to the "decadents" as to the general public.

She is tall – oh, so tall and thin – oh, so thin! Her skin is chalky white and her figure slightly rounded, but she has no bosom to speak of and her chest is quite extraordinarily narrow. She has long – too long – thin arms clad in high black gloves that resemble flimsy streamers, and a bodice that seems to be about to slip from her shoulders. The great originality of this very modern singer lies in her almost rigid immobility, the "English" appearance of her long, thin, overgrown body, and the absence of gesture which contrasts strongly with the almost diabolical rolling of her eyes, and the grimaces and contortions of her bloodless face.

Later in her career, when she had abandoned the *chanson réaliste* for historical ballads which she sang in costume, Yvette Guilbert lost the lean and hungry look which had so fascinated Lorrain. In fact she became quite plump. But even when she was reviving little-known songs of the Renaissance and the Middle Ages, she still retained the long black gloves which had become her personal trademark.†

In the 1890s, however, it was her personalized versions of the "realist" material popularized by the *chansonniers*, the sung poetry of the Parisian "other half," which stirred the literary world and the public alike. Nor was this success restricted to Paris or even France. In 1894 she was treated to a standing ovation at England's Leicester Square Empire, then it was an equally rapturous reception in Germany, and finally,

★ **Curiously, for one so sensitive, Yvette Guilbert never recognized the artistic worth of the Lautrec designs which immortalized her. She much preferred Chéret's posters, perhaps because she was, after all, a little vain. "My God," she would say when her managers commissioned a Lautrec, "what will the little monster do to me this time!"**

† **Her trademark was familiarized throughout the world by the Chéret and Lautrec posters – but in fact Yvette Guilbert first adopted the long black gloves, not as a "gimmick" or piece of stage "business," but simply because she was appalled, coming from a poor home, at the cost of laundering the white gloves then traditionally worn by singers.**

in 1897, she crossed the Atlantic to star at Koster and Bial's music hall in New York. Her success there, and during the nationwide tour that followed, astonished even the critics who had praised her. "Not only were most of her songs in French," one of them wrote in bewilderment; "they were also in an idiom only a sophisticated Parisian could understand. It was wholly due to her finesse in putting them over – the expression, mannerisms, and gestures that made the meaning clear – together with a personality unrivaled in the music halls."

The tour even survived the unwise insistence of Yvette's American manager, Ted Marks, that she include in her act a number of popular "coon" songs, as they were called, and, by special permission of the English star, Vesta Victoria's "Poor John" – perhaps because (in the words of Douglas Gilbert) "she was a tall redhead with beckoning features and a stage personality of ineffable resource: La Guilbert – the incomparable." (Marks recovered some of the lost ground when, in New Orleans, his artist became inconsolably homesick and pined for her mother. She was so unhappy that the misery became contagious and the company almost broke up. Marks and his assistant, John Loeffler, wired frantically to Paris and had Mama record a greeting on a Columbia phonograph cylinder. Then they persuaded Yvette to do the same thing, and the problem solved itself with the subsequent exchange of cylinders.)

Back in France, Yvette Guilbert, by now the biggest name in the business, was able once more to concentrate on the type of song which had made her famous. "My only aim was realism," she wrote in her *Memoirs*. "I tried to do in song what de Maupassant, de Goncourt and Zola had done in fiction." For this, her talents were admirably suited, for she was basically what the French call a *diseuse* (a reciter) rather than a singer, and she was at her greatest performing material which gave free rein to her dramatic gifts. In such numbers the words were more important than the music, and her acting genius, her skill in evoking atmosphere or creating a personality more important than her singing voice. She followed the melodic lines of such compositions, but the performance as a whole was more of a recitation with music than a song.

This is not to say that tragedy was the only component of Yvette Guilbert's stage presence. Like so many great music hall stars, she had a chameleonlike quality allowing her to perform sentimental or even comic songs with equal success. Similarly, although

she was tall and inelegant, she could radiate an air of beauty and an aura of boundless sex appeal. It was for the tragic songs, nevertheless, that she is remembered. These included a handful of Xanrof specialities, her own "*La Pocharde*," an anti-capital punishment dirge entitled "*Ma Tête*," and "*La Soularde*," generally held to be her masterpiece. Written by Jules Jouy, on the suggestion of the singer herself, the lyric pictures one of those decrepit female winos, one of the meths-drinking hags who still reproach our civilization today among the backstreet trashcans of the affluent society. Translated from the Parisian argot, the first two verses of "*La Soularde*" set the scene:

Prostitutes waiting for clients in the Moulin-Rouge garden. The archivists tagged this photo "around 1880," but since the famous Bal didn't open until 1889, and the stucco elephant was acquired from the Universal Exhibition the same year, the date is unlikely to be accurate. The pavilion sheltering the ballet dancers was a later addition still – so the picture is more likely to have been taken in the early 1890s.

> From morning on she's stumbling
> Haggard faced and mumbling
> From street to sidewalk on her own
>   The drunken crone.
> A threadbare shawl next to her skin
> Hat skewered with a rusty pin
> She slurs her muttered monotone
>   The drunken crone.

Even in the French, the lines themselves are of slight poetic worth – but Yvette's special genius, like that of the American blues singer Billie Holiday, was to invest everything she sang with that "terrible beauty" that transcends the material. The song reaches its climax with children and passers-by taunting the human derelict as they pelt her with overripe fruit. In London, *The Yellow Book* found this denouement immensely moving. "At the end," wrote the reviewer, "Yvette Guilbert throws her head back and breaks the final syllable of the refrain *La Soularde* into a cry of two notes. It would scarcely be too much to call this the greatest moment that has ever been brought off in executory art. It takes your breath away."

The description again recalls Billie Holiday – in the antilynching masterpiece, "Strange Fruit," and especially in the line where the black man's body, the "strange fruit hanging from the chestnut tree," is left "for the sun to blacken and the wind to rock." For in Langston Hughes's sung poem the artist also breaks the final syllable to soar up a despairing third, and then down again in a moment of unbearable poignancy.

Although she shared many qualities with other music hall stars, Yvette Guilbert more than any of them touched familiar chords in the lives of her listeners when she sang. It was hardly surprising, therefore, that she preferred the intimacy of a small *boîte* called the Divan Japonais to the impersonal wastes of the big new Moulin-Rouge auditorium when the music hall was inaugurated in 1903. For a long time she doubled both dates, hurrying down from the Place Blanche to the Rue des Martyrs after the show at the Moulin was over. At the Divan, she wrote later, "there was a platform at the back of the hall about four-feet six-inches high, which meant that I dare not lift my arms unless it was absolutely necessary, for then my hands would hit the ceiling – a ceiling to which the heat of the gas footlights rose so fiercely that it was like putting one's head into a suffocating oven!"

In spite of the discomfort, she nevertheless found in these cramped quarters the interrelation between audience and performer so characteristic of early music hall. Here, under the low ceiling, in an atmosphere that other singers could only tolerate for ten minutes at a time, she would sing for an hour on end to a crowded house of up to two hundred painters, writers, sculptors and assorted Parisian night birds – while outside in the dark waited a crowd of fans who had accompanied her from the Moulin-Rouge, might accompany her later to Les Ambassadeurs in the Champs Elysées, and would still follow her cab when

it took her home in the early hours of the morning. She was the best-loved entertainer in France, because to the public she represented the spirit of Montmartre – and Montmartre in the Belle Epoque was the spirit of Paris.

With La Goulue and the quadrille stars plus Yvette Guilbert, the Moulin-Rouge in the nineties had been assured of a head start over all music hall opposition. The place had everything. There was the atmosphere, there was the artistry of the great singer, there was the romantic garden, where on summer nights the strolling crowds could pause between dances to watch conjurors and balancing acts, ventriloquists and jugglers. And then inside, when sufficient space had been cleared and the orchestra had worked up to a crescendo, there was of course the rumbustious *quadrille naturaliste* itself. Sometimes this by-now-traditional finale was referred to as the *quadrille réaliste*. Perhaps this was because of its connection with the songs of Bruant and Guilbert; perhaps it was to distinguish the original, basically amateur version from the regimented, commercialized chorus dance later using the revived name of the cancan.

Aubrey Beardsley's portrait of Madame Réjane, the famous tragedienne. Réjane was taught a "respectable" version of the Moulin-Rouge quadrille by the dancer Grille d'Égout. She then introduced it in the salons and drawing rooms of socialite Paris.

103

LEFT:
Music and marvels were in the air – and among the marvels at "speciality houses" such as the Olympia, on the Boulevard des Italiens, were these Japanese acrobat-jugglers whose expertise unfailingly drew the music hall audiences. The troupe were equally popular in the U.S.A. where this poster advertised their art.

RIGHT:
The cancan quadrille was soon identified with other halls besides the Moulin-Rouge – Parisiana's program cover in the 1890s.

It was nevertheless the cancan – lace petticoats frothing around the daring, dangling, black-stockinged legs of its shrieking girls – which was to become the rage of all Paris and sweep far beyond the confines of music hall itself.

Apart from Zidler's own Jardin de Paris, many other music halls adopted the dance as a traditional finale, notably the Alcazar d'Eté and the new Parisiana in the Boulevard Poisonnière. The concept was particularly welcome at halls such as the Parisiana, and later the Bal Tabarin, which devoted more than half their entire program to the dance. Some of the other attractions emanating from the Moulin-Rouge and its neighbors, however, found less favor with managements outside the brawling Montmartre orbit. Among these was that bizarre physiological specialist calling himself Le Pétomane, from the French verb *péter*, meaning to explode or, colloquially, to break wind or fart – surely the only artist in the whole history of entertainment entitled to call himself truly unique.

According to Yvette Guilbert, a pale, sad-faced man had one day asked to see Zidler and explained to the impresario that he had discovered during a Mediterranean swim near Marseille that he possessed the singular muscular gift of being able to ingest or expel water from his body at will. Experimenting later in the privacy of his home with an enamel bowl, he found that this surprising faculty extended also to air. Furthermore – such was the nature of his gift – he could so regulate and control the expulsion of air that notes of different pitch could be obtained. He had been endowed with what medical specialists later termed an "aspirating anus."

Assiduous practice with this orifice had enabled him to master a repertoire of simple tunes such as might be performed on a bugle (without, he was quick to point out, giving offense to those in his immediate proximity, the air being freshly drawn). It remained only to coopt the third element, fire – he had mastered the technique of extinguishing a candle flame accurately from a distance of several feet – and he was in business.

The coarse vulgarity of late nineteenth-century humor, as broad in Paris as it was in London, was ready-made for this kind of anatomical peculiarity. After an audition before the astonished management, Joseph Pujol (as he was named) was hired to perform at the Moulin-Rouge – "*In* the garden, if you please!" as Dylan Thomas's Mrs. Ogmore-Pritchard would have said. And there, on the small stage within the bowels of the elephant, wearing a sober jacket and pants with a suitable vent, he would go through his act to such delighted laughter from the patrons as could be heard two hundred yards away on the far side of the Place Blanche.

His performance received a great deal of publicity and was well reviewed in the press (the critics' only difficulty being to find words that would describe the act without giving offense to lady readers). The king of the Belgians paid a special visit to Paris to witness the phenomenon. Le Pétomane's billing made much of the fact that he was "the only man to pay no author's royalties." Contemporary records report that he leaned unctuously forward toward his audience each time he refueled his reservoir, turned in profile to blow the tunes, and used the candle-flame routine as a finale. *Ars gratia artis!*

It must not be thought that Montmartre was the sole influence on popular entertainment. The last ten years of the century saw the new music hall established as a way of life as Parisian as the brasserie, as French as hot croissants and coffee, as familiar as the plane trees lining the *grands boulevards*. And Zidler and the Ollers were not the only innovators on the scene. Managements chopped and changed, names altered, programs broadened to include an ever wider selection of talent – but throughout all the complexities of the period the form flourished and strengthened, thrusting its roots deep into the fabric of the society which in certain ways it mirrored.

In October, 1890, Lointier and Demange had opened the present Casino de Paris in the Rue de Clichy – at that time a huge premises, including an oriental garden and a theater, extending all the way to the Rue Blanche. Built on the site of an old skating rink, the "new" Casino had nothing to do with the oversized former *café concert* in the Rue de Lyon. Two years later, the vast Palais Chinois was acquired by Monsieur Paris, former director of the Café du Géant, completely modernized, and reopened as the Ba-ta-clan with Paulus as the star and a long bill of supporting attractions.

The years 1893 and 1894 were significant. In the first place, both Zidler and the Oller brothers widened their interests. Joseph Oller, the inventor of the "*Pari-Mutuel*" (later developed into pari-mutual betting in the United States, tote betting in Britain), had founded the first "boulevard" music hall, Les Fantaisies Oller, back in 1875. Three years later he transformed the hall, which was on the Boulevard des Italiens, into a theater, Les Nouveautés, where he enjoyed a huge success with Feydeau's early farces (at that time, oddly enough, called *vaudevilles*). When the building was pulled down as part of a city redevelopment plan in 1886, he built the Nouveau Cirque in the Rue St.-Honoré. This was provided with a sophisticated (and typically nineteenth-century) plant, which could at the touch of a button metamorphose the orchestra stalls, open a series of sluices, and flood the lower part of the auditorium for aquashows.

Two more years passed and then Oller, as indefatigable as Goubert before him, bought a huge plot of land off the Boulevard des Italiens and erected an extraordinary edifice called Les Montagnes Russes. This rambling novelty, constructed mainly of wood, had been purchased in England and imported in its entirety. It was condemned as a fire risk by the Paris

Préfecture in 1892, and Oller was forced to demolish it. Within twelve months he had built on the same site an entirely new music hall theater which he called the Olympia.

The curtain rose for the first time on April 12, 1893, with La Goulue and the quadrille stars from the Moulin-Rouge (of which Oller was still a director) as the main attraction. Strangely, in view of its later history,★ the early bills at the Olympia were almost exclusively composed of specialty acts, singers only rarely being featured there. Other music halls, keeping closer to the old *café chantant* formula, presented little else but singers. Among these were the intimate Petit-Casino in the Boulevard Montmartre, which was known as a proving ground for new talent, and the Scala on the Boulevard de Strasbourg. Here, under the artistic direction of Brigliano, the brightest stars of the vocal firmament appeared in one glittering program after another. Here were Paulus and Yvette Guilbert again, her clown face pleading from posters all over Paris. Here were the great Max Déarly, unsmiling Claudius with his deadpan delivery, Baldy in his role as the unrepentant old rake, tremulous Moricey and long, tall Morton with his fatalist's phlegm. At the Scala too were some of the newer names: Harry Fragson, inimitable creator of *The Music Hall Shakespeare*, who spoke French when he was with his Belgian father† and good, honest cockney to audiences in London; Paulette Darty, the queen of the waltz; Polaire, all beehive hair and huge eyes, who was one day to rival Yvette Guilbert and who "shook like an infuriated wasp" when she sang.

There was fresh talent at the Concert Parisien as well. After the season which had given La Guilbert her break, the new director, Saint-Yves Corrard, starred Dranem – "the king of the idiots" – in his diminutive hat and yokel shoes. He was followed by another equivalent of the *lion-comique*: the elegant Félix Mayol. This dandyish figure, fastidious of gesture, precise of diction (though still guarding his native Toulonnais accent when he sang), was a cartoonist's joy with his quiff of hair and his inevitable lily-of-the-valley buttonhole. He was to become the model for a whole generation of music hall *boulevardiers*.

Not far to the north, at a music hall called the Cigale in the Boulevard Rochechouart below Montmartre, the comedian Nunès produced a revue titled *La Cigale Ayant Chanté*. This in its small way was a trailblazer, in that it was in fact a series of acts welded together

★ Since the end of World War II, the Olympia has been almost the only major variety theater in Paris to present regular programs starring top pop singers.

† Fragson's promising career had a tragic end. His father, a retired music hall artist, shot him dead in a fit of senile jealousy over a girl. According to contemporary newspaper reports, Fragson had been dining with his friend Bosc, director of the Bal Tabarin, and returned to the apartment he shared with his father to collect his clothes for that evening's performance. The old man refused to open the door. "Don't be an idiot!" Fragson expostulated. "Come on – open up, of I'll be late picking up Paulette" (his current mistress). Fragson Senior shouted that he hated Paulette; she was stealing his son's affection; he would shoot himself. Fragson broke down the door; but in the ensuing struggle his father's loaded gun went off and it was the son who died. A mourning crowd estimated at between one and two hundred thousand are said to have jammed the Place de la Madeleine for the popular star's funeral. And the unfortunate Bosc was beaten up on the mistaken assumption that he was Fragson's father.

to evoke, Montmartre-style, the events of the year. It was followed by *T'y Viens-t-y?* and *Voyons Voir, Oh Venus!*, two comic revues in the so-called "concert music hall" form which were among the first in Paris to use girls just *because* they were girls – and not because they could act or sing or dance.

Both departures were significant. The first because it presaged the modern "theme" revue with a specially written book, the second because it did for France what *The Black Crook* had done for the United States – invited an audience to appreciate the female form for its own sake.

There was at the same time an expensive revue at Les Ambassadeurs in the Champs Elysées which brought together Bruant and Yvette Guilbert with the remarkable jugglers Serverus Scheffer and Cinquevalli. Guilbert's electrifying performance, her superb diction and mastery of an eclectic choice of material, were celebrated in a poem by Arthur Symons which was translated by Verlaine. It was, nevertheless, the title of the show rather than the performances, brilliant though they were, that linked "Les A" to the Cigale and acted as a signpost to the future. It was called *La Revue Déshabillée* – the undressed revue.

Repeating the British syndrome, the music hall in France was undergoing a stylistic dichotomy: on the one hand, stemming more from the dance than the song, the "physical" approach with its implicit exploitation of sex, that was to lead to the voluptuous "spectacular"; on the other, the older tradition with a more cerebral approach which was to work through "intimate" revue and end ultimately in the series of unconnected acts termed "variety."

In 1894 Zidler severed his connection with the Moulin-Rouge, and from that time on – established though it was as an entertainment Mecca – the famous *bal* in the Place Blanche lost a little of its magic. Without Zidler's passionate interest and enthusiasm, without his genius for encouraging artists who worked more for love than money, the place naturally lacked a certain charisma. Under Joseph Oller's direction, it remained highly successful – but a little mechanical, a little commercialized. Oller himself was a naturalized Spaniard. Perhaps his tastes veered more toward the specialties appearing at the new Olympia. At any rate Jane Avril left soon after Zidler to go to the Folies-Bergère. La Goulue handed in her notice a year later,★ and the Moulin-Rouge company became what one critic at the time described as "complacent and unoriginal."

★ La Goulue's fame – due more to Lautrec and Valentin than to her own talent – had gone to her head. She fancied herself a "star," lived in a huge house on the Champs Elysées and drove in her own carriage. Frequently photographed, she was less often employed and, despite her previously huge earnings, by the end of the century she was reduced to becoming a circus performer in a lion's cage.

"A small, spindly girl, with teeth like piano keys" – Mistinguett at the beginning of her career in 1896.

This is not to say that an original talent was unable to blossom there. In 1895 a slender young woman of twenty had made her stage debut in *Madame Sans-Gêne* and Victor Hugo's *Les Misérables*. The actress, whose name was Jeanne Bourgeois, was at once applauded as a comedienne of unusual skills. But her personality was too strong to be confined within the limits of a fictional character invented by someone else; she had things of her own to say and she knew how she wanted to say them – mainly in the role of a raucous underworld gamine. The music hall would provide the opportunity she craved. Deserting the academic theater, she joined the cabaret at the Moulin-Rouge and adopted the stage name of Mistinguett.

109

Marchand, the Folies-Bergère director, acquired the Eldorado in 1896, rapidly turning it into one of the most popular music halls in Paris. Pacra, Dranem and Polaire starred in the first of a series of successful revues there, and the "Eldo" was soon the nursery of a great deal of budding talent. Two years later the Alcazar d'Eté entered the revue field (its sister hall had been transformed into a theater in 1889). And again the old Champs Elysées favorite was pioneering a new trend. For not only did the Alcazar shows now unify their attractions in decorative themes; they were also furnished with a coherent book, much of the material being written by such specialists as Héros, Flers, Gavault, and the poet Raoul Ponchon. For the stars – they included Lise Fleuron, Mathias and Baldy, the eternal sugar daddy – the "homogenizing" effect of the innovation did nothing but good; for the music hall as a whole, it paved the way for the sophisticated, witty and streamlined spectaculars to come.

Among the theater folk who had noted with interest this new trend, and that of the Cigale revues a little earlier, was Alexis Pitron d'Obigny de Ferrières, descendant of a general killed in battle whose name embellishes the Arc de Triomphe. Monsieur d'Obigny de Ferrières – who was known in the business by the simpler name of Paul Derval – had been musing on the viability of the unclad female form as one component of the stage extravaganza ever since he had witnessed the world's first public striptease in Montmartre a short time before.*

If the concept of the undraped lady could be allied to that of the revue with a specially commissioned book, Derval thought, then the music hall should have a success formula on its hands which could spread far beyond Paris and keep everybody rich and happy for ever. The debonaire, six-foot aristocrat had already served an apprenticeship at the Palais-Royal and had toured with the Barret stage company. Shortly afterward, he decided to put his ideas into practice and became artistic director of the Folies-Bergère.

Another man with similar ideas, but a great deal less taste, was the self-styled *chansonnier-poète* Gaston Habrekorn. So far as he was concerned, the wit, the book, the skill and the décor could go out the window, just so long as the sex was left in. After a season at the Ba-ta-clan, this high-class pornbroker took over a small Montmartre *boîte-à-chahut* in the Rue des Martyrs – none other than the old Divan Japonais, those cramped premises, half-music hall, half-cabaret, where Yvette Guilbert had once sung with such zest and enthusiasm.† Here, Habrekorn initiated the suggestive type of show by featuring his own *chansons sensuelles*, and then producing a whole *Revue Sensuelle* ("the programs of which," says Jacques Feschotte with prim reticence, "are curious documents").[31] To put it baldly, smut had sidled on from the wings. A first step had been taken on that downward path which was to lead ultimately to the commercialization of sex without finesse, sex without elegance or imagination – and the trend itself, resulting in the "naughty" nude show, the strip joint, the clip joint, and finally the skin flick and the blue movie, would do as much to kill music hall as the motion picture or television.

But in 1899 that was too far ahead to see. The music hall was booming. Paris, scintillating with talent, was getting ready for the next universal exhibition. Music and marvels were in the air. The British were fighting the Boers in South Africa, Millie de Leon was learning how to take her clothes off in New York, but in France the talk in the cafés centered around the retrial and condemnation and final pardon of Captain Dreyfus. Marconi was experimenting with a machine that could telegraph a song without wires. Men could travel at more than thirty miles an hour in the Marquis de Dion's horseless carriage, and Clément Ader had already raised himself from the earth in a heavier-than-air flying machine. Designers of fireworks were planning breathtaking displays to celebrate the coming of the new century. Best of all, Bruant, the great Aristide Bruant, had at last definitely quit Montmartre and installed himself at the Grand Concert de l'Époque in the Boulevard Beaumarchais.

Since it was a *Belle* Époque, who could doubt that the golden days of French music hall lay ahead?

† After a checkered history as cabaret, fringe theater and nude show, the premises of the Divan Japonais subsequently became Madame Arthur's, the transvestite night club.

A Glance at the Program

BY THE TURN OF THE CENTURY, the music hall in France had developed to the point where it was ready to take the definitive step that would set it apart from its English prototype. The satiric had gradually been displaced by the spectacular; now the review was to be ousted by the revue. Unlike the cabarets of the *chansonniers*, whose performances really were a sardonic review of the social scene (and whose stars, with such notable exceptions as Bruant, Roger Fursy and Salis, rarely impinged on the music hall), the *revue à grand spectacle* featured acts that were closely related to present-day attractions at such halls at the London Palladium, the Olympia in Paris, or the old New York Palace.

For the public, there were advantages and disadvantages in the change. They could now see and hear their favorites in lavish settings, with splendid costumes and imaginative décor, surrounded more and more as time went on with troupes of beautiful girls. The music, and the orchestras playing it, became better and better, tailored to each particular show as it was written. But because of the tremendous financial outlay involved in this kind of production, each one had to run for many months – sometimes even years – before the overheads were amortized.* And this was why the topicality which had spiced the earlier music hall shows had necessarily to be lost. With it went a certain almost amateurish rapport which had previously united audience and performers – the very element which had so attracted the French directors to the music hall in England in the beginning, and which existed still in the cabarets of the *chansonniers*. At the revue proper, the footlights were now definitely a barrier, physical and mental, with the audience firmly installed on the "other" side. Instead of their own world, satiric, angry, or just humorously distorted,

* A typical Paris revue required the design and construction of fifteen sumptuous sets, many of them equipped with expensive stage machinery, and the manufacture of two thousand pairs of custom-made shoes or boots and four hundred costumes, some of which needed fifty pounds of ostrich feathers and sixty yards of costly material.

they were presented with a world of fantasy in which exotic tableaux, ensemble spectacle seasoned with eroticism, and the production as a whole were as important as the stars whose names were in lights outside the theater.

They *were* theaters too. After the construction of the larger halls – Ba-ta-clan, the Casino de Paris, the Scala, the Gaieté and, later, the Moulin-Rouge and the

Speciality acts shared the second part of the program with the stars until World War I. A French historian lists fifty-four different categories of speciality. Judging by this page from an early nineteenth-century gymnastics manual, most of them were taught in school.

113

Empire– programs had established themselves in a familiar formula. The first part was largely devoted to the introduction of new talent. After this came a succession of "name" artists, singers, dancers and specialty acts, with the best spots reserved for the stars (who were usually, though not invariably, singers). Finally, there was a short play or operetta, or even a series of sketches, featuring comedians from the show sometimes allied with big names from opera or the "legitimate" theater. Cécile Sorel, Cornélie, Chaliapine, Yvonne Printemps, even the great Bernhardt herself at one time or another appeared on a music hall stage. Some, like Judic, Paulette Darty, the incomparable Mistinguett, came to stay.

One of the best Sarah Bernhardt stories centers on the tragedienne's performance at a Paris music hall. She had just played a scene from Edmond Rostand's *l'Aiglon* and was returning, exhausted, to her dressing room when someone who had escaped the vigilance of the stage doorkeeper ran down the corridor, seized her hand, and began kissing it. The visitor was a woman of middle age, dressed in deep mourning, layers upon layers of it, enough to make her look like the rail in back of a second-hand clothes stall. As she appeared to know the star, Bernhardt replied with her customary greeting:

"Hello there, my treasure." At the same time, out of the side of her mouth, she hissed at her dresser: "Who is it, for God's sake?"

The dresser shrugged helplessly. "No idea, madame."

Bernhardt escaped to the dressing room, that holy-of-holies to which nobody was admitted without authorization. She began to remove her make-up. The door opened. In the mirror loomed the image of scores of yards of black crepe. "Well, treasure," the actress said, hoping to gain a clue to the unknown's identity, "what's new?"

"Oh, madame, I've had so much trouble . . ."

"Evidently," the divine Sarah sighed, trying to guess from the yardage of crepe how many had died.

"You knew that Papa had gone?"

"He was a splendid man," Bernhardt sympathized, one eye desperately pleading with her dresser: "Who *is* it?"

"And then . . . and then I lost Mama."

A tear rolled down the actress's cheek. "A sweeter woman never lived. Oh, my poor friend!"

"After that it was Cousin Lily . . ."

"Dreadful!"

". . . and now," gulped the unknown tearfully,

"now Grandma's gone!"

"How *terrible!*" Bernhardt said, picking up a pot of cold cream.

"I don't know *what* I'm going to do."

"Neither do I."

"I . . . I can't see any way out. . . . I think I'll kill myself."

A relieved smile irradiated the star's features. "Now that," she said happily, "is an idea!"

Certain music halls, notably the Folies-Bergère before World War I, staged the sketches at the beginning of the evening. And then gradually, as the lavish revue established a formula of its own, these more dramatic sections of the entertainment shortened and disappeared, to be replaced only by two or three very short sketches embraced within the framework of the show itself and played by members of the company assisting one or more of its comic stars.

"Flying trapeze, high wire and ladder acts performed without nets immediately above the heads of unconcerned diners seated in rows" – an engraving executed soon after the London Alhambra was turned into a music hall, complete with proscenium arch, in 1860.

Within this broad formula, however, the variety of talent employed was astonishing. Before Zidler left the Moulin-Rouge, the breathless attractions of Jane Avril and the quadrille stars were varied by a collection of "genuinely nude" *poses plastiques* in the foyer, a three-legged man, waxworks, and – before half the garden was lost to the new music hall auditorium in 1903 – jugglers, acrobats, conjurors, Zelaska the belly dancer and the inimitable Pétomane, all performing on a small roofed stage beside the hollowed-out elephant. The parallels between this kind of entertainment and America's "museum" shows, between the emerging revue formula and that of the early burlesques, is evident.

The Folies-Bergère also planned its attractions along the same lines. In the 1889 edition of *Plaisirs de Paris*, Camille Débans described it as "a theater which is not a theater, a promenade where you may sit down, a spectacle which you are not obliged to watch – with two thousand men all smoking, drinking and joking and seven or eight hundred women all laughing, drinking and smoking, and offering themselves as happily as you could wish. . . . An overture, a polka, is played . . . and then you can watch in succession an indiarubber man, English lady singers, a crazy cyclist, seven acrobats, three clowns, a juggler. . . ."

The attractions at other music halls were equally diverse. Among them, the show business historian Adrian cataloged:

> *Tumblers* (with ladders, tables, chairs, etc.); *Clowns* (White Clowns, Augustes, Contra-Augustes, Musical Eccentrics); *Cyclists* (Single and in Troupes, Unicycles, Cycles on Plinths); *Dancers* (Classic, Ballet, Exotic Ballet, Ballet Fantasy, Soloists, Girls in Duos, Trios, and Troupes); *Trainers* (of Wild Beasts, Elephants, Monkeys, Dogs, Seals, Birds); *Equestriennes* (High-Stepping, Cavalry, Balancing, Bareback Juggling); *Wirewalkers* (Tight and Slack); *Gymnasts* (without props); *Gymnasts* (with props: Fixed Bars, Trapezes, Spheres, Flying Trapezes, Ropes, Rings, Trampolines); *Jugglers* (Classic, Parodist, Plate-Breakers, Foot Jugglers or Antipodeans); *Marionettists* (Glove and Wire); *Skaters*; *Conjurors* and *Illusionists*; *Phenomena* (Physical: Ventriloquists, Limbless Artists, Fish-Men, etc.); *Phenomena* (Mental: Hypnotists, Thought-Transferers, Memory Acts, etc.).

And among the more spine-chilling circus acts

transferred to the music hall before 1900, Adrian listed:

Looping, Double Looping, The Human Comet, The Flying Torpedo, The Infernal Globe, The Wall of Death, The Devil's Wheel, The Death Leap, The Gyroscope, The Human Brake, High Divers [into a stage tank], The Living Smash-Up, and The Neck-Break.

Such eccentricities rely more for their effect on the sense of imminent peril they communicate than on any special skill exercised by the performer. But the true specialty acts in the former list, most of which can be traced back through centuries of fair and marketplace performance, are all in their different ways miracles of control and timing, the end-product of years of painstaking effort. Such artists never stop working. They cannot afford to: in the first place, their lives may literally depend on it; secondly, they are always trying out new acts and different techniques. There has to be a first time for everything, whether it's a gymnast's lift or a back somersault onto a wire one hundred feet above the ground. As recently as the 1950s, when there were still variety "circuits" in England and real variety shows still toured the remaining halls, the stages of those theaters were open to the artists every morning for two or three hours. And every single morning each specialty act on the bill would be there for an hour or more, practicing, practicing, practicing the current act, perfecting what had been worked out already, experimenting with something new – a side of the profession that the public rarely sees.

Opinions vary on the exact relation of such enter-tainment to music hall as a genre. The French critic Legrand–Chabrier, who holds that the variety show deriving from the *café concert* is the only true expression of the medium, would put them in the same category as the spectacular revue itself – there, as it were, on suffrance. Jacques Feschotte, on the other hand, agrees with the famous revue producer Jacques-Charles that the music hall can assimilate and digest anything: it is this very amalgamation, they say, that has created, in the revue, music hall's one truly original contribution to the entertainment scene.

Theorizing apart, there is little doubt of the effective-ness of such performances. Unlike Dr. Johnson's dog walking on its hinder legs (of which the marvel was said to be not that it was done well but that it was done at all), they are applauded because what they do is done so brilliantly. And, as with many matters of skill, it is the simplest things that most impress – and are the most difficult to achieve. The juggler who circulates an egg, a silk scarf, and an empty cigar box has a far harder task than the one who keeps a score of Indian clubs of identical weight spinning through the air. Two of the most intriguing acts in recent decades – each deceptively simple in this way – were Gaston Palmer and the Australian, Rob Murray. Both of them were jugglers; each was a familiar at the London Palladium in the 1950s.

Each used the absolute minimum of props. Palmer's whole act revolved around a tray to which were glued twelve glass tumblers, and in the tumblers rested twelve spoons. All he did was jerk the tray so that the spoons flew up into the air, somersaulted, and then returned each to the same glass. By the time he had finished, the performance – spiced with a couple of sympathy-raising and well-judged near misses – had the audience as much on tenterhooks as a horror film or spy thriller. Twelve spoons, twelve tumblers . . . *all* he did? Just try it with two of each if you think it's easy!

Rob Murray was already juggling eight or a dozen simple balls made of rubber when he walked on stage. The comedy in his act lay in the fact that he apparently hated every minute of it. Scowling and mouthing profanities to himself, he would glare malevolently at the balls as they whirled like a pinwheel between his hands – and then, his animosity centering on one particular ball, he would pluck it from the stream and hurl it pettishly away behind him as the others continued to circulate. The rejected ball, which was of course very skillfully biased, would do a complete circuit of the stage behind Murray's back in a series of eccentric bounces. At the last moment, he would reach behind him without looking, the ball would bounce into his waiting hand, and he would replace it among the others without breaking his rhythm.

The equivalent of these two artists in the golden age of music hall was the Italian Enrico Rastelli, whose dazzling career, celebrated not only by contemporary critics but by academicians and poets as well, was tragically cut short at the age of thirty.* Rastelli's genius (says Feschotte in an enthusiastic passage enlivening *Histoire du Music Hall*) was such that his performance surpassed anything that had been done before him and has never been equaled since. "He was no less extraordinary in his 'frozen' balancing acts," the historian added. "This incomparable artist . . . enriched the memory of all who saw him with perhaps the most splendid sight ever to come out of the music hall or the circus."

* Rastelli was only one of a number of music hall stars of the period whose lives ended while they were still in their prime. The list includes Gaby Deslys, Fabris, Régine Flory, Harry Fragson, Yvonne Georges, and the impresario Oscar Dufrenne, murdered in his office when he was director of the Casino de Paris, the Alcazar and the Concert Mayol in association with Henri Varna.

Famous too, in their day, were the great clowns and eccentrics who transferred successfully from the circus ring to the stage, many of them confusing Adrian's definitions by combining elements of the tumbler, the wirewalker and the acrobat with more purely comic talents. The praises of such men are too seldom sung today; critics, on the rare occasions when they review variety or vaudeville, occupy themselves solely with top-of-the-bill attractions. But most readers must have seen, at one time or another, the archetypal red-nosed figure with baggy trousers, derby hat and wildly flapping umbrella, advancing tremulously along the whole length of the wire – only to take fright when the journey is almost complete and plunge frantically back to the platform which was his starting point. Or the high-wirewalker whose artistry consists in *almost* missing his footing, *almost* plummeting to the ground far below – and then, while the audience's single breath is still stifled in its collective throat, executing a back somersault to land perfectly on the wire (possibly while playing a popular tune on the flute).

Such a man was the French acrobat Germain Aéros, who continued working well into his seventies, punctuating each averted catastrophe with delighted exclamations of "*B'en, mon vieux!*" or "*Quelle aventure!*" Of such, too, was the immortal Grock, who would make a series of entrances playing a succession of violins which grew progressively smaller until the last was hardly bigger than his own big hand, while he shook his head in disbelief and murmured in German the only line he ever uttered on stage: "It's not possible! . . . It's not possible! . . ."

Grock was the sole circus star able to transfer his act direct to the music hall without altering it in any respect. To a greater or lesser degree, all the others were obliged to modify their performances to suit the changed conditions. Circus acts after all are designed for an audience-in-the-round encircling a wide arena with almost unlimited height, while the unilateral viewpoint of the theater audience, added to the limitations of stage area and proscenium height, impose a totally different set of conditions.

Nevertheless, a Beau Colleano in immaculate white tights, a green-wigged Boulicot, a Charles Rivels complete in Chaplin costume, or a performer like Henriette Lefèvre, the queen of that forgotten skill, diabolo, could still be relied on to electrify a music hall audience. In some cases the smaller working area actually heightened the effect of the performance. This was true, for example, in the case of the extraordinary comic juggler Bagessen, who reversed the routine of those artists who keep an impossible number of plates spinning at the tip of a flexible cane. Bagessen built a tottering pyramid of unstable china-ware which the delighted audience *knew* would inevitably end up in fragments on the floor. (Bagessen has a parallel in the contemporary Tommy Cooper, a six-foot four-inch English ex-guardsman purporting to be a magician whose tricks infalliby go wrong – "Hah! . . . Which cup hides the missing coin? . . . Ha-ha! . . . Ha-ha-ha! A child of five could do it!" – pause – "I wish he was here now! . . .")

It remained true more recently in the case of such internationally famed "whirlwind tumblers" as the Hassan Ben Ali Troupe, the Seven Volants, and the Wazzan Troupe. The speed and dexterity and skill of these breathtaking artists, most of whom come from North Africa or the Near East, is immeasurably emphasized by the confines of the stage. The whole lighted rectangle, immediately the curtain rises, appears to be filled with a dizzying multiplicity of figures leaping, bounding, vaulting, handspringing and cartwheeling one over another – and all of them over a second layer of bodies rolling speedily from one side of the stage to the other in the opposite direction.

And it has always been true of those more "classic" acrobats, each of whose feats is heralded by a prolonged roll on the orchestra's drums. The very proximity of a theater audience underlines the superb judgment of a man who somersaults off a springboard to land upright on the shoulders of a companion standing five yards away – and then himself receives with equal aplomb a third who has *double*-somersaulted off the board to land twelve feet above the stage precisely on *his* shoulders.

Some modern "novelty" acts use the audience's awareness of its own position for a sensationalist effect. A favorite trick among trios, where a girl is repeatedly flung and caught between two men, is secretly to substitute a dummy girl dressed in the same clothes. The dummy is then hurled out over the orchestra stalls – to snap back on powerful elastics as the clients scream. In the half century between 1860 and 1910, such legerdemain was played for real: contemporary prints of the Canterbury, the Oxford and other London music halls show flying-trapeze, high-wire and ladder acts performing without nets immediately above the unconcerned heads of diners seated in rows.

Trick cyclists like El Did (who remained balanced

immobile on one wheel at a great height) and Joe Jackson (who was the first to dismantle his machine while he was riding it), escapologists such as Houdini and Steens (who could extricate his head from a real guillotine while the blade was actually falling) are equally at home in the ring or on stage. But some acts are peculiar to the theater: marionettes like Podreca and his Piccoli, for instance, and their present-day counterparts, the Salici Puppets. Ventriloquists and illusionists also require the immediacy of an enclosed audience to demonstrate paradoxically that there is "no trickery" in their deceptions. Maskelyne and Devant, the master illusionists of the years immediately before and after World War I, positively relished the close attention of those they so successfully bamboozled. Advertisements for their magic show at St. George's Hall, Oxford Circus, described the performance as "the Cemetery of Superstition and Imposture," boasting: "All Theories Utterly Exploded . . . Vendors of Bogus Imitations Checkmated." There followed the promise that "*Psycho, the Greatest Dynamic Problem ever submitted for Solution, will be Introduced at Every Performance!*" Maskelyne and Devant offered the sum of $8,000 (£2,000) to any member of their audiences who could come up with "a genuine automaton" capable of reproducing "Psycho's" movements.

Like their Parisian contemporary Ryss, who billed himself as "The Barman of Satan," they closed their stage performance with a multiple delusion involving a selection of different drinks. Ryss used a carafe, Maskelyne and his partner an ordinary 1½-pint tin kettle, but the principle was the same. At the request of members of the audience, the magician would pour out an endless succession of wines, spirits, fruit juices, beverages, all of which were drunk by the people who had "ordered" them, all of which came from the same apparently empty vessel. Tea and coffee presented no difficulty, the hot infusion and the cold milk alternating as often as required. If the gallery became restive, Maskelyne would serve a couple of dozen pints of beer – still from the same 1½-pint kettle, which never left the spectators' sight – and send them up there. Then he would toss the empty kettle into the stalls for the audience to examine – and, of course, it was just an ordinary tin kettle. Magicians, amateur and professional, are still trying to work out how it was done.

Some specialties defy classification. Any list of these oddities compiled over the past fifty years should include Nino, the Wonder Dog; Inaudi, the man who knew the Paris telephone directory by heart; the Italian comedian Fregoli; Gautier with his "Excess Baggage"; and a nameless brown bear about nine feet tall which used to ride solemnly around the stage on a vintage motorcycle.

Nino was a smooth-haired terrier. The curtain rose on an empty stage. Then, from the prompt side, a beach ball about a foot in diameter would slowly roll across behind the footlights, propelled by Nino, who would be standing on top of it and "walking backward" on its revolving surface. The ball would vanish into the O.P. wings – and Nino would reappear at once, footing a ball *two* feet in diameter back to his starting point – only to make a third entrance on a ball that was larger still. No trainer appeared during or after the act, which was performed in a silence broken only by the laughter and applause of the audience. At the end of half a dozen such traverses, the dog would stop what had now become a gigantic sphere many times his own height, spin it round in the center of the stage, jump down, and advance to the footlights on his hind legs to take a solitary bow. Whether or not Dr. Johnson would have approved, audiences always loved it.

Fregoli was what the French call a transformist, in other words a quick-change artist. His specialty was to play all twenty roles himself in a somewhat over-populated sketch – miraculously changing costume, make-up and personality in the couple of seconds it took to exit by one door and reenter by another. Britain's unforgettable Sid Field performed a similar tour de force in the postwar Prince of Wales revue *Piccadilly Hayride*. He played nine characters in a farcical melodrama entitled *The Convict's Return*, alternating Convict, Policeman, Gamekeeper, Rascally Squire and other stock melodrama types in a wild perplexity of exits and entrances while Roberta Huby, the only other artist in the sketch, sat helpless with laughter on stage. But here, of course, the comedy lay in Field's immaculately pretended confusion between the various roles as the plot staggered on.

Gautier's "Excess Baggage" comprised a set of medium-sized suitcases with which he was discovered on stage – and out of which, to his own feigned and the audience's undisguised astonishment, he would produce what appeared to be large ragdolls but were in truth live contortionists incredibly doubled up in that improbable space. The high point of the act, after the contortionists had been berated, scolded and thrown about as limply as real ragdolls in a kind of

In Paris after 1900, specialties gradually became incorporated into the general scheme of a revue, the artists being costumed in keeping with the sets in which they performed. An early photo of Cléo de Mérode in Balinese costume.

eccentric dance, was when he tried to fold the rebellious "dolls" back into the suitcases and close the lids.

In Paris after the turn of the century, the specialties became incorporated into the general scheme of each spectacular revue, the artists being costumed in keeping with the lavish sets and tableaux in front of which they performed. The same thing happened with the dancers, who created special choreography – sometimes with specially commissioned music – in the idiom of the various production numbers in which they appeared. Always an important, indeed an integral element of music hall, the dance nevertheless played a curiously fragmented role in its development. The quadrilles and the cancan, which originally formed a link between performers and audience, were prettified and drilled once the footlights became a barrier separating them. At the same time, directors started to experiment by presenting soloists like Jane Avril and Cléo de Mérode; specialists such as the celebrated gypsy Pastora Imperio and Argentina, who starred at the Olympia; ballerinas of the quality (much later on) of Ludmilla Tcherina and Zizi Jeanmaire; pioneers like Loie Fuller.

Miss Fuller was art nouveau in three dimensions, the

original psychedelic girl. Born and trained in the United States (where she had the enviable reputation of never paying a debt yet never making an enemy), she was the first stage artist to experiment with moving lights as part of the choreography of a dance. Her innovations made use of light sources that were at first gaseous, then electrical, and, finally, photographic. As a dancer she was a forerunner of Isadora Duncan, her style barefoot, free and flowing.

Paris audiences first applauded her whirling arabesques at the Moulin-Rouge, where they saw her as a human flame among special effects of luminous gases, wreathed in incandescent veils. Later, inspiring posters from Chéret, Lautrec and others, she appeared at the Folies and in the Champs Elysées *café concerts*. During the 1900 Universal Exposition, she had a miniature theater to herself in the "Rue de Paris" entertainment section near the Trocadero.

As for the ballet as a whole, whether it was classical, modern, folk or exotic, this was an integral component of the spectacular from the time of its inception. Indeed, many admirable short ballets have been composed especially for the medium. Adagio and acrobatic dancers also have always featured in revue: the performance heightens the atmosphere of the set pieces. Such specialized dances as the cakewalk, the black bottom, the Charleston, and the exotica of Mata Hari and Isadora Duncan herself also found their places alongside the soft-shoe and tap routines of the period. All these forms had – and have – an existence of their own independent of music hall; the one dance concept created by the medium is the leg show chorus line. And this, with its underlying erotic content, only made its appearance gradually – by way of vaudeville out of burlesque, with the help of showmen like Ziegfeld, Cochran, Earl Carroll, White and Charlot.

By 1900 organization had imposed some kind of pattern on the sprawling American entertainment scene. Those spiritual descendants of Tony Pastor, E. F. Albee and B. F. Keith, had already inaugurated their United Booking Office, which was eventually to control four hundred theaters coast to coast and incorporate such show business diversities as the Western Vaudeville Managers' Association and the Orpheum chain, which boasted seventeen houses between Chicago and San Francisco. Even before the First World War, an act "given a route" on the Keith circuit could look forward to anything from forty to eighty weeks straight work.

The circuit's showplace was the New York Palace

at Broadway and 47th Street, which Keith and Albee opened in 1913 after buying out Oscar Hammerstein's Victoria Theater – because the Palace would have broken the "zoning" agreement which they themselves had imposed. But the partners had "made an honest woman" of vaudeville twenty years earlier, when they spent nearly a million dollars on the Colonial in Boston, running special trains to bring the celebrity first-nighters from Washington and New York and (as Albee put it) "clean the air of that tainted variety."

It was Keith and Albee more than anyone who established the schism between "respectable" family vaudeville and burlesque, that sleazy stag refuge whose hallmark was rhythm allied to the risqué. The prudishness of what performers termed "the Sunday School circuit" was said to have derived from Keith's wife, who would tolerate no profanity, no suggestiveness, no sexual allusions of any kind, no off-color "business," and very little slang. The holier-than-thou attitude nevertheless came strangely from a partnership which had originally been rooted on both sides in trickery and deception. Keith and Albee each rose from a circus background: Albee had been a tout selling tickets at inflated prices to mugs before they got to the show – on the grounds that it would save them time waiting in line when they arrived; Keith had been a "grifter" – a concession-holder with the right to con hicks into buying quack remedies and fake do-it-yourself medical equipment. Their first joint big killing was a pirated production of Gilbert and Sullivan (not copyrighted in the United States at that time) with which they were able to undercut seat prices for the "official" version by 400 percent.

Thereafter, "they made of entertainment a specialized, regimented industry; they were products of their time – in organization and development for financial gain this pair was to vaudeville what Frick and Carnegie were to steel, the elder Rockefeller to oil, the elder Morgan to banking."[32] Even at the height of their success, both were traditionally tight-fisted, though Albee was always prepared to spend money to make money.* This did not, however, extend to exaggerated salaries for his performers, and he lost a number of headliners through his refusal to pay the going rate. One manager who fancied himself as a tough negotiator emerged from an Albee-Keith conference and exclaimed: "I'd take on either of those birds alone – but God forbid I should sit between them! They act like conjurors: I came out with my eyeteeth, but they got my watch and my shirt and my pants!"

* Albee laid out $5 million for the twenty-one story Cleveland Palace, which opened in November, 1922, with seating for 3,680. Paintings by Corot, Lely, Bougereau, van Marcke and others hung in the marble lobby, which was floored with a rug said to be the largest single piece of weaving in the world. Backstage conditions were like a luxury hotel, with a handsome greenroom, individual boudoir-style dressing tables for each chorus girl, and showers for all, including the stage doorkeeper, usherettes and porters. There was even a separate chamber of special design for animal performers. Albee said the theater had been erected as a memorial to his "lifelong friend and associate," Keith, who had recently died. But by that time vaudeville was dying too, and the investment was never recovered.

There were, of course, advantages to this clean-up-and-rationalize campaign. Bouncers, private cops patrolling, and even more the bullying attitude of Keith, Albee and their managers, succeeded in suppressing those gallery thugs who came purposely in many cities to break up the show. After that there was no smoking in U.B.O. theaters, hats and caps had to be removed, whistling was forbidden, and any patron who spat on the floor, stamped or crunched peanuts was ejected.

Apart from this, the actual conditions of working were greatly improved. There might be restrictive aspects, but, once vaudeville was put on a business footing, a stage became at once more effective and more agreeable. Away went the suffocating gaslights, lit by an alcohol torch on a long pole; away went the hissing flames sputtering against fragments of calcium to produce the "lime" lights in the center of the balcony; away went the gaudy make-up and crude costumes the garish gaslight demanded. With proper equipment, electrical lighting, and money available to smarten the show, acts could afford to splash-out on their own gear instead of relying on the property man at each separate theater for everything from "breakaway" furniture to seltzer siphons, from slapsticks to lycopodium torches.★

Once efficiency was allied to initiative, it was hardly surprising that vaudeville, already oriented toward dance acts, should lift the chorus line from the sleazy burlesque house and transform it into the regimented, high-kicking formation that was finally exported from the United States, seasoned with a spice of elegance from London's Gaiety Girls, to the flourishing music halls of Paris.

Yet the French revue, however attractive *Les Girls*, however splendid the specialties, relied for its impact on the star holding the show together. And that star, in the early days, was almost always a singer. The entire production would be designed as a setting in which this particular jewel could glitter. Links were largely dispensed with, and the high point of the evening was the top-of-the-bill spot at the end of the first or the beginning of the second part of the program when the star performed his or her *tour de chant*.

A *tour de chant* (which is really just in-group jargon for the bill-topper's spot, the star turn) required the solo artist to fill the stage for eight, ten or twelve numbers. To hold the traditionally critical Parisian public, he or she would need to combine the gifts of singer, actor, comedian, mime and even dancer or

★ Lycopodium was a herbal powder which, when blown through a glass tube at an alcohol torch, produced an instantaneous, brilliant flash about four feet long. It was used with "quick match" – a witches' brew of powdered sugar and potash which flamed immediately if touched with a rod tipped by cotton soaked in sulfuric acid. Both devices were used in military sketches, for stage "fires" and "explosions," as a means of frightening clowns, and by fire-eaters making a sensational entrance. They were also handy for the revels of gnomes in spectaculars, according to a contemporary manual.

impressionist, peopling the set with diverse personalities and often presenting a selection of numbers so varied as to form a miniature show-within-the-show.

The qualities required for success in this arduous role as *meneur* or *menuese de revue*,[33] as the stars were called, have been listed by Jacques Feschotte as, first the perfection of diction. "The music hall public wants to hear what it is being told . . . it is more important than the quality of the voice and as important as the interpretation (which in any case naturally depends on the diction). This is the main reason why artists cradled in the music hall so often succeed in the legitimate theater, and even rise there to the top of the tree – while it never seems to happen the other way around. Next to the quality of diction, the other major elements required are the art of the actor, a sense of rhythm, and stage presence."[34] To which could be added that indispensable attribute of the star in any medium: charisma.

Within that broad formula there was room for singers basically of many different kinds. These too have been listed – French music hall critics are very fond of cataloging – and the categories include: romantic singers, "big voice" singers, comic singers (rustics, peasants, drunks, tramps, old rakes, etc.), folk and ballad singers, eccentrics, reciters and imitators, and singers of the *chanson réaliste*. Practically any kind of singer, in fact, except the modern pop or rock artist, who would have been ruled out on grounds of diction alone.

Three names stand out above all others as *meneuses de revue*: Yvette Guilbert, Josephine Baker, and Mistinguett. Below these empresses of the music hall, the minor royalty includes Emilienne d'Alençon, Jane Aubert, Louise Balthy, Gaby Deslys, Fréhel, Anna Judic, Suzanne Lagier, Nina Myral, Polaire, Anna Thibaud and, of course, much later, Edith Piaf.

Insofar as they acted as stage partners, the consorts of these great ladies of the music hall included Maurice Chevalier, Fernandel, Max Déarly, the American dancer Harry Pilcer, and such future movie stars as Raimu and Jean Gabin. Of these, only Chevalier and, to a lesser extent, Fernandel were capable of holding a revue together on their own – for it was not sufficient merely to be a great artist per se; it was necessary also to possess a certain team spirit coupled with a very particular personality offstage as well as on. The great *meneurs*, as in England and the United States, were comics more often than singers or dancers – although the formula naturally required of them an act in the

PHOTO: LIPNITZKI-VIOLLET

ABOVE:
The comedian Dranem – "one of that sacred band of music hall grotesques who were also clowns of genius." Phonograph cylinders of the star singing show him as an artist of infinitely flexible technique, punctuating his act with quickfire comments and bursts of infectious laughter at his own lunacy. Offstage (as this photo demonstrates) he was, like so many great comics, a serious and thoughtful man.

OPPOSITE:
Contrasting programs from an English music-hall and its American equivalent. To be noted: the appearance of the Americans Blanche Ring and and Collins and Hart on the British bill; the fact that Marie Lloyd's star spot was soon after the intermission; the inclusion of burlesques in the original sense of the term.

form of a *tour de chant*, however rudimentary or nominal the musical element might be. The big names here were Claudius, Dranem, Fragson, Georgius, Félix Mayol, Pacra, Paulus, Polin and Vilbert.

Not all of them were of the same "weight" when it came to filling a theater. Jacques-Charles recalls a season at the turn of the century when "Dranem was the big star of the day. The smart public flocked to see him at the Eldorado, where his single presence was enough to bring out the house-full notices, while across the road at the Scala, the director . . . was forced to hire Polin, Fragson, Maurel, Max Déarly, Sulbac, Claudius, Moricey and Polaire to compete with Dranem on his own."[35]

Dranem was one of that sacred band of music hall grotesques (it will be recalled that he was billed as "the King of the Idiots"), which includes Red Skelton, Jerry Lewis, early Danny Kaye, Herb Williams, Frank Tinney and perhaps even Britain's Norman Wisdom when he was a solo act trying to play a recalcitrant Sousaphone on ice. Dranem was also a member of that more exclusive group, the clowns of genius. Such rare talents as those of Jacques Tati, Buster Keaton, W. C. Fields, Jack Benny, Frankie Howerd and Sid Field rely entirely for their effect on the persona of the artist: without his indefinable brilliance to illuminate it, the material in script form would seem slight. Dazzling professionals like Bob Hope, the Marx Brothers, Mort Sahl, Max Miller, Arthur Haynes, Tommy Handley, and Morecambe and Wise are in a different category: their technique is inseparable from good material, not necessarily created by themselves. In a third category are such teams as Olson and Johnson, the Goons, Rowan and Martin, and *Monty Python's Flying Circus*, where the material is all and the different roles could be filled by any competent clown.

A competent clown – but not necessarily a comic *actor*. The English theater critic John Barber draws a sharp distinction between the latter and the comedian proper. The actor, he points out in a perceptive survey headlined *Playing The Fool*,[36] remains essentially that: an impersonator of other people. But "a comedian goes to work in the opposite way. He sets out to represent only one character. The delight of the great comic for us is that he is always the same." Barber cites as an example Frankie Howerd, "who has built up a public persona by devising the character pragmatically, in front of many audiences, keeping and developing those aspects that proved amusing, jettisoning the rest." And he adds: "A great comic is the result

✤ PROGRAMME. ✤

Monday, January 11th, 1904, & Every Evening.

Reduced Prices to Saturday Matinees
Fauteuils 3s.   Other Seats 2s., 1s., and 6d.

1 Overture ... "The Gladiators" ... *Fucik*
2 Mr. Herbert Willison ... Vocalist
3 Miss Maggie Carr Banjoist and Comedienne
4 Mr. Tom Leamore ... ... Comedian
5 The Excelsior Quartette
6 The Bensons ... ... Musical Comedians
7 Mr. T. E. Dunville ... ... Comedian
8 Miss Ray Wallace ... ... Mimic
9 Collins & Hart ... The Tramp Hunters
10 Miss Vesta Victoria ... Comedienne
11 Mr. Gus Elen Coster & Cockney Comedian
12 Miss Blanche Ring American Comedienne
13   "THE FOLLIES"
In a Selection from their Celebrated Pierrot Entertainment—
1 Opening Chorus   2 A Coup'e of Coons   3 Cat Quartette
4 Burlesque of (a) A French Mimodrame.
           (b) An English Musical Comedy.
           (c) A German Wagnerian Opera.
Written and Composed by H. G. PELISSIER.
Misses Marjorie Napier, Lucy Webling and Ethel Allandale.
Messrs. Norman A. Blumé, Dan Everard and H. G. Pelissier.

14 Mr. Hamilton Hill ... In a New Song,
                              "GOOD LUCK, JAPAN"
15 Miss Marie Lloyd Queen of Comediennes
16 Selection ... "Czardas" (No. 1) ... *Michiels*
17 Mr. A. Bo Kon ... Continental Juggler
18 Mr. Joe O'Gorman ... Irish Raconteur
19 Mrs. Brown Potter will recite her famous
    Fiscal Poem, "THE PLEDGE OF A BRITISHER."
20 Mr. Will Evans In Sketch, "YACHTING"
21 Sisters Dacre ... Duettists and Dancers

Musical Director   ...   MAURICE JACOBI

The above Programme is subject to alteration, and the Management disclaim responsibility for the unavoidable absence of any Artiste announced to appear.
RONISCH Grand Piano used on stage supplied by Messrs.
METZLER, 41 & 43, Great Marlboro' Street, W.

SPECIAL NOTICE.—To meet the requirements of the London County Council—The Public can leave the premises at the end of the performance by all exits and entrances ; all doors, gangways and passages must be kept clear.

The fire-proof screen to the proscenium opening will be lowered at least once during every performance to ensure its being in proper working order.

MATINEE EVERY SATURDAY AT 2.15.

Manager ... ... PHILIP YORKE
Acting Manager ... ... JAMES HOWELL

EAGLE THEATRE
Junction Broadway, Sixth Avenue and 33rd Street.
PROPRIETOR AND MANAGER   MR. JOSH HART

Production of an Entirely New
Fairy Musical Extravaganza
By the World-Renowned Queen of Burlesque,
MISS LYDIA
THOMPSON
AND HER
MAMMOTH BURLESQUE COMP'Y
Comprising an Ensemble exceeding 60 Artists. INCREASED ORCHESTRA and POWERFUL CHORUS.
Musical Director   Mr. Michael Connolly

WEDNESDAY EVENING, NOV. 21st, 1877
Every Night Until Further Notice.
SATURDAY MATINEES!
And on Thursday, November 20th.
☞ A Special Thanksgiving Matinee
Will be presented in Two Acts and Five Scenes, a New Fairy Musical Extravaganza, by H B Farnie, after Clairville and Gastineau, entitled

PIFF-PAFF!
OR, THE MAGIC ARMORY!

Scenery by Mr GRAHAM. Machinery by WILKIE WALDRON. Costumes Designed by Miss LYDIA THOMPSON, and executed by Mrs. WILSON

Music Arranged by   Mr. MICHAEL CONNOLLY
Stage Manager   Mr. WILLIAM EDOUIN

CHARACTERS:

KING GRAMERCIE XXXVII	Importance Personified	Mr. FRED MARSHALL
GATTIVO	his Generalissimo	Mr. W H LEIGH
SIR RATCLIFFE		Mr. THEO BONNER
SIR HAYNE	the Army Champions	Mr. W H HARPER
SIR DE BROADWAY		Mr. W H ANDREW
SIR DE BOWERY		Mr. J D. SMITH
OLDEST INHABITANT		Mr. HARRY HARRAWAY
CHERUB		Mr. WILLIE EDOUIN
HAUT VOL	Knights of Prince Diamond	Miss MARIE WILLIAMS
HOOP LA	Chief Verderer	Miss EMILY DUNCAN
BAM BAM	Court Messenger	Miss ELLA CHAPMAN
	A M E S.	
PRINCE GLAMOUR	Heir Apparent of Diamonds	Miss LYDIA THOMPSON
QUEEN POLLYBONNE	Gramercie's Second Wife	Miss ALICE ATHERTON
PINNETTE		Miss LINA MERVILLE
MIMILITY	The Princesses her Daughters	Miss KATE EVERISSON
FANFAIT AMOUR		Miss IDA LEE
JACUMDE	Pet Page	Miss ADA NEWVILLE
HORTENSE	a Quakeress	Miss MARION ELMORE

Misses IDA LEE, ANNIE DRAON, CLARA GREY, LAVINIA HOGAN, MISS LYSTON, MISS M LIND, CALLA PEARSON, BASSIE TEMPLE, SMITH, CALDWELL, M. HOLDING, SWAN, HOWE, ORRISTER, FOSTER, CLARK, BOYD, LANE &c.

ACT I.
SCENE 1.—The Old Castle at Gramercie
SCENE 2.—Refectory of Castle Gramercie
ACT II.
SCENE 1.—Vaults of the Magic Armory
SCENE 2.---Ivy Nooks.
SCENE 3.—The Royal Bleaching Grounds

LYDIA THOMPSON *1836?-1908*

ON SEPT. 28, 1868 A GREAT SENSATION WAS CAUSED IN NEW YORK BY THE APPEARANCE AT WOOD'S MUSEUM OF LYDIA THOMPSON AND HER "BRITISH BLONDES" IN "IXION". SHE WAS A CHARMING AND VERSATILE ACTRESS FOR WHOM THE YOUNGER BURKE HAD ALREADY WRITTEN A PLAY. FOR MANY YEARS SHE TOURED THIS COUNTRY AND HAS BECOME A LEGEND. SHE IS SHOWN IN THIS PICTURE AS ROBINSON CRUSOE, ONE OF HER MOST POPULAR PARTS.

of years of intensive public work on one character. It has been noted before that actors always talk of playing, and comedians of working. . . ."

The music hall does not, of course, have a corner in great comics. Many, like Herb Williams, started in vaudeville and stayed there all their lives. Williams was a pianist who accompanied the acts on a small Ohio circuit too poor to afford an orchestra. He improved every turn for which he played by improvising cadenzas, interpolating suitable themes and inventing trills and runs to build up the performance. Then he developed his own routine and became the most hilarious "nut piano" specialist in vaudeville. Douglas Gilbert described the act thus: "He had trouble with the piano stool, which kept sinking until he could scarcely reach the keyboard – adjusted, it would raise him almost above the piano. Certain keys produced clacks, gong beats, and plunks; trying to avoid them got him into more trouble – fearsome faces would arise and objects appear from the piano's insides. At the finish of a long and difficult cadenza, a hand reached out and smacked him on the head. Finishing his piece in spite of handicaps, he drew a glass of beer from a tap on the side of the piano, and went into another number."

Some of the great pre-World War I comedians pioneered the near-surrealist approach adopted half a century later by the Danny Kayes and the Lennie Bruces. Fred Allen, who was a star in vaudeville long before he was "created" by the radio show, was a master of this improvisory technique. Sometimes he would break off slap in the middle of a routine, sit flat on the stage by the footlights, and read his press notices aloud to the orchestra leader. Much later, "Professor" Irwin Corey would deliberately start his act with a "dead" microphone. Loping on stage in a rusty black, oversized dress suit, he would mime a ferocious harangue in total silence, complete with grimaces, sweeping gestures and frequent references to notes. When – after what seemed an age – the uncooperative loudspeakers boomed to life, the first word the audience heard was a shouted: "*However . . . !*"

Turn-of-the-century audiences in the United States were especially fond of "sight acts" or "bone crushers," some of which could be incorporated as specialties into a revue – although this did not become a custom in the French music hall until after 1910. Among the most famous of these were Collins and Hart, Rice and Prevost, and Hickey and Nelson. Most of these teams worked up a succession of pratfalls, acrobatics, and

A genius for the right thing at the right time? This slightly "spicy" studio study – labeled "Gaby Deslys in her dressing room" – shows that even the stars contributed to the popular image of an Ooo-la-la! Paris derived from the "Naughty Nineties."

gymnastic excesses into a continuous routine that had the customers rolling. The male half of the team was usually the kind of guy who got everything wrong – and the more the girl tried to help him, the worse it got.

Bill Hickey, for example, wore shoes that were so big that, every time he leaned down to pick up a scrap of paper from the floor, the approaching sole fanned it out of his reach. If he was shifting a chair from one side of a table to the other, one of the chair legs would become entangled in a leg of his pants. Trying to free it, he would contrive to get both his own legs into one of his pants' legs. And then, discovering the empty pants' leg, like Buster Keaton in the movie *Limelight*, he would milk the audience for laughs, searching desperately everywhere for his own "missing" leg.

The finale of the act was typical. A contemporary description (early Douglas Gilbert again) sets the scene with Hickey sitting on a chair placed on a table, holding a hat as a target for Sadie Nelson's high kicks.

She did several good kicks. Then, as she was about to do a hitch and kick, Hickey leaned over to look into the hat; the kick jammed it over his head and face and Hickey fell from the chair, landing on the back of his neck. Unable to see, he scrambled under the table, attempted to rise, and upset chair, table and himself. After Sadie pried him out of the hat, he put a barrel on the table, the chair on the barrel, and managed to climb into the chair and hold out the hat. At this point something in the gallery would interest him and he'd lose balance and do a shoulder fall to the stage. Then, deciding to do some kicking himself, he'd get Sadie to hold out the hat. With a run, jump, and a kick with both feet he'd turn completely and land in a split on the floor. Intensely angry, he set out to kick the hat to pieces, but Sadie had surreptitiously placed a brick under it. Measuring his distance carefully and making elaborate preparations, Hickey finally kicked the hat. It exploded with a loud report, throwing him into the air and landing him in a headspin. Exit.

Such catalogs of disaster do not happen by mistake. As in the clown routines and specialties described earlier, every part of each move has been worked on and perfected and rehearsed a hundred times – the "sight acts" with their limbs as the stand-up comic with his voice; the dancers with their arabesques and pirouettes as the trainer with his dog. But there still has to be a first time, even for getting your head out from under a falling guillotine.

It was just this kind of daring added to perfectionism, this genius for the right thing at the right time, on the part of a great number of dedicated people, that brought the music hall to its full glory in France in the early years of this century.

CHAPTER SIX

Chorines and Courtesans

THE TRANSITION TO spectacular revue in Paris did not happen overnight. In 1899 and 1900, it was "the *café concerts* alone which presented revues (the first revue at the Folies-Bergère dates from 1908)."[37] Most of the better-known music halls at that time were offering a program very similar to those produced by provincial English variety theaters before World War II: a kind of music hall stock or repertory, with a permanent company changing the whole show each week or two. This is why those period postcards showing the stars of the time, so popular as tourist souvenirs on the riverside stalls along the banks of the Seine today, always carry the name of a theater printed below that of the artist: the job was semipermanent and it was worth the management's while to have throwaway pinups printed.

Basically the programs were still a series of *tours de chant*, seasoned with specialties and followed by a comic playlet, the whole in some cases still being linked together with specially written material. Comparison with the standard American museum show or burlesque is inescapable. But once more the parallel is misleading. The *form* of the entertainment might have been similar; its content was not. Turn-of-the-century burlesque shows were described by Fred McCloy, press agent for the Columbia Amusement Company, as:

> ...a conglomeration of filthy dialogue, libidinous scenes and licentious songs and dances with cheap, tawdry, garish and scant scenery and costumes ... in or near the slum spots in the larger cities ... dirty and unkempt, dismally lighted, and with no attempt at ventilation. They were allowed to exist without police interference along with the bawdy houses that infested the neighborhoods.

Variety stock companies staffed most of the better-known Paris music halls at the turn of the century, and managements encouraged the sale of postcards "plugging" their artists. This one – showing the ex-opera star Judic costumed as a White Auguste when she was part of the team at the Théatre des Variétés – was posted at St. Elix, in the Garonne, in 1905.

VARIETES

JUDIC   M.J.S.

No woman ever crossed the thresholds of their doors, and male patronage was confined to shameless degenerates and to that other species of degenerate that sneaked in with concealed faces. This describes 90 percent of the burlesque business up to about 1900.

On the American entertainment scene, in fact, variety – as one commentator put it – transformed itself into vaudeville and opted for talent; burlesque continued the way it was going and opted for dirt. By now the mainstay of the burlesque show, the attraction to which all the other acts served merely as appetizers, was the suggestive dance which became known as the hootchie-kootchie. Sometimes its exponents were euphemistically billed as oriental dancers, exotic interpreters, shimmy specialists or tassel dancers; but the effect they produced was always the same. Whatever it said on the program, the enthusiasts in the auditorium knew that they would see a succession of "bumps" and "grinds" which in effect amounted to a public representation of the sex act.

The hootchie-kootchie, or, as it later became known, the cooch, was supposed to have been introduced at the St. Louis Exposition in 1904 by a nautch dancer billed as "Little Egypt." ("A relatively normal routine of gyrations of the torso. 'Bumps' were added to this; also the spinning of the breasts and the rump."[38]) In fact the burlesque queen Millie de Leon had already been performing a similar act for some time.

A writer in the Philadelphia *North American* reported that de Leon was "unspeakably frank" in the way she made up to men in the audience. As for the dance itself, he wrote:

> Slowly, in a manner hardly noticeable even through the transparent net which constituted the middle portion of her gown, the muscles of her body took on a wavelike motion. The undulations increased in rapidity. A purely muscular side to side movement, generally deemed the peculiar gift of horses, complicated the pattern and introduced a chaotic activity that probably lasted five minutes. . . . From knee to neck she was convulsive. Every muscle became eloquent of primitive emotion. Standing suddenly erect, with a deft movement she revealed her nude right leg from knee almost to waist. A strut to the right, a long stride back, and the abdominal "dance" was resumed. . . . Streaked and sweaty, her face took on the aspect of epilepsy. She bit her lips, rolled her eyes, pulled fiercely at great handfuls of her black, curly hair. Indescribable noises and loud suggestions mingled in the hot breath of the audience. Men in the orchestra rose with shouts. A woman – one of six present – hissed. Laughter became uproarious. And then, sensing her climax, Millie de Leon, gave a little cry that was more a yelp, and ceased.

Burlesque, in short, was, to quote one columnist, "concocting its shows purely out of the physical differences in human gender." Vaudeville was aiming a little higher. Room could be made for a Cornélie, a Bernhardt, a Lillie Langtry or a Lillian Russell★ – whose variety appeal lay more in the observance than

★ Lillie Langtry's sole claim to headliner status lay in the fact that she was known to be the mistress of King Edward VII; Lillian Russell's in the much quoted observation that she regarded life as a confection – and life made haste to return the compliment. A jewel in a satin setting, Miss Russell's most generous vaudeville critic could say no more than that "she sang all right and looked nice." As for Langtry, she was "England's loveliest woman and its most awful actress."

Lillian Russell – her appeal lay more in the observance than in the act.

in the act – but the majority of the performers, like their English music hall counterparts, were hard-working specialists of particular talent. Such differences as there were revolved more around the format of the show than the composition or quality of the acts. The reasons for this were partly geographical. The "wheels" and circuits of American vaudeville (and burlesque too) were vast enough to permit far longer tours than could be envisaged by a British manager. In fact, a favorite show business story concerns a blackface comedy musical act, Bryant and Saville, who met and became friendly with the comedian Jack Murphy while playing the same theater in Philadelphia in 1878. Yet, such were the vicissitudes of booking, although they toured ahead of or behind each other constantly for thirty-three years, they didn't in fact meet up again on the same bill until 1911.

British bills tended as a result to stay longer in the same place, with a smaller number of performers playing a greater variety of roles. An American vaudeville program of unrelated acts could bring together as many as thirty-five specialties in one week, whereas English music hall artists, with more time together to work out routines, could get by with as few as ten or fifteen. And the balance in the United States tipped more toward the dance than in England – a circumstance which was to have a profound influence later in France. At the turn of the century, there might be six or even twelve song and dance acts on a single American bill. But there was such a variety of these, due to the immensely varied pattern of immigration, that they scarcely conflicted one with another.

Bookers and agents listed dancers as: Dutch, Irish, Slav, Blackface, Whiteface, Neat, Rough, Plantation, Acrobatic, Rival and Clog. The latter were further subdivided into Lancashire, American, Hornpipe, Trick, Pedestal and Statue. An American clog dancer named Queen caused a sensation when he toured the English music halls at the end of the nineteenth century. "They found his triples, rolls, and nerve steps uncanny, refused to believe he accomplished them unaided by tricks, and caused him no end of embarrassment by demanding to see his shoes. Queen stopped all that by making his entrance in slippers and passing around his shoes for the audience to examine, as proof that he used no clappers or other Yankee gadgets. When the shoes were returned, he put them on in full view of the audience and went into his act."[39]

The programs presented by music halls in Paris relied more on team activity than those in London or the United States. A stock variety company obliged, as they were, to rehearse and perfect an entirely fresh revue each week while the current one was still being played, demanded a high degree of professionalism on the part of performers, stage hands, musicians, writers and director – and the season during which this activity was required could be for many months. Often enough, changes had to be made more frequently than once a week, for the Parisian public was notoriously hard to please, especially in the case of the playlets or sketches – the *petits vaudevilles* which closed (and sometimes opened) the show. One of these which was booed or whistled off the stage at its first performance was immediately replaced. The writer of a *petit vaudeville*

In French music halls as in English, the part of the audience most difficult to please was the crowd in what would now be called the gallery – the poulailler *or "hen roost" at the back of the house. This painting by J. E. Harris, exhibited at the Paris Salon of 1897, with its laughing, whistling regulars, its gas lighting and fans and seltzer siphons, recaptures the atmosphere at the Eldorado, heavy with "the thick fog of cigarette smoke swirling against the ceiling, the sauve smell of mandarin oranges, and beads of moisture pearling the walls."*

which played the whole week had good cause to congratulate himself.

As was the case in the English music hall, the customers in the cheapest seats were the hardest to please. This was particularly true of the "neighborhood" *café concerts* and halls strung out along the northern sector of Paris from Montmartre to the Place de la Bastille. Plusher theaters such as the Folies, the Moulin-Rouge, the Olympia and the Casino de Paris catered – like the Champs Elysées *caf' conc's* – to an audience that was cosmopolitan or international. But the artists at these local houses were playing to a crowd drawn essentially from the poorer citizens in their own district. And, money being scarce, they wanted good value when they spent it.

The jokes therefore had to be at the right level. Allusions must be topical, preferably local, and not too highbrow or literary. Songs and sketches must be geared to the tastes – and the mores – of the audience.★ Above all, the performers had to make themselves heard, and heard clearly in the *poulailler*, the upper gallery at the back of the house.[40]

The crooner, or "singer of charm," did not exist: the Charles Trenets, the Tino Rossis, the Jack Smiths and the Jean Sablons had to wait for the invention of the stage microphone before they could make their bow. At the turn of the century, even the love songs had to be belted out in a voice that could be understood distinctly at the back of the gallery – "that old-time paradise (Francis Carco wrote a year or two later) whose luxury recalls the waiting rooms of provincial stations and government offices . . . with the heat of the gas lighting, the thick fog of cigarette smoke swirling against the ceiling, the suave smell of mandarin oranges, and beads of moisture pearling the walls."

When an act displeased the *poulailler* – that was the one time that French music hall and American burlesque found themselves on common ground: the field of raucous laughter, ironic applause, the catcall and jeering whistle, scabrous repartee between actor and audience, and empty bottles rolling down the aisles.

In France, as in the United States, favorite acts were categorized. There were therefore many different classes of song in Paris, and the artists at that time tended each to concentrate on one particular genre. Dranem, who carried the Eldorado show on his broad shoulders, appeared in a clownish get-up complete with red nose and tiny hat, singing with eyes closed and a rapt expression such inspired pieces of lunacy as "Taste the Mint, Petronella!" and "There's a Hole in My Platform," songs of such apparent stupidity that only a comic of his genius could get away with them. He was supported at the "Eldo" by three men and three girls, and that was it.

Montel, tall, thin and horse-faced, specialized in humorous monologues. "His comic force," according to a contemporary reviewer, "resided in his enormous chin." Sinoël was a master of that peculiarly Gallic crazy song classified by music hall historians as "epileptic." And Bérard was the house singer, under contract to the management season after season, who bawled out romantic lyrics in a hoarse, stentorian voice that endeared him to the crowd in the *poulailler* even if it caused some discomfort to those in the front row of the orchestra stalls.

On the distaff side, there was Gaudet, a brunette *diseuse* skilled like the comedians of the London music hall in the art of innuendo, and Angèle Moreau, who sang apache songs wearing a black skirt, a red apron and a red neckerchief. The third member of the female trio was Mistinguett, still at the threshold of her career, who was later to adopt the same costume and a similar gamine role on her way up to the top of the bill. When Dranem was king of the "Eldo," she appeared in the

* French morals, especially locally, were not always as free as the "Naughty Nineties" image of "Gay Paree" would suggest. The author Colette, who also appeared in music hall, was once indiscreet enough to play a sketch at the Moulin-Rouge with her lesbian lover, the Marquise de Belbeuf – the latter dressed as a man, playing the role of a painter infatuated with his model. The intrusion of life into art scandalized the audience. Whistling, booing and shouting broke out; the curtain had to be rung down as coins, cushions and even opera glasses were hurled at the stage. A similar scandal (recalling the notorious Marilyn Monroe calendar) raged around the dancer Cléo de Mérode when the sculptor Falguière exhibited a statue of her completely nude. Public outrage subsided only when Falguière pointed out that Mlle. de Mérode had posed just for the head, the rest being that of a studio model. Neither the Monroe nor the Mérode career suffered from the resultant publicity.

unenviable spot at the beginning of the show – "a small, spindly girl, not at all pretty, with teeth like piano keys," who bustled about the stage and, like Fred Allen and Danny Kaye after her, "pushed eccentricity to the length of performing half her act seated astride the prompter's box."[41] The musical director at the Eldorado was a large and very dark black man named Dédé, whom the gallery regulars – again echoing the humor of their cockney counterparts – christened Whitey.

At the Scala, on the opposite side of the Boulevard de Strasbourg, Polin, Fragson and Polaire were the

Paulette Darty – reigning dreamily over the romanticism of the waltz.

headliners. The company (bolstered by extra talent to counter the draw of Dranem, as has been noted) also included Max Déarly, the conjuror Morton, Sulbac, Anna Thibaud, Paulette Darty and a collection of beauties comprising Alice de Tender, Elise de Vere (the Jane Russell of the epoch), Lise Fleuron and Marion d'Autrey, who had taken the place of Anna Held.★

Harry Fragson, as big a name in England as he was in France, owed his success to a simple stratagem: when he was playing Paris, he sang, suitably adapted, the current London successes; and when he was on the other side of the English Channel, he sang the songs that were the rage of Paris. In this way, pounding out the melodies at the piano, he was certain of having no imitators wherever he was. Fragson was always billed as "the singer of the *Entente Cordiale.*" Max Déarly also used a cross-Channel gimmick, although his was from a different angle. Like a male Petula Clark, he sang French songs with a heavy English accent – which came naturally enough to him since he had passed his apprenticeship touring Britain with a circus. Polin, on the other hand, was a star whose brilliance never shone beyond the frontiers of his own country. His stage persona was that peculiarly French creation, the comic *troupier* – the slovenly baggage-train G.I., complete with oversized trousers and kepi, whose repertoire of songs and patter nevertheless reached far beyond the confines of mere military humor. In this role he was an innovator – Fernandel, Raimu, Bach and Vilbert all made successful debuts copying him – but his originality did not end there. Such was his breath

★ When Anna Held returned to the United States, and before she married Florenz Ziegfeld, she took with her the eighteenth-century affectation of a black "beauty spot" on one side of the face. Her sisters in vaudeville and burlesque thought the idea cute and followed suit – either to look "exotic" or to hide facial blemishes. The spots, bought ready-made or put on with black plaster, grew larger . . . and larger. Finally theater managements vetoed them – "before," as one director put it bitterly, "we have the whole damned chorus line in blackface!"

PHOTO : HARLINGUE-VIOLLET

Polaire as "Claudine" – "a small, vibrant body brimming with talent . . . a dress that hid a rainbow under its skirt and spread it wide about the slim, black, silky legs and their exotic strength and elegance."

control and vocal technique that, microphone or no microphone, he was able to murmur, almost to whisper his songs in a fashion that still sounded crystal clear in the furthest corners of the theater. It was also Polin who founded the weekly periodical *Paris Qui Chante* (*Paris Sings*), a sixteen-page illustrated glossy which sold for twenty-five centimes (five cents) and reproduced the words and music of variety hits.

The three female stars of the Scala couldn't have been more different. Paulette Darty reigned dreamily over the romanticisms of the slow waltz, although despite the sentimental stage image, her private life was a trifle less submissive: contemporary publicity photos show her, very daringly for the period, smoking a black cheroot. Like Gaudet across the street, Anna Thibaud masked the most outrageous innuendo with the façade of a healthy, tennis-playing blonde. A gossip column in the weekly edition of *Gil Blas* records that she had a nose and chin giving her "a slightly nutcracker appearance" – and that, to heighten the effect of the doubles entendres, she would lower her eyes at the appropriate moment in mock modesty. This gave the impression that she was constantly checking up on her own breasts as she sang, and one night a wag in the gallery broke up the house by shouting out: "All right, love – we know they're both there, but which one is the ripest?"

Polaire's publicity concentrated on the fact that her waist, when tightly corseted, was an incredible fifteen and three-fourths inches. In fact, although she had no "voice," her small, vibrant body was brimming with talent. What she lacked in tone and power, she made up for in superb diction and a burning sincerity. Passionately intense, privately as well as in public, she was the only artist of her time likely to rival Yvette Guilbert. Her repertoire, which was highly personal, included many songs caustically flaying the affectations and drug-induced vices of the decadents. If she was obliged to sing a song she considered trite or inferior, she would "screw up her body and smile convulsively as though she had been sucking a sour lemon."

Colette knew her well, for when the famous *Claudine* books became stage successes, it was Polaire who created the name part and gave it depth beyond anything the author had conceived. Admiring "the harmony between the long line of the eyes and the long line of the mouth," Colette described the star as "a strange young woman who had no need of true beauty to put all other women in the shade, an inspired actress to whom training and study were equally unnecessary." The authoress added:

> Except for the bistre shadow on her lids, the mascara of her wonderful long lashes, a faintly purple rouge on her lips, she glowed with her own radiance that flashed and faded, flashed again, a shining that seemed near to tears in her eyes' sad infinity, a long-drawn, unhappy smile, all the pathetic appeals that contradicted her diabolic eyebrows, her dancing ankles, restless as a moun-

Despite his reputation for entente, Harry Fragson (left) was a difficult man, quick to take offense and, according to a close friend, "more jealous than Othello." When he was on tour, he would insist that his current mistress report to him by telephone ten times a day, often calling them at home himself at all hours of the night to check on their whereabouts and fidelity. When he was married to Alice Delysia (right) he taught her everything he knew of stage-craft – but he was too jealous to allow her to perform. It was only after their divorce that she was able to put this acquired skill to use, with the help of Jacques-Charles and C. B. Cochran becoming a music hall star in England in her own right. It was a supreme irony that jealousy should have been the motive behind Fragson's tragic death at the hands of his own father.

tain goat's, the sudden jerks and snake-twists of her tiny waist, and that proclaimed, luminous and moist and tender, that the soul of Polaire had got into the wrong body.[42]

For the music hall songs and dances that made Polaire famous, the couturier Mme. Landolff invented amazing dresses: "A paper doll's dress in little loose frills of changing blue and green taffetas; a dress the color of Polaire's skin with a Prairie Indian's diadem of purple feathers; a mulatto's dress of purest white, all froth and snow; a dress that hid a rainbow under its skirt and spread it wide about the slim, black silky legs and their exotic strength and agility and elegance."[43] Frequently, however, the character of the dress was at variance with the mood of its wearer. A favorite Scala story centers around Polaire's nervous trick of jigging impatiently up and down while waiting for someone to finish speaking. During a rehearsal in which the star was swathed in yards of romantic tulle, the director suffered this fidgeting for some time without comment, but finally he burst out: "For God's sake, Polaire! Can't you keep still? You look like a flower that wants to pee!"

The name, of course, was a stage name – but nobody ever called her anything else. Why did she choose it? Because she wanted to be a star and, one night in Algiers when she was very young, she saw a star brighter than anything in the sky. It was *l'Étoile Polaire* (the Pole Star) – and the name in French seemed so romantically apt that she adopted it then and there.

Perhaps the most revealing anecdote about this tempestuous young woman whose passion for her art made her neglectful of love concerns a simple goodnight at the end of a pleasant evening. Colette (whose story,[44] again, this is) and her husband leave the star at the door of her apartment. "Sleep well, Popo," says the authoress.

"Oh, I don't sleep much, you know," replies Polaire. "I lie and wait."

"Who for?"

"Nobody! I wait and wait for tomorrow's performance."

When that performance was due, Polaire and her co-stars had the advantage of a fine stage at the Scala. Less enviable was "the abominable unventilated basement where, in tiny wooden cubicles which Mme. Marchand called dressing rooms, the unfortunate artists were imprisoned from eight o'clock until midnight."[45] Variety theaters and music halls have never been noted for the luxury of the performers' quarters. But the Scala seems to have ranked low even in this dubious company. The description continues:

Just before the entrance to the auditorium, a steep neck-breaking staircase led down to the toilets on one side and the dressing rooms on the other. A blind man guided only by his nose would have found it hard to determine which was which. At the same time, as you came in, you were greeted by improper noises from Reiter, the house comic, whom the laurels of the Pétomane prevented, not from sleeping, but from digesting, in silence. The next-door dressing room was occupied by Fragson who, to annoy visitors, would nonchalantly

Little Tich – an early example of the international variety star. Continental audiences loved his burlesque tilts at jingoism.

drink the water from the basin after he had scrupulously washed his hands. On the other side, Max Déarly would be reciting through his nose to practice his English accent, Morton would be conjuring and Sulbac standing on his head with his feet on the ceiling.

The company at the Folies-Bergère was housed in slightly more salubrious conditions. Every night there, making their way into the wings one after the other, came the Griffith Clowns, Cinquevalli – the king of the jugglers – La Tortoyada, the first genuine Spanish dancer to stamp on a Parisian music hall stage, England's Little Tich and, to close the first half, Anna Judic with a selection of songs from current operettas, including her favorite "*Piouit.*"

Little Tich was an early example of the international variety star. A forerunner of the modern radio and television comic, he "did not so much sing songs as present characters, and he was able to do this in several languages, becoming as popular on the Continent as in England."[46] The nonsense element in his gallery of eccentrics was presented deadpan, in a subtle burlesque of the dramatic monologue so popular in that period, punctuated with illogical absurdities, wordplays and innuendo. One of his acts was a British parallel to the comic *troupier* in which, his voice heavy with mock sententiousness, he would ridicule the jingoism of the time. The French audiences especially enjoyed "Since Poor Father Joined the Territorials," with its tilts at British amateurism:

He puts poor Ma in the trashcan, to stand on
   sentry guard,
     And me and Brother Bert
     In his little flannel shirt
He keeps drilling in the old back yard . . .

To an audience accustomed to automatic conscription and obligatory military service for those through with school, this was both alien and richly comical. French newspaper readers laughed even more at an apocryphal story printed by a journalist whose regard for the truth was outweighed by his sense of a good angle. According to the story, the diminutive comedian dressed himself in the clothes of a six-year-old boy and went to a public park where he was discovered crying piteously by a kindly lady. When she asked him what was the matter, he replied in his best French: "*J'ai envie de faire pipi . . . et Nounou n'est pas là!*" ("I want to have a pee . . . but Nanny isn't here!")

La Belle Otéro – about as genuine as a chestnut seller from the Auvergne. But the twelve-string pearl choker was real.

"Poor little lad," soothed the lady. "Don't worry: I'll take her place." And she solicitously unbuttoned his shorts. A moment later she started back and gasped: "But . . . but goodness gracious . . . I mean . . . how old are you, my child?"

"Thirty-five," Little Tich replied cheerfully, hauling up the pants and running off as fast as his short legs could carry him.

(The story is unlikely to be based on fact, if only because Little Tich, like so many comics, was a serious and tormented man offstage. Although his act was essentially one long laugh at adversity, M. Wilson Disher points out – in *Winkles And Champagne*, published in London in 1938 – that he very seldom "saw the joke" outside the theater. "He was painfully conscious of his physical peculiarities. . . . Nor was he happy in exciting laughter. He wanted higher tribute than that. He wanted to be praised for his art, to be taken seriously – a desire not altogether unlike Dan Leno's ambition to play Hamlet.")

The second half of the show at the Folies was opened by the Barrison Sisters, the very first troupe of *Les Girls* to be presented in France. There were only six of them. They were not, of course, sisters – but they were all of the same height and build, each wore identical make-up, and they all performed in similar

Otéro caught unposed and unaware: an unusually informal shot from the Reutlinger studio, which photographed every belle of the Belle Époque, from crowned head to courtesan.

⁂

★ Jacques-Charles, who always swore that her accent was more Auvergnat than Spanish, made a lifelong enemy of Otéro when he published a skit satirizing her lisp. The piece was supposedly recounted by a barrow boy with a similar impediment who alleged that the star was his cousin and came from a long line of chestnut sellers in the Massif Central. Colette, on the other hand, thought Otéro "presumably boasted Hellenic blood."

strawberry-blonde wigs. To a public for whom the dance so far had meant the languors of Italian-style ballet or solo Spanish stampings, they were a sensation – the six heads turning as one, the legs all raised to exactly the same height, the regimented gestures cued in precisely to the music. And their little-girl voices, equally drilled and automated, oddly at variance with their ripe young bodies, brought a touch of the better-class New York burlesque house to Paris that rapidly increased the number of stagedoor johnnies in the alleyway off the Rue Richer at the end of each performance.

The top of the bill was La Belle Otéro – Otéro of the magnificent eyes and dazzling teeth; Otéro whose figure was so beautifully sculptured that it drew the attention away from the flawless symmetry of her features; Caroline Otéro who alone was splendid enough to carry off the pretentiousness of her stage name; Otéro the temperamental, the tempestuous and the trying – whose Spanish blood made her the most difficult of all music hall stars to deal with.★

The Americans (according to Douglas Gilbert) held that Otéro's "magnificent torso and tendril legs were her only appeal" when she appeared at Koster and Bial's music hall in New York. Europeans were less critical. With a voice that was "major in tone, true in pitch," and a dance style that "exploded across the stage like dynamite," she was, in the words of a contemporary reviewer, "from her arched brows to her greedy chin, from the point of her velvety nose to her famous, softly curved cheeks, a masterpiece of convexity."

Those who knew her at home among "certain fine old pieces of furniture anchored in a sea of blue satin" (the description is Colette's again) were frequently privileged to watch her working for love rather than money. For Otéro was selfish as well as greedy – and the self-indulgence extended from the acquisition of jewels to gastronomy, from the condescension with which she treated her lovers to the pleasure she took in her art.

There are not many beautiful women who can stuff themselves without loss of dignity. Otéro would not leave the table until she had cleared her plate four or five times. A strawberry sorbet, a coffee, and up she would leap, fixing a pair of castanets to her thumbs. . . . It would hardly be ten o'clock. Until two in the morning she would dance and sing – for her own enjoyment; she cared little for ours. . . . There was nothing base in her violent, totally selfish pleasure; it sprang from a true passion for music and rhythm. She would seize a sauce-stained table napkin, dry herself vigorously, face, neck, moist armpits – and then dance once more, sing again. . . . Her fine lawn petticoat clung to her hips, drenched with sweat . . . the muscles of her waist rippled over her powerful loins; the savage, swaying furrow of her naked back had triumphed over sickness, ill-use and the passage of time. [Otéro was already in her forties when Colette met her.] It was a well-nourished body, sleek sinewed, skin bright, amber in daylight, cream at night. I have always told myself that I would some day, with proper care and objectivity, describe it and its arrogant decline.[47]

The foregoing, a modern reader might decide, would do quite nicely for a start.

Otéro, of course, was not alone as a "character": music hall bred ladies that were in every way larger than life – and even then there were publicists to make sure potential audiences knew about it. In the first few years of the century, Polaire affected an ankle-length chinchilla coat to set off her vast Edwardian limousine and its black chauffeur. Otéro replied (it was an era when automobile designers worked in collaboration with milliners, accommodating bodywork to the size of hats) with a blue Mercedes – "a hatbox for egret and ostrich feathers so narrow and so high that, when it rounded a corner, it drooped and sank gently on its side."[48]

Then as now, publicity could at times work against its subject. When Polaire visited the United States, not content with her astounding fifteen and three-fourths-inch waist, her promoters advertised it as *less* than fifteen inches – and offered $1,000 to any lady who could produce a measurement that was smaller. In addition, they billed her as "the Ugliest Woman in the World" and announced that her songs had "a universal appeal." The Americans thought she was cute rather than ugly, found her material incomprehensible, and were unable at any place on the tour to win the $1,000. As a result they felt obscurely cheated all along the line, and the tour was a flop.

Later, after she had "graduated" via the *Claudine* plays to the theater, Polaire lost with advancing age the line which had made her famous. Women who had for years laced themselves daily into garments of whalebone and leather resembling medieval torture instruments cast them angrily aside when they discovered that their idol no longer lived up to the exacting standards she herself had set. Almost overnight, Polaire became as out-of-fashion as the corset itself.★

Otéro too was once a victim of her own publicity. She was in Berlin, on the same bill as Yvette Guilbert, fresh from her triumphant appearances in London and New York. Naturally, neither of the superstars was prepared to cede the top-of-the-bill spot to the other. The theater director ("unquestionably a descendant of Solomon," comments Jacques-Charles) decided to solve the problem by allowing each to close the show on alternate nights. One evening, when it was Guilbert's turn to fill the star spot, Otéro's fabulous twelve-string pearl choker, itself a jeweled corset reaching from her collarbone to her chin, broke in the middle of her act. The matched gems (of priceless value, according to the press handouts) pattered down all over the stage – and the show was stopped while they were recovered.

By the time the curtain rose on Yvette Guilbert, the audience had grown bored and restive, and her entrance was greeted with applause that was barely loud enough to be termed polite. Halfway through her first number, sensing the coldness of the house, she made a brilliant impromptu riposte. Interrupting the song, she walked to the footlights, pretended to find a pearl that had been overlooked . . . and then, with a wicked glint in her eye, she bit the "gem," crunched it up, and swallowed it.

The public were delighted, Otéro was furious – and from that day on, Yvette insisted on appearing before her rival. It was more satisfying, in effect, to let the closing spot go and say "Follow that!" rather than risk another debacle.

Otéro, Guilbert, Polaire, Cléo de Mérode – their stage personae in one way or another exteriorized, reflected, dramatized, or made fun of the experiences common to the great mass of the people; their lives offstage on the other hand, were inescapably allied to that glittering round of pleasure indulged in by le tout-Paris which has lent to the city and the period such imperishable glamor. And if the fraction of the population contributing to that "Naughty Nineties" image was insignificant, the effect varied inversely as the cause – for it was this more than anything else that made Paris the pleasure capital of the world. In the maintenance of that reputation, the music hall had one of the most important roles to play.

★ The tyranny of the "long corset" was exemplified in the case of Germaine Gallois, wife of the actor Guy, who refused any part which required her to sit. Clinging to the fashion which pushed up the breasts, lowered the buttocks and hollowed the abdomen, she was sheathed in stays that started under the arms and finished near the knees, equipped with two iron springs down the back, two more down the thighs, and a leather centerpiece firmly strapped between the legs to keep the structure in place. The laces required to tighten this device were more than six yards long. When she was working, Mme. Gallois remained on her feet from 8:30 a.m. until midnight at the Théatre des Variétés, intermissions included.

Anna Held, the Scala star who caught Florenz Ziegfeld's eye and then married him after a successful season in London.

Predictably for France, the great courtesans of the era were responsible for the tone and direction of this exuberant social scene as much as the brilliant artists, writers and *bon vivants* who celebrated it. Some of them were music hall stars. Others, more numerous, certainly appeared on the music hall stage. But – like the wine room girls in American honky-tonks – they were there for what the French delightfully call their *plastique* rather than their talent. Many of these *grandes horizontales* found it convenient to have a spot in a show. Men did not advertise their mistresses as widely then as they do now. They had them, but there was a certain discretion to be observed. The rich, noble or otherwise eminent "protector" would dine at home with his family, after which it was permissible for him with decorum to go out to his club or to a theater – from which he would collect his *petite amie* and then take her to supper at Maxim's, the Café Anglais, Paillard,

Liane de Pougy. One of the most sought-after – and the highest priced – of the grandes horizontales, *she possessed emerald rings for all her toes. But she only wore them when she was in bed.*

Durand, the Café de Paris or Weber's, where they could sit side by side with such notables as Marcel Proust, Guillaume Apollinaire, Débussy, Tristan Bernard or the young Cocteau. At the same time, the stage provided a showcase in which the lady herself could display her charms before future lovers who might be even richer or nobler.

The true courtesan had been defined as "a venal, public, pretty woman of enormous social influence who was kept by a kind of cartel – three millionaires or two dukes or one royal – and who, if she knew her business (which she usually did), had no private life or loves." (One of the better bon mots of the period concerned a once-famous courtesan who had finally married well and become Paris's leading literary hostess. Many years later, when she died, a wit consoled a grieving friend: "*Ne vous inquietez pas. Elle s'en est allée dans un meilleur demi-monde.*")

The kept women followed an invariable routine. In the morning they rode, sidesaddle and in top hats, in the Bois de Boulogne. In the afternoon they skated at the Palais de Glace, their multi-colored and many-layered skirts of silk and lace and embroidered satin rising and falling, swirling around the high-laced boots that the pastime had made fashionable. The blonde demimondaine Liane de Lancy was the best skater of all. Next to her came Polaire, gliding on the ice with a chinchilla muff ("Mink is only worn by common tarts!"). At five o'clock the rink cleared as if by magic to make way for the "respectable" predinner crowd, and everyone went to Maxim's for an apéritif. Here the girls who had no *rôles à maillot*[49] to fill in the theater would spend the evening waiting for their lovers.

According to Jacques-Charles's *La Revue de ma Vie*, Maxim's at the turn of the century was a specifically Parisian in-group meeting place and had yet to become the international merry-go-round into which it later developed. Among the clients then, there were "as many grand dukes as there are *nouveaux riches* today." In an almost family atmosphere, there was a politicians' table, a painters' table at which such artists as Caran d'Ache, Sem, Forain and Boldini would group themselves, a literary table, and a special table for the playwright Feydeau, thinking up the plots of ever more complex farces behind his eternal cigar. "In 1900 at Maxim's, in that macaroni-style room decorated by Mucha, the Rumanian painter who designed posters for Sarah Bernhardt, one came straight in through the bar to the 'omnibus' – as we called the wide corridor leading to the big dining room where the orchestra played. With its face-to-face banquettes each side of the gangway it reminded one irresistibly of the famous 'Madeleine-Bastille' bus which gave it its name. The omnibus was the chic place to sit then, and Cornuché, the headwaiter, took care to place well-known Parisian personalities there to create an exciting atmosphere as people came in."

Among the *grandes cocottes* who frequented Maxim's were the music hall stars Emilienne d'Alençon, Otéro, Gilda Darthy, who was the girlfriend of a Baron de Rothschild, and the outrageous Liane de Pougy, who later became the Princess Ghika. Along with Liane de Lancy, she was one of the most fascinating – and the most exaggerated and therefore typical – courtesans of the period. According to Janet Flanner, Liane de Pougy "was launched at the Folies-Bergère by Edward VII, then Prince of Wales, to whom, though he did not know her, she sent a note saying, 'Sire: Tonight I make my debut. Deign to appear and applaud me and I am made.' He did and she was."[50]

Soon, says Miss Flanner, every Parisian who could afford it fell in love with her. She possessed a fabulous collection of jewels, including emerald rings for all her toes, which she wore only in bed.★ "In order to humble a rival, she once entered the Opera bare of any gem except the flashing of her eyes and teeth. But she was followed by her maid, her shoulders sagging beneath her mistress's necklaces: in her hands on a red cushion lay all the tiaras, brooches, rings, and other jewelry the lady had decided *not* to wear. . . ."

A contemporary story delighting the malicious told of a dinner party at which the clasp of one of Liane de Pougy's diamond necklaces broke, sending several strands of the brilliants cascading into their owner's lap. A young man, involuntarily reaching forward to catch the errant gems, was restrained by an older friend: "Don't bother: it is just the river returning to its source."

Liane de Pougy and her jewels, Emilienne d'Alençon and her waiting line of lovers, Polaire with her temperament and Otéro with her diamond breastplate and pearl collars, Yvette Guilbert surrounded by intellectual admirers – they were all an integral part, an indispensable element of the glamor and glitter of *fin-de-siècle* Paris. Below them in the night-life hierarchy came the nontheatrical demimondaines: La Belle Martelli, who became a princess; Angèle Delinière, Paris's first platinum blonde; Suzanne de Behr, the voluptuous daughter of a rabbi; Manon Loti,

★ Liane de Pougy was known to have more than one sexual eccentricity. Marchand, the Folies director, once took the young Jacques-Charles to dine at the de Pougy apartment. The other guests were Oscar Wilde, Aubrey Beardsley, the homosexual journalist Jean Lorrain, and two well-endowed young wrestlers. Jacques-Charles, yet to become a revue producer, was looking for copy to spice a Hedda Hopper-style column he had just started in <u>Gil Blas Illustré</u>. His description of the dinner – and the gay frolics succeeding it – earned him the lifelong enmity of Liane de Pougy to add to the wrath he had already sparked from La Belle Otéro.

In the early 1900s, promoters were already alive to the possibilities of "merchandising." These two Reutlinger photos – on postcards again – show two of the beauties from Maxim's underwriting the benefits of a tonic wine. At left, Gilda Darthy; at right, Arlette Dorgère.

★ **Dinner at Maxim's in 1900 cost 5 francs (the equivalent of 35 cents or 20 pence today) per head. A Paris apartment could be rented for about $5 a week if the neighbourhood wasn't too chic. In the same period American vaudeville specialties were paid an average $40–$70 per week.**

pale-haired mistress of a grand duke; Chouchou and Féfé; Tica La Rousse – table after table of them among the laughter and the champagne, taller and fleshier and more full of fun than the good-time girls of today, the least of them provided with an apartment, a mink coat, a row of pearls, a hired carriage and fifteen hundred francs (about $240) a month spending money.★

Their less fortunate sisters worked in the famous bordels of the day – Mme. Kelly's Chabanais; No. 6, Rue des Moulins; No. 14, Rue de Monthyon – or else they tried their luck in the Moulin-Rouge garden or around the Folies and Olympia *promenoirs*. At the Folies-Bergère every night, under the limpid eyes of the barmaid immortalized by Manet, several hundred girls peddled their own attractions as the attractions on stage competed for their clients' attention. They were a far cry from the booted and bare-breasted beauties of the Paris side streets today. Each paid a small subscription (20 francs per month – $3.20 or 80 English pence) to Marchand for the privilege of being there. Marchand insisted that every girl should wear gloves and a hat with feathers, and that she should not appear too many times in the same dress. It was, after all, a high-class establishment. If a girl was not sufficiently well dressed to please him, he would advance her money to buy a new outfit. Selling back flowers and candies that had been bought for them at stalls in the foyer was strictly forbidden – and Marchand himself stood by the fountain under the Moorish ceiling roofing the lobby during each intermission to see that his orders were carried out. If the girls hadn't been successful by the end of the show, they met equally disappointed friends from the Olympia at the American Bar of the Restaurant Julien behind the Opera. By this time the crowd at Maxim's had broken up into pairs or groups setting off for the late dancing at the Moulin-Rouge or the *chansonniers'* cabarets in Montmartre. The routine was invariable throughout the winter, but as soon as the hot weather arrived, the pattern changed.

The atmosphere in the stuffy, gaslit *boîtes* became insupportable. The "theater" music halls, in what today is their busiest tourist period, closed their doors for the summer season. Tall hats and tail coats were put away, to give place to dinner jackets and straw boaters. And "one" transferred "one's" nocturnal activities – if one was poor to *guingettes* like the Moulin de la Galette, if one was rich to the Champs Elysées, where the *caf'conc'* stars entertained under the trees in the lamplight at Les Ambassadeurs, the Jardin de Paris or the summer Alcazar. The night of the Grand Prix at the Jardin de Paris marked the end of "the season." *Le tout-Paris* strolled around and around the bandstand, exchanging delighted greetings with those they had already met two or three times before in the Bois, at the Palais de Glace or at Maxim's, the ladies uttering shrill cries of pleasure, their escorts raising their hats above their heads at arm's length in the manner of Boni de Castellane★ (for to sweep off the headgear and hold it low was to invite ridicule and receive a crown full of coins).

At 11:00 P.M. the promenade ceased while the strollers watched the *quadrille réaliste* which Joseph Oller still brought down every night from the Moulin-Rouge in a three-horse omnibus complete with postilion. And at midnight the place emptied as quickly as it had filled. "Everybody" was on their way to the fair at Neuilly.†

Victorias, broughams, dogcarts, coupés, *urbaines* full of cocottes – perhaps Liane de Lancy in an *Americaine* drawn by two trotters, a notorious prostitute who had imported a hansom cab from London, or even Mme. Réjane behind the mules given to her by the king of Spain – they would form a double line on the

★ Comte Boniface de Castellane was, with Comte Robert de Montesquiou (Proust's original for Baron de Charlus), one of the playboy dandies who set the fashion pace in fin-de-siècle Paris. He was said to have won his American heiress wife from a friend in a game of cards.

—————— · ——————

† Everyone went to Neuilly. Unless someone who was "someone" was giving one of the grand balls for which the Paris season was famous. Boni de Castellane once held one in the Bois which cost 300,000 francs (almost $50,000 or £12,500) of his wife's money, employed the entire ballet company of the Opéra, and ended with the release of a multitude of flying swans among eighty thousand Venetian lanterns illuminated by fireworks.

—————— · ——————

outskirts of the crowd thronging the sideshows and stalls. Costly perfume from the Rue de la Paix would spice the feral tang of wild beasts in their cages and the odors of frying potatoes and naphtha flares. Among the cries of barkers and the wheezing steam organs, the crowd would divide their attention between the shrieking occupants of merry-go-round horses and the fabulous creatures in their carriages on the roadway (it was not chic actually to "descend" at Neuilly). Every night, though, some gallant blade would leap from his Victoria to impress his lady and shoulder his way to Marseille's wrestling booth, where odds were laid against any amateur who cared to take on the Terror of Beaucaire, the Negro from Martinique, or Mademoiselle Adèle (and curiously enough the man-about-town always beat the professional, for Marseille was a good businessman and knew how to keep a client). But finally, far into the small hours of the morning, it was all over and "one wended one's way back to Paris a little drunk with the lights, the shouts, the noise and the music, leaving *la Fête à Neu-Neu* behind as the illuminations faded one by one like streamers subsiding after a parade."[51]

The social whirl of which the Paris music hall was a component had no counterparts in London, New York, Rome or Berlin, where in each case the divisions between the monde and the demimonde were more pronounced – and therefore less bridgeable. But Paris itself in 1900 and 1901 provided a rival to the Neuilly Fair: the gigantic *Exposition Universelle* which sprawled across a huge area on each side of the Seine embracing Les Invalides, the Champ de Mars and the Eiffel Tower, the Trocadéro, and even a corner of the Place de la Concorde. Among the grandiose pavilions from many countries displaying artistic and technical achievements, one Left Bank section was devoted to reproductions of architecture typical of the contributing nations. And here, in the Cour-la-Reine, was a kind of *Fête à Neu-Neu* on an even grander scale. Here, dining to the sound of castanets and guitars at Spain's La Feria, or sipping tea from onyx cups in an imitation trans-Siberian railway coach while panoramas of the steppes unrolled past the windows, Parisians could see Liane de Pougy and Jean Lorrain, Boni de Castellane and the Marquis de Dion, Coquelin and Réjane, and enough kings and queens and knaves (to say nothing of the grand dukes) to make a poker player blush. Away from the tinkling balalaikas, in the nearby Rue de Paris, there were attractions of another kind – comedians at the Maison de Rire (a witty parody of "official" architecture), marionettes and mimes, dancers like Loie Fuller and the extraordinary Sada Yako, singers and acrobats and sideshows, even a tiny theater for the sole use of La Belle Otéro.

But if this early world's fair drew heavily on the music hall for the lighter side of its entertainment, at least the traffic was still two-way – for there were two displays at the exhibition that were to have a profound influence on the formation of the spectacular revue, one of them concerned with dressing and the other with undressing.

The latter, modest indeed by present-day standards, was an embryonic striptease act entitled *Le Coucher de la Parisienne (A Parisienne Goes to Bed),* presented by Louise Willy. Although it caused a furor at the international exhibition (the lady actually stripped down to her camisole, hose and bloomers before the blackout), this mild bedroom disrobing scene had in fact been performed by Mademoiselle Willy at the Olympia five years previously, under the title of *Le Coucher de la Mariée (A Wife Goes to Bed).* And even then the act was not entirely original: in 1894, an unnamed neo-stripper had appeared in *Le Coucher d'Yvette* at a Rue des Martyrs cabaret called the Divan Feyouac. There appears to have been some doubt as to whether it was more seemly for *fin-de-siècle* voyeurs to gloat over the private movements of married women, anonymous shopgirls, or named maidens – but another step had been taken, hesitant though it might be, in the direction of the nude revue and the skin flick.

The second influence, less specific but more far-reaching, was an entire pavilion entitled the Palais de la Femme. And it was the revolutionary fashions in clothes and jewelry and décor exhibited here, with their reliance on the free-flowing arabesques of art noveau, that were to condition the designers of music hall revue for the next decade and a half.

CHAPTER SEVEN

Something Sweet, Something Sour

MANY INFLUENCES CONTRIBUTED TO the development of the spectacular revue between 1900 and the First World War. The artists of one kind or another involved in this evolution were equally numerous. But the fantastic success enjoyed by the form was due to only a handful of men: the impresarios and directors whose foresight and faith and imagination acted as catalysts to fuse these diverse talents into a coherent and dynamic whole.

Zidler, Marchand, Goubert, Auguste Mussleck and, above all, Joseph Oller had laid the foundations in the years before the turn of the century. Each in his way was a solo pioneer. Now it was the turn of the team. Chauveau and Cornuché, Dufrenne and Varna, Rip and P. L. Flers, the brothers Isola, Volterra and the great Jacques-Charles – together with Paul Derval of the Folies-Bergère, they modeled the lavish revue into the breath-taking, exotic, fast-moving spectacle that was to reach its apogee in the roaring twenties. Some of these men were administrators, some were artistic directors, others were mainly writers or simply businessmen – but they all had one thing in common: as impresarios, they gathered around them the most brilliant designers, costumiers, choreographers, lyricists and composers of light music that Paris could offer. And it was in welding together the gifts of these artists that they created in *la revue à grand spectacle* what Jacques Feschotte calls "music hall's most original contribution to the entertainment world."

Chauveau and Cornuché concentrated on the smaller, and more fashionable, *café concerts* like Les Ambassadeurs and the Alcazar d'Eté, streamlining their short programs, seasoning the ubiquitous *tours de chant* with specially created dancing acts and specialities. Derval, following up his theories on the attraction of the undraped female form, blazed the exotic-erotic

trail with inflammatory troupes of gorgeous girls once he was artistic director of the Folies. Flers was principally a revue writer (although at one time he did direct the Moulin-Rouge). A dry, thin-featured, professorial man with a lorgnette, he employed a team of "ghost writers" and churned out the book for music halls all over Paris on the production-line system. Once a week he would summon his "ghosts" and brief them:

"Henri – a four-minute sketch from you on an English girl who's lost her way and falls for the policeman giving her directions. Mayer – I want four verses, with lines of seven feet, in the style of Georgius, on *Figaro*'s second lead this morning. You there – do me a blackout gag on two eunuchs who jump the harem wall. Five girls. Forty-five seconds . . ." In this way many aspiring writers, including Rip and Jacques-Charles, learned the mechanics of their trade.

Specialty dancers taking a bow during a performance of Florence Mills's "Blackbirds" revue at the Casino de Paris in 1924.

159

PHOTO: ROGER-VIOLLET

After the big music halls in Paris switched to an extravaganza format, audiences were introduced to "a world of fantasy in which exotic tableaux, ensemble spectacle seasoned with eroticism, and the production as a whole were as important as the stars whose names appeared outside the theater." This particular tableau formed part of a later revue at the Folies.

Léon Volterra, Oscar Dufrenne and Henri Varna all thought big. With Derval, they were among the first to see that the future of French music hall lay not with parochial Parisian material but in the sumptuous, "international" superproduction which would attract tourists to the pleasure capital. Dufrenne and Varna were at one time or another connected with the Casino de Paris, the Concert Mayol, the Eden-Palace, the Empire and the Folies-Marigny in the Champs Elysées. Volterra, who started his professional life selling programs outside a theater and bequeathed his widow France's most illustrious string of racehorses, directed Les Ambassadeurs, the Apollo, the Casino de Paris, the Cigale and the Olympia during his career.

The tortuous story of how these music halls changed hands time and again is too complicated to follow in detail. The case of Emile and Vincent Isola must serve as an example. "The Brothers," as they were known in the business, left school at a very early age to become apprentice carpenters – but ran away and transformed themselves into a conjuring and juggling act. After a disastrous appearance at Amiens, they arrived penniless in Paris and talked themselves into a spot at the Folies-Bergère in 1886. In 1901, by then the owners of the "legitimate" Théatre des Capucines, they went back and bought the Folies from Marchand. In 1903, inauguration year of the Moulin Rouge's music hall, they leased it, together with Parisiana, which they had also acquired, to a promoter named Ruez. In the meantime, although Joseph Oller remained overall proprietor, the Isolas had also taken a lease on the Olympia. This too they sublet to Ruez. But Ruez was no genius. Business was falling off, and he was unable to meet the payments as they fell due. The Brothers went to law and repossessed all three halls.

By this time, however, their eyes were fixed on a richer, more prestigious prize: their ambition would be content with nothing less than the Paris Opera itself. They sold the Folies to Clément Bannel (it was he who installed Derval as artistic director), made a gift of the Olympia lease to Jacques-Charles, and finally – because they sensed the music hall image might spoil their chances of getting the Opéra – they returned Parisiana to Ruez.★

Jacques-Charles, then working as general secretary for the Isolas, received the Olympia as a gift because the Boulevard des Italiens rent was so high that the lease was virtually unsalable. Having acquired the Folies' goodwill for a capital sum, for example, Bannel paid an annual rent of 78,000 francs (about $12,500 or £3,120 at the exchange rate then current). The Olympia, with far less accommodation in a smaller space, cost 360,000 francs ($56,000 or £14,000) a year – a prohibitive sum at a time when an income of 25,000 francs ($4,000 or £1,000) gained a senior French executive a large house in the country with a carriage, horses, a gardener and several living-in servants.

Jacques-Charles, who accepted this heavy commitment because it would give him the chance to stage his own revues (and because he had private information that a street-planning change would make the Olympia a more desirable site), was a complete man of the theater. Some of his contemporaries worked like producers of movies, assembling the finance, the

The genius of the spectacular – Jacques-Charles, once an illustrator himself, caricatured by cartoonist-turned-revue-writer Rip in 1912.

creative talent and the performers, and letting them get on with it; others confined themselves to the director's role, imposing their own artistic concept on a prepared package. But Charles had to be in at every level of the production, advising, suggesting, insisting. In his books on the music hall,[52] he describes how the Isolas would make informal and unexpected visits to their theaters on most nights – but this was just to check that everyone was on his toes and earning his money. It had nothing to do with the *quality* of the show. He recalls his astonishment when, shortly after he began working for "The Brothers," P. L. Flers came into the office one day carrying three bound manuscripts. "I have brought you the new Folies-Bergère revue," Flers announced. Shortly afterward, Landolff, the famous costumier, and Menessier, the set designer, were ushered in. Jacques-Charles expected the five men – the author, the two designers and the Isolas – to sit around a table and go through the book together, scene by scene, line by line. But Vincent Isola simply stood up, handed a copy to each of the new arrivals, and said: "Here, Messieurs, is the new revue. We open in one month. Be sure everything is ready. So far as money is concerned, pray discuss this with our cashier, Boucheron." The third manuscript was then given to Charles to pass on to the musical director – and the "conference" was at an end.

Jacques-Charles himself, formerly a cartoonist, a theatrical gossip writer for *Gil Blas*, and then a press agent, favored an approach that was very different. His passion for personally supervising every detail of a production infuriated many of the people he worked with when first he began to direct. Costumiers were affronted when he insisted on accompanying them to choose materials; décor specialists became irritated at his perfectionism. Even on first nights, unlike his fellow impresarios, he was never to be seen, resplendent in white tie and tails, accepting congratulations in a stage box. He was backstage in his shirtsleeves, overseeing the show himself. "*Pace* is everything in a revue," he would say. "When *I* am in charge, I find on average that I can cut six minutes from the running time established by a stage manager."

In *La Revue de ma Vie*, Charles devotes a chapter to the analysis of what goes on behind the scenes before the curtain can rise on a revue premiere.

Once the stars have been signed and the opening date set, the first task is the choice of subjects for the tableaux around which the show will revolve – not forgetting that the first meaning of *tableau* is "picture."

From the sheaves of notes he always carries, the director selects twenty or thirty ideas which between them should appeal to all tastes – "always a cocktail: something sweet, something sour; something strong, something effervescent."★ The first choice is usually directed towards Madame, "because in most households it's the woman who decides anyway." Headings for these tableaux might read something like "Fashion through the Ages," "Perfumes from Paris," or simply "Lace," "Furs" or "Frills." Then, if Monsieur is to be permitted to gaze longingly all evening at ranks of half-naked lovelies, Madame will scarcely be indifferent to the charms of a few well-endowed dancers or musclemen, so a place must be found for these within the emerging framework of the show. Masculine tastes are pandered to with the inclusion of tableaux glamorizing the race-track, the roulette wheel, the "live" chess game, or anything of a sporting nature that lends itself to color and movement. Add a few scenes that can be sumptuously dressed ("Châteaux of the Czars," "Waltzes of Old Vienna," "Beau Brummel at Bath") for Her – and a few undressed ones ("Venus Arising," "The Judgment of Paris") for Him – and all that remains is the collection of crowd-pullers, the more sensational tableaux for the masses. These follow a fairly constant pattern, with recurring Balinese temples, oriental forests, Russian Cossack festivals, pagan dances, and an occasional Daphnis and Chloe pastorale, according to the finance available for special effects. For those music halls with a strictly French audience, the patriotic production number (the taking of Algiers, some heroic defense, Napoleon entering anywhere) is always a winner.

Once these visual highlights, which determine the broad outlines of the revue, have been settled, writers are called in to fill out the book. Then it is the turn of the designers. These have to be chosen with great care. Some costumiers are better at lavish effects, others excel with the simple and fashionable; some score with period costumes, others with fantasy or novelty. It's the same with scenic designers: this one will be successful with exteriors, that one specializes in eighteenth-century ballrooms; one is a master of the set piece, another finds his genius among stage machinery and revolves. Each of them is furnished with details of the scenes in the revue affecting him and asked to produce his sketches by a certain date.

While this work is going on, the director chooses the music. Some will be semiclassical "evergreen" material selected to tie in with the tableaux. Some will

★ Paul Derval's revue formula was: "Il faut donner à rêver et à rire" ("You must give them something to dream about and something to laugh at"). Perhaps that was why Josephine Baker once described the Folies-Bergère as being "like Ziegfeld with a heart."

In the few days between the closing of one revue and the opening of another, chaos reigns in the theater as costumes, sets and lighting are modified in last-minute rehearsals. Here, electricians at the Casino de Paris take the long view of a stage problem with the house lights up.

comprise contemporary hits that he hopes will last the run of the revue. But a large proportion will still be original – and for this there will be auditions, conferences, try-outs, in the hope that one of the sixty-odd songs in the production may take the public's fancy. Much depends here on the stars who have been signed and the numbers *they* like. "If a single song from a revue takes off, that's not bad. Two is fantastic. More would be a miracle."

When the production has reached this stage, the remainder of the company is hired – featured performers, dancers, specialties, and of course the showgirls and the chorus – which means more auditions.

Once the designs have been approved (and sometimes they have to be changed four or five times before the artist's ideas coincide with or express the director's), the two go together to choose the materials for each costume. Satins, silks, velvets, lamés, metallic weaves and decorative laces – all are minutely scrutinized, separately and together, always in artificial light, "because colors change like a bastard under the

spots." Often specialist dyers have to be called in to make sure that the many shades in ensemble tableaux harmonize.

The final selection of materials, each sample pinned to the relevant costume design, is then sent to the set designer so that he can make sure his décors will either complement or contrast suitably with the performers in front of them. He then produces a *maquette*, a scale model of each set, complete with entrances, exits, staircases, revolves, etc. Once these are approved, the designer sends scale plans of each element and every component in all the sets to the *chef machiniste*, so that the necessary machinery can be constructed, and flats, chassis, podiums and structural units built, fireproofed, and sent back to the studio for painting. Except in England the scenery is always painted flat on the floor.

Now, with the book written, the music chosen, the company hired and the designs approved, the preliminary work is finished. It will have taken two or three months. Next comes choreography and the rehearsal period, which will continue for a further

Showgirls and nudes receive as much attention as the principals – the dresser at the Folies makes a last-minute adjustment.

165

eight weeks. As is the case with any theater, this is made much more difficult by the fact that nobody can set foot on the stage until the very last minute – there will be a few days at the most between the closing of whatever is currently running and the premiere of the new show. For the spectacular revue, this brings design problems unknown to the director of straight plays or even musicals. Plays require three sets at the most, musicals seldom more than six. For a revue of this kind, *twenty or thirty* complicated sets have to be surveyed, measured, built to precise specifications, dismantled and numbered ready for reassembly – without a single chance to check that they accurately fit the stage for which they were designed. Small wonder, as Jacques-Charles claims, that so many stage managers die at their posts!

At the first rehearsal, the showgirls and chorus are divided into groups according to size and type. Each is then allotted the costumes most suitable to her looks, and the costumier, the wig specialist and the bootmaker are called in to take measurements. The choice of the right costume for the right girl is "a very delicate job requiring a great deal of experience and a specialist's eye. You have to know exactly how to display each girl's good points – and above all, above all hide the bad ones. There is no such thing as a perfect woman. To show off a girl to her best advantage, to know how to present her, is an art in itself. Mme. Rasimi possessed it to a high degree when she was directing the Ba-ta-clan. *All* the girls there looked pretty!"

Once rehearsals are in full swing, a routine establishes itself: dancers in the morning from 10:30 to 12:30; showgirls from 1:00 to 3:00 P.M.; the two troupes together from 3:00 until 5:00 – after which selected members of the cast are sent to the costumier for fittings. When a tableau has been finalized and the movements keyed in with the choreography, the music is sent to the arranger for scoring. The orchestra starts rehearsing eight or ten days before the last performance of the existing show.

Then the headaches start: major alterations to costumes, dances which for space reasons have to be rethought, orchestrations which have to be rescored, sets that require extensive amendment because an eye-line from one side of the circle penetrates the wings, or there's not enough room for twelve girls to enter at once from the O.P. side in the Arabian Nights number – all of which consumes time, time, time. And this is the one commodity with which the director cannot afford to be lavish.

PHOTO: ROGER-VIOLLET

At last the final performance of the outgoing show arrives. Traditionally, to lighten the sadness of the occasion, the performers pull outrageous gags on stage – and nobody complains. The girls don't go back to their dressing rooms to change: they switch costumes in the wings and throw the discards into huge hampers which are taken away by the cleaners. Later, along with the dismantled sets, they will be hired out or sold to touring companies (costumes and scenery from Paris revues have been known to turn up, years later, in places as far apart as Alexandria, Hongkong, Buenos Aires and even Blackpool or Atlantic City). The footwear will be put into stock at the costumier's or used for rehearsal work.

The following day, while the old sets are dismantled and the new scenery is delivered, the stage is left free and the incoming company assembles in the auditorium for the allocation and fitting of costumes. For two days and two nights the theater is in chaos. The artists

When the curtain finally rises on the opening night, chorus and stagehands alike watch anxiously from the wings. Will the public vote the show a hit or a miss?

become irritable and exhausted, standing for hours on end surrounded by dressers and fitters and gesticulating designers pinning up hems and taking in tucks – for every single costume has to be tried on, inspected, checked against the design, and probably altered. The costumes themselves look awful, because there is no proper lighting and the cast wear rehearsal tights and leotards under them to keep out the cold. Temperaments fray. The director is tearing his hair and one of the designers is in tears.

But at last it is all done and everyone is sent home – to return on the third day for the first band call, when all the musical members are rehearsed with the orchestra. On the fourth day, the first half is run through on stage with the sets in place – though the cast are still in rehearsal costume because the costumier hasn't delivered the alterations yet. The day after that, the second half is rehearsed. During these two run-throughs, the electricians familiarize themselves with the show. Each has been supplied with a detailed lighting plan charting the colors and intensity for each tableau, but there are many subtleties to add. The chief electrician sits beside the director, jotting down his instructions for each entry and exit. Much will depend on the accuracy with which he passes them on – especially in the case of the spotlight operators posted in isolation at each wing of the circle and gallery. A spot which "opens" too soon, to reveal the shifting of scenery or massacre a blackout sketch, can kill the momentum of a revue stone dead.

Only on the seventh day, when even a deity would be resting, can the director finally run through the entire revue from beginning to end – on stage, with costumes, with scenery, with music . . . and with luck. That is when he starts the most trying part of his own work. In the three or four dress rehearsals which remain before the opening, which are nerve-racking for everyone, but particularly for him, "he has to think of everything, correct everything, bring everything up to scratch in the tiniest detail. Specifically, he must summon the full potential of his own nervous energy to galvanize, electrify the whole company in order to give the revue the pace on which its success will depend."

After that he has only to sit back and keep his fingers crossed. Once the curtain goes up on the first night, it's up to the others.

The curtain did not rise on Jacques-Charles's first revue at the Olympia until 1911. Before that, all the Parisian music halls with properly equipped stages had

switched to the extravaganza formula. Thus between 1901, when the Isolas took over the Folies-Bergère, and 1906, when Chauveau and Cornuché transformed the Alcazar d'Eté and reopened with the revue *Vive Paris!*, the city was scintillating with talent of all kinds.

The Scala led the way with a dazzling succession of *tours. de chant* featuring Polin and the faithful Max Déarly; Fragson, Sulbac and Claudius; Yvette Guilbert, Polaire and Paulette Darty. Parisiana riposted in 1903 with Anna Thibaud, Edmée Favert, Otéro, Marguerite Duval, Méaly, Vilbert, Carjol, Dutard and a young comic named Maurice Chevalier. Mayol was a hit at Les Ambassadeurs (and was immediately booked by the Isolas to head a revue at the Folies); Dranem starred at the Alcazar. In the same year, at the expense of half the famous garden and a portion of the *bal*, the new Moulin-Rouge music hall opened in a blaze of publicity – though here as elsewhere spectaculars were sometimes varied with successful operettas. The Moulin-Rouge itself staged *The Geisha*; Léhar's *Merry Widow* followed its Berlin and London triumphs with a run at the Apollo; both *The Quaker Girl* and *The Arcadians* were produced at the Olympia (the latter disastrously because the star, Max Déarly, lost his voice on the first night, and only the first few rows of the orchestra stalls could fathom how the hero could be an aviator in the first act, a jockey in the second, and a restaurateur in the third – all the explanations being croaked by the actor).

In 1904 the Alhambra took over the vast auditorium of the old theater at the Château d'Eau, off the Boulevard de Strasbourg, which had for a long time specialized in historical drama and popular opera, including such Wagnerian successes as *Tristan and Isolde* and *Götterdämmerung*, directed by Alfred Cortot. The Apollo installed a costly invention christened the *Basculo* which became the talk of Paris. This was a device whereby the entire stalls, including the seating, could be revolved on a horizontal axis to transform the auditorium into a dance floor. There was a "dancing" at the Olympia too: it was installed in place of the old "hall" at the back of the theater when the *promenoir* was dispensed with to make way for extra seating in the pit. Pedestrian traffic on the nighttime sidewalks of the Boulevard des Italiens increased accordingly.

Before Chauveau and Cornuché reopened the Alcazar with *Vive Paris!*, the old Champs Elysées *caf' conc'* had for years been featuring revues with books by "quality" writers like Héros Gavault and the poet Raoul Ponchon. After the success of the new production, which starred Fragson, the intellectual content dwindled at the expense of spectacle. The same thing was happening all over Paris. With the disappearance of *compère*, *commère* and linking theme, with only the new Moulin-Rouge, the Bal Tabarin and Les Ambassadeurs clinging to the formula of *haute cuisine* allied to high-class entertainment, the era of song and dance was in. But it was song and dance in a sophisticated setting, as the Jacques-Charles description of the planning of a revue shows. This was a long way from the routine of the seventies and eighties, when the average variety theater – in France as in Britain and the United States – boasted no more than four or six stock sets;* when anything more complex was run up by the property man with the help of friends in a nearby lumber yard; when next week's flats were often painted during this week's show – on burlap sized with glue, by part-timers high up in the flies, working in the light of gas flames reflected in polished dishpan lids.

It wasn't only the décor that was new, however. There were, as has been noted, many other influences at work to mold the new form. Loie Fuller was still experimenting with revolutionary techniques making use of luminous gases and colored lights;† in another area of the dance, Isadora Duncan was pioneering the Greek approach, barefoot and with her soft body uncorseted. At the Folies-Bergère, the Fred Karno troupe from London brought a new angle on slapstick to music hall comedy. With them was a droll youth named Charles Chaplin, who gave an impersonation of Little Tich. Designers of scenery were raving about the Russian Exhibition, which had been organized by an eccentric called Serge Diaghilev.

But it was three years later, in 1909, that Diaghilev stunned Paris with the explosive effect of his opera and ballet seasons at the Chatelet.§ The costumes and décor of Bakst, Golovin, Bénois and their colleagues, added to the dazzling choreography, the matchless expertise of soloists and ballet companies, plus the music of Rimsky-Korsakov, Stravinsky and Prokofiev, literally took the city by storm. Overnight, *le tout-Paris* became Russian-crazy. Diaghilev, now exiled from his homeland, was wise enough to skim the cream of French talent too, and add it to the artistic confection he presented nightly just across the river from the Sainte-Chapelle. Satie and Les Six among the composers, Matisse and Dérain among French painters, Picasso, Max Ernst and de Chirico among the expatriates, all contributed to the czarist balletmaster's shop window

* Stock sets customarily included a kitchen interior with a "breakaway" window; a "dark" woodland scene – gothic and sinister, for villainies in unhand-me-sir sketches; a "light" woodland scene – probably with stream, for love songs and romantic pieces; a standard "respectable" interior with two entrances; a rustic cottage and village street "in one," before which drop-curtain acts and comics could perform while the scenes were shifted behind; and possibly a gypsy encampment, desert fort or Persian market, according to country.

—————— • ——————

† The story is that Loie Fuller's inspiration for the use of moving light in the dance came to her when, sitting penniless in Nôtre Dame cathedral, the reflections of one of the fabulous stained-glass rose windows fell like multicolored gems across her lap.

—————— • ——————

§ In London, Russian ballet was first introduced to the public through performances in the music hall by Pavlova, Karsavina and Lydia Kyasht, some time before the epoch-making Chatelet season. Diaghilev had also been invited to display his troupe to British music hall audiences, but declined the offer. Later, however, he was obliged to do so in order to honor debts to the theater magnate Sir Oswald Stoll.

—————— • ——————

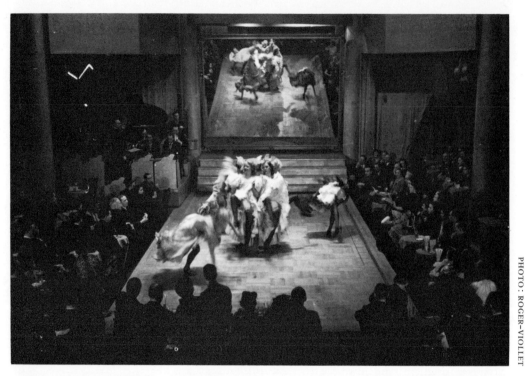

PHOTO: ROGER-VIOLLET

*Cancan dancers at the Bal
Tabarin – among the few places
offering gourmet food with
high-class entertainment. The
huge inclined mirror ensured a
perfect view for the unlucky
ones at the back.*

for the avant-garde. And the music hall designers, rendered speechless by the brilliance of the settings at the Chatelet, followed his example. Hesitantly at first, and then with more and more confidence, the involvement of modern fine arts with the popular stage progressed. So far as revue was concerned, this meant that mere sumptuousness and extravagance was now enlivened by wit and panache.

The transition was not without its problems. Landolff is said to have been outraged when a revue director insisted that he must go and see the Ballets Russes so that he could learn just how a show could and should be dressed. "But, Monsieur . . . !" the costumier protested. "Monsieur forgets, perhaps, that it is *I*, Landolff, who has been leading the fashions for the past thirty years!"

The director smiled. "My dear friend," he said, "if you wish to continue working, *you*, Landolff, had better make up your mind, as of today, to follow them. . . ."

After the epoch-making Salon des Independants in 1911, fauvists, futurists and cubists added their talents to that theater-art amalgamation which had begun over a decade before with the posters of Lautrec, Bonnard and Chéret: as designers, Matisse and Picasso were joined by Braque, Chagall and their disciples. But oddly enough it was through another costumier that the effects of these trends were to be felt in the music hall. His name was Paul Poiret – and he would have been as enraged as Landolff to see himself referred to as costumier rather than couturier. For if Boni de Castellane was the archetypal playboy of the Belle Époque, Poiret was his updated successor: the playboy eccentric who indulges his extravagant whims, not through inherited wealth but with money he has earned himself. Brought up in a bourgeois Catholic background, he started his professional life selling umbrellas in a boutique, served an apprenticeship with Worth and Doucet, and then branched out on his own. By the time Diaghilev's Slavic orientalism was revolutionizing the theater world, he was the best-known dressmaker in France.

Poiret was the right man at the right time. After the rigidities of the nineteenth century, the world was ready for extravagance and exaggeration – and Poiret was more exaggerated than most. Believing himself to have been an Eastern prince in a previous incarnation, he too, as if to surround himself with suitable companions, "persistently dressed his clientele, whether from Chicago or Berlin, in the beads, gilt, and scarlets of the gorgeous East."[53] Ignoring the theory that fashion is based on change, "year in, year out, his clientele looked like Asiatic princesses or Tartar priests in scarlet, black, tassels, and magnificent gold. . . . With the grand obstinacy of a dictator and an artist, Poiret egotistically designed dresses he liked as if he were the one who had to wear them."

"Swooning mauves and lilacs," he wrote, "soft hydrangea blues, honey and corn and straw – everything pale and washed-out and insipid had been the rage. All I did was let loose a few wolves among these lambs: reds and purples and royal blues that made the rest come to life and begin to sing."

Poiret's love of the East and Near East was reflected in his extravagant life. As famed as de Castellane for his luxurious parties, he once gave a costume ball entitled *The Thousand-and-Second Night* at which three hundred guests in garments designed, made and paid for by their host stayed to watch the dawn gild the roofs above his Faubourg St.-Honoré mansion. "Black slaves served dishes at tables seventy feet long. Paler female slaves lay feigning sleep on an immense golden staircase erected beneath the trees. In one salon lay Mme. Poiret, dressed in aigrettes. De Max, the actor, in another, recited poems, his costume shivering with the shaking of thousands of pearls. Among electric blossoms, live parrots were chained to the bushes; their

Reutlinger's famous study of Mata Hari, one of the revue performers to appear in early movies, who eclipsed such small show business kudos as she had by becoming perhaps the world's most notorious spy. Of Dutch-Javanese origin (her real name was Gertrude Margarete Zelle), she was in fact neither beautiful nor particularly dangerous as an agent. Her regular features and thickish, unexceptional body were of more interest to the ladies of the then fashionable lesbian cult than to men. In 1904 she was one of the amazones to be seen riding in the Bois de Boulogne in top hat and veil, and subsequently she was more successful as a nude dancer at gay parties and in certain select private salons than she ever was in the music hall. For public performance of her quasi-oriental dance specialties, she affected harem trousers and concealed her bosom beneath circular metal plates. ("So would I, if I had breasts like hers!" Colette once remarked acidly.)

companions were monkeys and cockatoos. Rug merchants, beggars, and sweetmeat sellers, hired to whine, strolled among the crowd. Thousands of shrimps were consumed; three hundred each of lobsters, melons, goose livers; and nine hundred liters of champagne. To contrast with the delicacy of this scene and to show that the color of the East really is red, behind the table laden with dead lambs stood a butcher."[54] Poiret himself, sultan-fat and smiling through his dark beard, sat on a throne wrapped in a gold robe and a white silk turban.

To these exotic details, Jacques Chastenet adds that Mme. Poiret was in fact locked in a vast golden cage, playing the court favorite, while "a battalion of odalisques dressed in transparent muslin lay at Poiret's feet."[55] A blue and gold canopy had been stretched between trees in the garden to diffuse the electric light, and beneath it was a white carnelian urn surrounded by pink ibises. "Twenty Negroes and Negresses kept frankincense and myrrh smoking in precious incense burners, and the music of flutes and zitars trembled from a grove at the far end of the garden." Boni de Castellane, himself an amateur of luxury that was a trifle less flamboyant, pronounced the party "satisfactory."

It must have been quite a party at that: if the figures are correct, every guest must have drunk three liters – i.e., four bottles – of champagne.

Nevertheless, it is a little sad to have M. Chastenet and others confide that the ball was really no more than a gigantic public relations exercise, designed to launch Poiret's "Persian look." Whether or not this is true, such an individualist was a natural for the world of extravagant revue. Like Diaghilev, Poiret had already moved in on the turbulent fringe of the avant-garde. He employed Iribe as a designer, Lepape as a publicist; he commissioned Dufy to create fabrics; and then, in 1912, he began the association with Erte – the most famous revue designer of all – which was later to bring a new and exotic dimension to the music hall spectacular. With Erte, in addition to dressing exotics like Cora Laparcerie, Isadora Duncan, Mata Hari and Mistinguett, he became the first designer to conceive décors *and* costumes for a show as an integral whole (this was *Le Minaret*, at the Théâtre de la Renaissance in 1913). He was the first couturier to use live mannequins as a means of displaying his creations to future clients.★ And when these models received, as it were, a public showcase via the revue stage, he anticipated the postwar emancipation of women through his daring use of slit skirts, "harem" trousers, hot colors, transparent materials and the "free," corsetless styles advocated by Isadora Duncan. "Let the bust be freed and the legs fettered!" he decreed while his seamstresses were hastening to ready his first hobble-skirt collection.

Many of these trends were the products of Poiret's own imagination; some he adopted from Max Reinhardt's Arabian Nights extravaganza, *Sumurum*, designed by Ernst Stern, which opened in 1912 at the Vaudeville. The production, whose voluptuous orientalism was of course very much "in" at that time, was breathtakingly original too. The principals made their entrances along an illuminated gangway over the heads of the audience in the orchestra stalls. The critics were enraptured. The house was full. Reinhardt was decorated with the Légion d'Honneur – and the impresarios were losing 30,000 francs ($4,800 or £1,200) a month. Even in 1912, stars' entrances were not the only overheads which had to be taken into account.

COLLECTION VIOLLET

When Poiret began his trend-setting association with the brilliant costume and set designer, Erte, the young Mistinguett was one of their first customers.

★ Later in his life, Poiret branched out into other professions with equal vigor. He designed a windowless room for Isadora Duncan, introduced black carpets, wrote one-act plays, and gave an exhibition of paintings in the manner of Cézanne. During the art-déco exposition, he ran a floating restaurant on the Seine. In 1926 he made his bow as an actor, playing opposite Colette in her own work, La Vagabonde. Traditionally enough, at the end of his life he lived penniless and friendless in an attic, fleeced of his business interests by the banks and lawyers whose exigencies he had found too boring to heed – or to read – "the aesthetic nineteenth-century individual gobbled up by the twentieth-century corporation plan."

Eight weeks before their short-term lease of the theater expired, the impresarios took off *Sumurum* and replaced it with Feydeau's farce, *Le Dindon*, which recouped their losses and made a handsome profit as well in the remaining two months. In those days, that was show business.

With Erte's décors and costume designs bringing a new look to the lavish revue and even to the near-naked beauties of the chorus line, Mme. Rasimi, who had taken over the big Ba-ta-clan music hall between 1910 and 1911, launched a series of productions rivaling in sumptuousness the spectaculars at the Folies and the Moulin-Rouge. At the Scala, the Montmartre *chansonnier* Roger Fursy had opened with an English-style concert party. The Jardin de Paris was becoming famous for its glittering nighttime galas. Félix Mayol, who had invested money earned from his triumphs at Les Ambassadeurs and the Folies in the little Concert Parisien, leased the hall to Dufrenne and Varna. Here, under its new name of the Concert Mayol, they were to produce miniature revues starring Marie Dubas, Lucienne Boyer, Jane Aubert and Fernandel which equaled the attractions at the established music halls.★

Among the latter, only the Casino de Paris was having a hard time. Having lost a quarter of its length when the garden was cut in two to enlarge the classical Théâtre Réjane, the auditorium no longer pleased the public. A huge and beautiful new stage had been installed (it is still there today) – but now the gallery was too far away from the performers because the rebuilt theater was at right angles to its former position;

★ **The Concert Mayol, originally a** <u>café chantant</u> **built on the site of a disused nunnery, cradle of the talents of Dranem, Mayol and Yvette Guilbert, is still in business at No. 10, Rue de l'Echiquier – as one of the homes of nude revue.**

there was no rake to the stalls; and, worst of all, the seats were villainously uncomfortable. It was only by staging wrestling bouts and then boxing matches that the Casino was able to avoid bankruptcy – perhaps because such exhibitions could be relied on to keep spectators on the edge of their seats.

At the Olympia, after a successful opening with a revue written by Rip, and two less rewarding shows featuring Fragson and Déarly, Jacques-Charles staged the first production starring and written especially for Mistinguett. She was already famous through *La Valse Chaloupée*, which she had popularized two years before with Déarly at the Moulin-Rouge. But, in the Place Blanche, she had been simply the partner of a big star, lending her talents to a dance composed and created by him. Here she was the jewel for which the setting had been designed; here, for the first time, people began speaking of her as "the Queen of the music hall." Among songs, dances, monologues and impersonations, Mistinguett brought the house down every night with a wicked pastiche of Forzane – a beautiful and eccentric Parisienne who had by sheer personality imposed on the ladies of *le tout-Paris* a style of dress peculiar to herself. For years they had been sedulously favoring the back bustle, aided (despite the defection of Polaire) by stays, busks, corsets, cushions and other invisible machinery of whalebone and leather. Forzane neatly turned fashion back to front by adopting *le ventre en avant* (literally "belly forward," i.e., the front bustle), with which she launched as accessories Poiret's hobble skirt, boots laced to the knee, an umbrella tucked under the arm and a peaked hat based on the Austrian army shako. With such a mixture of the *mondaine* and the military as material, the new star's irreverent genius for burlesque blossomed and matured.

Maurice Chevalier, who had first partnered "Miss" in a Folies revue in 1909 (and started their long love affair there by kissing her on stage, rolled up in a carpet at the end of a sketch), was at this time doing his military service in Alsace. His three-year contract with Bannel had guaranteed him 1,800 francs a month the first year, 2,000 francs the second, and 2,500 the third (an increase from $288 to $400, or £72 to £100) – more than he had ever earned during his debuts as a red-nosed comic in suburban music halls, but rather less than he was able to command only half a decade later when, reunited with Mistinguett, he became a star in his own right and the partnership was the toast of Paris.

In 1914, when Parisians could still eat a first-class

Erte's costume for Mistinguett in the revue L'Orient Merveilleux, *which was staged at the Fémina theater during World War I. The cloak was in ultramarine velvet with indigo and green appliqué and a gold lining. Ermine tails formed the collar. From a close-fitting helmet made of pearls, blue and green egrettes fanned out like the rays of the sun, and the tassels on the cloak were silver and gold.*

dinner watching the sparkling revues at the Moulin-Rouge or the richly costumed dance routines at the Bal Tabarin, a whole new generation of music hall performers was waiting in the wings. Some of them, like Arletty, Fernandel, Raimu and Jean Gabin, were destined to eclipse their revue fame with brilliant careers in the movie industry; others, such as Jane Aubert, Henriette Bépoix, Florelle, Jane Marnac, Yvonne Printemps and Viviane Romance, successfully transferred to the legitimate theater. A few, among them Gaby Deslys, Damia and Fréhel, were to rival Mistinguett as *meneuses de revue* in the magnificent, audacious and extravagant costumes and headdresses designed for them in the studios of Poiret and Erte.

But the Moulin-Rouge was destroyed in a disastrous fire. The Jardin de Paris was forced to close down in spring of that year. Parisiana – ominous portent for the future – had been turned into a movie theater. And

The Bal du Moulin-Rouge was remodeled and reduced in size to make way for the new music hall in 1903. This photo, taken three years later, shows the second generation of quadrille stars approaching the finale of the dance. . . .

. . . but the famous hall was burned down during the war, in 1915, leaving a plaster cupid as the sole witness to its former glories.

the dust of battle was to shroud Europe for four long years of austerity before this dazzling potential could be realized.

CHAPTER EIGHT

The Age of Superlatives

THE AGE OF POIRET and of Erte was an age of superlatives. No apology is made for the frequent occurrence
in this account of such words as lavish and spectacular
and sumptuous and glittering. They are used in their
literal sense: music hall revues *were* remarkable visually;
they did use vast amounts of costly materials; they
were indeed extremely expensive to produce; and the
end product certainly gleamed, scintillated, coruscated
– or glittered. Nor was that glitter a tinsel effect. This
was the period when chorines at the Folies sported
G-strings covered in genuine diamonds, when the
mime Ida Rubinstein spent 30,000 francs (nearly
$5,000) in gold each month on sets of silk underclothes
destined to be worn only once, when the rough
sketches for Erte's costume designs were executed in
flakes of silver and real gold leaf.

The summer of 1914 naturally halted the flow. With
death in the air, even brass buttons were no longer
shined. During the "war to end wars," as in the war
that succeeded it, there was, nevertheless, a boom in
the entertainment business as a whole. Troops on leave
flocked to Paris to forget the rigors of the trenches;
wounded recuperating from the hell of the front line
needed rehabilitation; factory workers, with money in
their pockets, were eager to replace "the reign of Mr.
Bloom, when the loud machines beat on our mind"
with something more musical; the civilian population
were happy to turn their backs on the somber world of
shortages and casualty lists, trading reality for make-
believe. There was in fact no business like show
business. From the beginning of 1915, once govern-
ments realized the propaganda effect on morale, the
show, traditionally enough, went on. In Paris, as in
London and Berlin, blacked-out theaters, cabarets and
music halls functioned normally, and it was not until
1917, when air raids from marauding Gothas and the

threat of shells from "Big Bertha" became acute, that the undertones of war made themselves heard in the French capital.

Naturally enough in a time of national austerity, the lavish revue suffered: the music hall was obliged to veer more toward the variety formula than the spectacular. Yet it was in 1917 that Mme. Rasimi of the Ba-ta-clan contrived to stage a *revue à grand spectacle* at the little Fémina theater, near the Rond-Point des Champs Elysées. The production was notable not only for the splendor and imagination of the settings on the small stage. It also established Mistinguett and Maurice Chevalier as a duo. The new queen of music hall had found a worthy consort.

Chevalier as will be recalled, had been doing his military service near the German border on the outbreak of war. He had subsequently been wounded and taken prisoner. Then, after repeated pleas from Mistinguett (already a popular star in Germany) and a personal intervention by King Alfonso XIII of Spain, he was repatriated at the end of 1916.

After his convalescence, Chevalier made a hesitant comeback at the Folies-Bergère, as though still a little dazzled by the bright lights. But it was at the Fémina with "La Miss" that his talents finally matured, and the

An age of superlatives – but a close study of this picture, taken during the lean war years, will reveal that not every revue tableau was sumptuous or glittering or spectacular.

enraptured public acclaimed a new star of infinite versatility. Chevalier was the complete entertainer – singer, dancer, mime, clown, impressionist, comic actor and charmer – the perfect *meneur de revue.* Many of his successful numbers, moreover, were peculiarly personal to his own brand of humor.

Two examples remained in his repertoire when, in the late 1950s, he was still capable of packing a theater as large as the London Hippodrome with a remarkable one-man show. Among such favorites as "Louise" and the Willemetz-Christiné jazz-age hit, "Valentine," were a syrupy German love song whose romantic, sentimental words were screamed out in the hate-filled voice of Hitler addressing a Nuremberg rally, and a piece of his own entitled *"Accents Melodiques."* The latter, a genuine tour de force, was simply a series of impersonations of people of different nationalities each speaking his own language. Every vignette was utterly convincing: Chevalier *became* the Italian, the Russian, the Spaniard, the Englishman, his stance, gestures, intonation and facial expression perfect in each case. It was only when one heard one's own language "done" that one realized with incredulity that there was not a single genuine word in the whole tirade – each impression was a string of nonsense vocables delivered with consummate assurance.

While Chevalier and his beloved Mistinguett were at the Fémina, Léon Volterra took over the Casino de Paris and completely refashioned the auditorium which the public had so decisively rejected. There, in association with Jacques-Charles, he mounted the historic succession of splendid revues which started in 1917 with *Laissez-les Tomber!*, continued with *Boum!*, *Pari-Kiri*, *La Grande Revue*, *Paris Qui Dance*, *Cach' Ton Piano*, *Paris Qui Jazze* and *Avec le Sourire*, and finished in 1924 with *La Revue Olympique*. But before the first of these could open, there were problems to overcome – repeated delays in the work, strikes, anonymous letters threatening the stars, denunciations to the préfecture of police that the structure was unsafe, everything which seemed to support Jacques-Charles's contention that a conspiracy of rivals was determined to kill the show before it started.★

Nevertheless, the revue did open – and it was an immediate success. The star was Gaby Deslys, at that time a close rival of Mistinguett's, fresh from a personal triumph in an operetta at London's Globe Theater. Her partner was the American dancer Harry Pilcer, whose dynamic neo-Gene Kelly style was a revelation to Parisian audiences. The hit of the show was the

★ Préfecture building experts insisted on a number of tests before the Casino de Paris could open – among them that the new circle, designed on the pillarless, cantilever principle, must support a load of sandbags (readily available in wartime) <u>ten times heavier</u> than the maximum weight of any audience it could seat. The circle survived, but the "experts" nevertheless demanded the addition of two thick wooden pillars below it. These "provisional" supports are still there today.

famous "ladder" tableau, in which the two stars jazzed up and down a complicated arrangements of steps and staircases to the music of the Ragtime Band led by Pilcer's brother, Murray. Predating by two years the Original Dixieland Jazz Band's debut in London, this was the first time America's contribution to modern music had been heard and seen on a European stage.

When air raids increased in severity at the end of the year, Volterra closed the Casino and transferred the whole revue to Marseille where, in addition to the ebullient southerners themselves, there was a ready-made audience of Parisians who had already fled from the bombs. Later, when the raids abated, Volterra reopened the Casino with a second edition of *Laissez-les Tomber!* (which literally means "Let 'em fall!"). This time he signed Chevalier and Mistinguett to play the Deslys–Pilcer roles, with the book suitably amended to fit their talents. It was the only time in their careers that the two stars consented to play in a revue which had not been specially written around them.

The second edition was as much of a hit as the first. On the opening night, all went well until Chevalier's boxing sketch, in which he pugnaciously challenged anyone in the audience who cared to take him on. Normally, there would be a "plant" in the auditorium, a tough-looking character who was hired to be worsted by the star. Once, to Maurice's consternation, the heavyweight champion, Georges Carpentier, strode up on stage – only to allow himself graciously to be "knocked out." But at the premiere, no sooner had Chevalier announced, "I'm not afraid of *anyone* . . .", than the sirens sounded, followed by the menacing drone of bombers overhead. Glancing briefly heavenward, the star muttered: "I wasn't talking to *you!*"

The audience loved it. And this time they really did "Let 'em fall": nobody left the theater, and the revue played right through the raid to a standing ovation.

In the last year of the war, Volterra took over the Apollo, continuing the successful series of operettas which had started with *The Merry Widow* and followed through with *Rêve de Valse* and *La Cocarde de Mimi Pinson*, based on the life of the famous courtesan. At the same time he leased the Olympia to Paul Franck, who was to remain as director until 1928. The theater by now had a fantastic reputation to maintain. Jacques-Charles's sensational revue debut during his tenure of the lease had showcased Polaire, Fragson, Balthy, Max Déarly, Mistinguett, the up-and-coming Yvonne Printemps, and Max Linder, the great silent screen comic from whom Chaplin and Keaton "borrowed"

Damia was one of Paul Franck's discoveries. She was said to sing as much with her arms as with her voice . . . and the voice itself "could only be maintained at the price of three packs of cigarettes a day."

so much. Franck, an enthusiast always eager to promote new talent, was equal to the challenge. He made stars of Lucienne Boyer, Fortugé, Yvonne Georges, Marie Dubas, Damia and Raquel Meller, in a series of productions also featuring the world-famous dancer Argentina and numerous jugglers, acrobats and clowns whose names were already household words.

Of all his discoveries, Damia and Raquel Meller went the furthest. Damia, dark, smoldering and intense, in looks reminiscent of the Portuguese fado singer Amalia Rodrigues, brought a new dimension to the *chanson réaliste*. Her vibrant personality, her expressive gestures (she was said to sing as much with her arms as with her voice), and a style described by the journalist Henri Beraud as "expressing the very soul of the people," all justified her label as "the tragedienne of popular song." A certain stunning sincerity, wrote Jacques Feschotte, "made her a real sovereign of the music hall, often imitated, never equaled." Yet Damia's dramatic stage persona might never have been created had it not been for an insulting remark by the young Sacha Guitry one day at rehearsal when she was still a beginner.

Damia, daughter of a policeman and alumnus of a reform school, had hung around the stage doors of theaters and *caf' conc's* since she ran away from home at the age of fifteen. She'd been taught to sing by the husband of her great friend Fréhel. Finally she had landed a small part at the Chatelet. Now she was rehearsing as a singer. Below a frizz of dark hair, she was tightly swathed in red velvet fringed with gold, and smothered in junk jewelry. "My God!" Guitry exclaimed. "Do you have to look like a performing flea trainer?"

Damia took the point. When she appeared for Franck at the Olympia, she sang against a black backdrop, wearing a long sheath of black silk, black gloves, and a hairstyle framing her face as sleekly as jet. The only relief to the sobriety of that presentation, the only touches of color, were the scarlet of her lips and the whiteness of arms "that moved with the grace of wings beating." From this vision of fashion and restraint, there issued a voice whose indefinable quality (Henri Beraud again) "could only be preserved at the price of three packets of cigarettes a day." Within months Damia was a star.

She sang songs like "*La Veuve*" (a slang term for the guillotine), like "*Pour en Arriver Là*," and like "*La Garde de Nuit sur l'Yser*" (a moving evocation of the horrors of trench warfare). Later, when that Greek-tragedy voice had assured her parallel careers in the legitimate theater and the film industry, she became one of Europe's first recording stars with more "popular" numbers such as "*Mon Matelot*," "*Tu Ne Sais Pas Aimer*" and that echo of the early music hall, "*La Guingette A Fermé Ses Volets*." Like Polaire, she led a solitary life, living only for her art, in the execution of which she was most frequently compared by critics either to a panther or a tigress. Her career continued through World War II and was only terminated by her hatred of the by then ubiquitous microphone.★

Raquel Meller, who came from a poor family in southern Spain, made her debut as a singer of risqué songs at the Arnao theater in the Parabello red-light district of Barcelona. Her first success was the near-striptease "novelty," "Song of the Flea" (which was evidently similar to Angèle Hérard's "Dance of the Flea" performed at the Casino de Paris in the 1890s, at least insofar as each provided a story line giving the performer an excuse to remove several layers of cloth-ing in search of the offending insect). The Spanish version was originally created by a singer named La Chilito, who also introduced "*La Violetera*." It was, however, the latter, along with "*El Relicario*," which brought Raquel Meller fame in France.

Senorita Meller, with her tempting mouth, slum-brous southern eyes and caressing voice, was a re-nowned beauty. She was also a very good singer. Unfortunately, according to contemporary accounts, these attributes made her so much in demand – and so spoiled – that she developed a temperament beside which La Belle Otéro appeared a model of restraint and reason. Her first tame songwriter was a painter, Martinez Abadas, who composed only to amuse him-self and to please her. Their affair lasted long enough for Raquel to become a star in Barcelona, but the relationship was stormy and soon afterward Abadas, unable any longer to tolerate her capriciousness, walked out on her and died, as they say, of a broken heart. José Padilla was the next. He was made of sterner stuff. The first time he brought a song to her apartment, she liked it so much that she insisted on learning it right away. She would introduce it in her act that very night. Padilla sat down at the piano and they ran it through. When she had finished, the song-writer shook his head. "Senorita Meller," he said, "that is not the way the song is written."

Raquel's eyes flashed. "It is the way I wish to sing it."

Padilla closed the piano. "It is my song," he said politely. "If it is to be sung at all, Senorita, it will be

★ Interviewed by French television in 1976, when she was eighty-seven years old, Damia remained equally enigmatic, equally solitary in her small apartment on the heights of Montmartre. Nor had her dislike of the microphone weakened. "Singers today have got no guts," she said. "They're lost without their micro – that little stick behind which a singer congeals into another stick! If you want to know what killed the music hall, you don't have to look any further than that." Damia died at the beginning of 1978.

sung the way *I* wish it to be sung, and not the way *you* wish to sing it." And he gathered up his manuscript and left.

Subsequently La Meller pleaded with Padilla, shouted at him, wept, insulted him, threw tantrums – and finally sent a messenger to say that, yes, she would sing the song the way he wanted it sung. That was the start of another relationship that brought each of the partners equal renown throughout the world. This time – perhaps because Padilla was the one man who refused to give in to her – it was Raquel Meller who broke it off. In so doing, she lost the chance to introduce "Valencia," the biggest hit Padilla ever wrote. But she continued on her tempestuous way, gaining fame and losing friends, until in the late 1930s she married for the second time and retired to Spain. When she was at the height of her career, she became so authoritarian and difficult to deal with that, on one U.S. tour, her impresario, exasperated beyond endurance, quit her private train at a wayside station and disappeared into the unknown – relinquishing his star, the tour, his lucrative percentage, and even his toothbrush, razor and personal baggage rather than continue.

Such behaviour was not unknown in the United States. Since the early 1900s, show business had been enlivened by the antics of the one-woman wave of destruction known as Eva Tanguay. This terrifying lady was "an electrified hoyden, a temperamental terror to the managers, a riotous joy to her audiences. A singing and dancing comedienne, it is easy to analyze her act: it was assault and battery . . . under the very nose of Albee she got more sex into her shouted numbers than could be found in a crib street in a mining town."[56]

Curiously enough, Tanguay was basically French too: she was born in Canada in 1878 of a Parisian father and a French-Canadian mother. She began her career working for George M. Cohan in the 1890s. A few years later her salary had leaped from the $40 a week class to $2,500 – an incredible sum for the time. It was, according to Douglas Gilbert,[57] "impossible to overestimate Tanguay's personality or her influence in vaudeville. In the years she was tops, this astonishing woman alone jolted the maudlin period of the early 1900s away from its eye-dabbing with the vigor of unashamed sex. Precisely when the vaudeville public was listening to such treacle as 'You'll Be Sorry Just Too Late,' Tanguay was screaming 'I Want Someone to Go Wild with Me'; 'It's All Been Done Before – but Not the Way I Do It'; and 'Go As Far As You Like.'" To the fury of Keith, who was forced to tolerate this deliberate flaunting of his puritan policy because she had such tremendous box-office pull, Tanguay developed "these naughtily suggestive numbers . . . in her brassy delivery almost to physical fulfillment."

Offstage, Eva Tanguay was just impossible. She missed matinees if she felt tired; she assaulted chorines if she thought they were making eyes at her man; she would bawl out an audience, calling them smalltown hicks, if her dressing room wasn't comfortable enough. Once she threw a stagehand down a flight of stairs because he "got in her way" when she was taking a curtain call. On one circuit the managers exacted a $5,000 cash bond from her in every town – to keep

Nora Bayes. She was prepared to settle for billing that termed her "The Greatest Single Woman Singing Comedienne in the World."

the peace, and the terms of her engagement. Eva paid the fines, settled the suits, shouted back. She was one of the first stars to realize the value of publicity – any publicity – and the number of times her jewels were "stolen," or she was "kidnapped" before an appearance in the sticks that would have bored her, became a press joke. Despite the brawls, she was nevertheless surprisingly honest. She once admitted to an interviewer that her success was entirely due to the publicity and the exploitation of her personality. "I am not beautiful," she confessed, "I can't sing, I don't know how to dance. As a matter of fact, I'm not even graceful."

It *was* a matter of fact. But Eva Tanguay was estimated to have saved more than two million dollars in thirty years of trouping. She lost it all in the 1929 Wall Street crash.

Tanguay was billed as "The Girl Who Made Vaudeville Famous." Nora Bayes, her biggest rival as a headliner, was content with "The Greatest Single Woman Singing Comedienne in the World." But then Bayes always was fussy over her billing: nearly all the quarrels she had with Albee, Keith, Ziegfeld, the U.B.O. and a dozen other managements were over the size of her name or her place on the program. She first drew the attention of the public at the Fifth Avenue Theater in New York in 1907 (where she was fortunate enough to have the untalented Lillie Langtry as top-of-the-bill). A year later, with Jack Norworth, she was drawing $2,500 a week. In 1909, two years after its first "edition," she starred in Ziegfeld's *Follies*, and by 1914 she was big enough to start a thirty-week vaudeville tour at the New York Palace.

Her material was very different from Tanguay's. She has been described as "the American Guilbert, mistress of effortless talent in gesture, poise, delivery and facial work." There was something of Damia's tragedy genius in her too. Gibert wrote[58]: "No one could outrival her in dramatizing a song. She was entrancing, exasperating, generous, inconsiderate – a split personality; a fascinating figure."★

One of Nora Bayes's numerous comebacks was at the London Palladium in 1926 (when she was down to $300 a week). Cissie Loftus was doing a Bayes impersonation – when the original came up on stage and helped her with it. The act went over well, and they repeated it in New York at the Palace. This got Bayes back on the Keith circuit at $2,500. Her last comeback was on the West Coast in a sketch – they were still doing afterpieces in vaudeville then. Her partner was a young man earning $350 a week as a singing single. Name of Jack Benny.

There were plenty of others waiting to make their bow. Between them, burlesque and vaudeville produced a galaxy of stars, many of whom were to cross the Atlantic and make their names in European music hall as well. Eddie Cantor and Jimmy Durante started out in the Coney Island equivalent of a *café chantant*, bawling out songs and wisecracks while the customers tucked into thick rye sandwiches and steins of beer. W. C. Fields, Fanny Brice, Al Jolson, Joe E. Brown, Leon Errol and Vinnie Henshaw learned their trade in the rough houses of burlesque's Columbia and Eastern wheels. Vaudeville cradled the talents of George Jessel, Marie Dressler, Weber and Fields, Blossom Seeley, Marilyn Miller, Elfie Fay, Marie Cahill, the Dolly Sisters, Florence Mills and others too numerous to mention. Except perhaps Elsie Janis and Sophie Tucker.

Before the First World War, however, both vaudeville and burlesque found themselves on a slight downgrade. Forgetting its rumbustious origins, vaudeville was hanging red velvet drapes behind singers in a doomed attempt to make a "classy" image for itself on a par with musical comedy. The thief, too, had been invited in the back door: instead of an afterpiece,

Jimmy Durante – bawling out songs and wisecracks while the customers tucked in to thick rye sandwiches and steins of beer.

THEATER AND MUSIC COLLECTION: MUSEUM OF THE CITY OF NEW YORK

★ **Much of the inconsistency in Nora Bayes's personal life, and the unevenness marring her work later in her career, may have been due to the cancer which was secretly ravaging her body and which finally killed her in 1928.**

many vaude shows now closed with a biograph flicker or short movie. The motion picture had also siphoned off some of the burly trade: since the circuits no longer featured travesties or genuine burlesques, melodrama fans who wanted their heroines trussed to railroad tracks or ravished by the rascally squire were forced to go to the movies for their entertainment.

Legitimate producers were the first to spot the danger. In 1911 Charles Frohman inserted a clause forbidding movie work in all his contracts. "There will be no welcome mat at Frohman's," he said, "for stage actors who fill out a summer wait before the cameras." Later, Keith and Albee joined with other impresarios barring film acts from their theaters – a veto subsequently extended to the radio too. None of them foresaw the day when superstars like Benny, Bob Hope, Frank Sinatra or Judy Garland would drag down $30,000 a week, year after year, alternating radio, television, screen, nightclub and occasional stage appearances.

Burlesque was cleaned up considerably around the turn of the century, many touring shows featuring a fancy book with special music, lyrics and production numbers. Business at once fell off; this equivalent of the European revue was bringing burlesque into disastrous competition with the smarter, more professional musical comedy productions. What was needed, the tycoons decided, was a return to the "real" burleycue – two pieces and an olio, with all the accents on smut. A lady named Odell performed the first striptease at New York's American Theater in 1907. By the end of the year, the grosses at burlesque houses were increasing in inverse proportion to the area of flesh clothed.

The real boom waited for the war years, but before that there was a spin-off, again based on the European music hall formula. It started with a cabaret revue, offered with food and drink at the Fulton Theater on New York's 46th Street in 1911. Jesse L. Lasky, later a big wheel in Hollywood, was the man behind the project, which he called the *Folies-Bergère*. But even with top-line stars and James J. Morton as master of ceremonies, the place never clicked with the public and folded in less than a year. Lasky lost a cool $100,000 as punishment for being ahead of the times.

But only just ahead. Ironically, the show aroused a latent interest in cabaret that only spread after it closed. There was nothing new about a "combined eye-ear-and-mouth feast" of course. Coney Island had been supplying them for years. Higher up the social ladder, vaudeville headliners gave impromptu performances three times a week at the Café des Beaux Arts on West 40th Street. But this was to an audience of professionals – and diners came by invitation only. The idea was nevertheless taken up elsewhere: Farbacher of New Orleans introduced "acts while you eat" in 1909, and a year later there were fashionable restaurants in Saratoga and Boston offering "vaude-ville between courses." By 1912, huge "cabarets" such as Shanley's, Maxim's and Louis Martin's were proliferating all over New York. They were so successful – and the takings, ranging from $20,000 to $30,000 a week, so huge – that show business managers began taking over from the restaurateurs. With the obvious result that, as more money was laid out to pay for the entertainers, the quality of the food declined. By the time the war was over, Europe had, as it were, lost out again – and the movement had channeled itself toward the plush nightspot on one hand and the Prohibition speakeasy on the other.

An exception to this rule – at least in the earliest editions – was Florenz Ziegfeld's *Follies*: the first few productions were staged in the roof garden of the New York Theater in a setting reproducing a typical Parisian café concert, complete with iron tables, striped awnings and trees in the lamplight. But then Ziegfeld was an exceptional man; few of his ventures followed any rules save those he chose to invent himself.

Son of a Chicago German immigrant who had awarded himself a European "degree" and then founded the city's musical college, young Flo made his show business bow outshooting the legendary Annie Oakley when she challenged the audience in Buffalo Bill's touring circus. He had perfected his aim gunning down tame pigeons in his parents' backyard. His own debut as a promoter featured a tent show presenting "The Dancing Ducks of Denmark." SPCA officials closed the show when it was discovered that the birds (in fact from a neighborhood farm) were "dancing" and "singing" to the music because a fellow conspirator was playing the flame of a spirit lamp on the underside of their metal "stage." Ziegfeld came back with "The Invisible Brazilian Fish" – an outsized tank filled with nothing more Latin than water.

The blend of callousness, invention and ruthless efficiency characterizing these youthful excesses con-tinued to color his actions once he broke into theater business proper. Ziegfeld's father had been appointed musical director of the Chicago Columbian Exposition in 1893 and he sent his son to Europe to book classical players for the great Hall of Music he had designed for the fair. But Flo returned with material more suited to a music hall than a hall of music – a bizarre selection of specialty acts which had taken his fancy in London, Paris and Berlin. The little music there was didn't go down so good with the crowds, so father was forced to season the concerts with aerialists and trick cyclists. But still they stayed away in thousands. What was needed was a good top of the bill. Flo went to New York to find one.

He succeeded at the Casino Theater, on Broadway and 39th Street (its similarity to the London Alhambra was emphasized by Moorish architecture, an onion cupola, and the vast 'buffet floor" from which the show could be watched). The star was Eugene Sandow, Apollo of the 1890s and the world's strongest man.

In Chicago Ziegfeld surrounded him with the specialties, added food and drink at tables served in the orchestra, and substituted skin-tight satin shorts for the traditional weightlifter's leopardskin and white tights. With his blond hair and his oiled body gleaming in a single spot, Sandow was a sensation . . . hoisting his accompanist in one hand and the piano in the other, opening a safe with his teeth, lifting an enormous dumbbell with a man concealed in each ball. Young Ziegfeld – he was twenty-six at the time – found himself pulling in a net profit of more than $5,000 a week.

When the fair was over, he took Sandow on a nationwide tour and made nearly a quarter of a million dollars. Later he persuaded Evans and Hoey, the biggest comedy duo in the business, to revive a burlesque called *A Parlor Match*, which held the record for Broadway's longest run – 2,550 performances. Ziegfeld's masterstroke, however, was to transform the comedy into a musical. And among the numbers were Charles Evan Evans's theme song, "The Man Who Broke the Bank at Monte Carlo," and a novelty based on the cycling craze sweeping Europe and the United States. It was called "A Bicycle Built for Two."

Evans was in some ways an American equivalent of a French *boulevardier* or a British lion comique. Ziegfeld too was a dandy, immaculate in London-tailored suits, tall hat and gold-knobbed cane. By this time he was also an adept at the shrewd publicity stunt, the attention-drawing gimmick, no matter how outrageous, and a style of living which combined egotism and panache in a manner inseparable from showmanship. Together with Evans, he went to London to look for a European beauty who could star in *A Parlor*

PHOTO: REUTLINGER

Anna Held at the time she first came to the United States to work for Ziegfeld.

Match and rival Oscar Hammerstein's success with Yvette Guilbert. It was there that he met Anna Held, who was appearing at the Palace music hall on Cambridge Circus.

She was gorgeous, "with ravishing, opalescent eyes, a perfect hourglass figure (her waist was eighteen inches), and an exquisite style, which consisted of perfectly timed shrugs, wriggles, and a tiny erotic laugh at the end of the stanzas of a song."[59] She was also, despite the apparent innocence of her looks, an artist who could put over a song with as much implied sexuality as Marie Lloyd. Ziegfeld determined to book her right away.

The only trouble was, Mlle. Held was already contracted to Marchand (who was still director of the Folies-Bergère at that time) for the winter season.

Ziegfeld's biographers (there are several of them) disagree about the origin of his romance with Anna Held. Some say that he was resolved to sign her at all costs – and that marriage was the price he paid; others claim that he was genuinely in love with her from the moment he saw her. At any rate, he bombarded her with flowers, invitations, gifts of jewelry, telegrams of adoration – and finally he persuaded her to break her contract and come back with him to the United States. *A Parlor Match* was a smash hit. It was followed by a season at Koster and Bial's, a nationwide tour, a starring role in *The Parisian Model* – the first show to highlight Ziegfeld's genius for presenting beautiful women in daring settings.

At the same time, Ziegfeld was "merchandizing" his wife as if she were a box of breakfast cereal. The profligate extravagance of their private lives was made public through the society columns of the newspapers; there was the $22,000 Anna Held railroad pullman, which had once belonged to Lillie Langtry; there was the five-piece band which accompanied her wherever she went; there was an Anna Held statue cast in $35,000 worth of solid gold; there were carefully arranged "thefts" of her fabulous jewels, Cleopatra-style milk baths wherever she stayed, a model farm in Maine – and of course the fabulous thirteen-room apartment at the Ansonia hotel in New York. This luxury suite, heavy with the scent of one thousand American Beauty roses, was "furnished in blue and gold, with exquisite antiques, paintings, sculptures, busts and lavish sofas."

> The boudoir was based on the style of Louis XIV, the bed of heavily carved ivory laden with Irish point lace and blue satin, its canopy made of satin and lace. The bath and dressing room were done in Dresden brocade and ivory, the screens covered in exquisite eighteenth-century woodland designs. The drawing room was of yellow moiré antique – walls, divans, chairs and sofas. The piano was stained a rich red-gold and embossed with solid gold; its keyboard was made of pure mother-of-pearl.[60]

Anna and her husband settled into an enviable routine: a fall season in New York, a triumphant tour of the United States, and then a few months relaxation in the pleasure capitals of Europe before the next autumnal opening stateside. The famous *Follies* were inaugurated in 1907, not at first to make too much of an impact on the show business scene. The initial production was little more than a prettied-up vaudeville show; the second, starring Nora Bayes and Jack Norworth, was more successful with the public; but it was not until Ziegfeld moved the series to the New Amsterdam Theater in 1913, and started his epoch-making partnership with the Viennese designer Josef Urban two years later, that the breath-taking spectacles for which the impresario became famous took shape.

He had shown his flair for imaginative settings when Anna Held played a short season at the Harlem Opera House in 1898. She sang in front of an immense blow-up magnifying the score of her song – and as she sang, the heads of black singers appeared individually from the relevant black notes in the music by way of chorus. Now, with the Pre-Raphaelite and art-déco extravagance of the New Amsterdam as a frame, Ziegfeld and Urban composed tableaux which for daring and originality rivaled the best that Paris could produce. The costumes too were superb. Ziegfeld insisted that his showgirls were clothed – or unclothed – in the costliest and most luxurious fabrics; Urban, who applied the theories and principles of the impressionists to stage design, insisted that the dyes harmonized completely with his sets. Even offstage, the two men agreed, their beauties must be able to compete with the most fashionable and chic of the socialites.

Where the *Follies* differed from its counterparts in Paris was precisely in this concentration on the physical charms of "Les Girls." There were of course chorus lines and nudes and showgirls at the Moulin-Rouge and the Scala and the Folies-Bergère and the Casino de Paris. Some of them even alternated work for Ziegfeld with contracts for Volterra and Jacques-Charles. But in France they were merely, as it were, the blue velvet against which the gems of the topliners glittered. At the New Amsterdam they themselves were the jewels.

Ziegfeld's public ambition, often stated, was "to glorify the American girl." Unfortunately it coincided all too frequently with a private ambition to glorify the Ziegfeld casting couch. Anna Held, who had at first turned a charitably blind eye to his infidelities, left him in 1908 when he urged her to have an abortion rather than allow her pregnancy to delay the opening of *Miss Innocence*. Greatly distressed, the actress refused. A bitter quarrel broke out, and finally Anna fainted. When she came to, the apartment reeked of chloroform and the abortion had been performed. Although she duly starred in the show and several later editions of the *Follies*, Anna Held never forgave him and they were finally divorced in 1912.

By this time he was firmly enmeshed in a scandalous liaison with the showgirl Lillian Lorraine (later, a similar entanglement with Marilyn Miller, the star of *Sally*, threatened to wreck his marriage to Billie Burke). A man whose driving force was "one of demonic sensuality and a passion for vivid artifice," Ziegfeld made his stage productions "direct expressions of his essentially primitive sexual character," Charles Higham wrote.[61] The *Follies* were "astonishing demonstrations of the mind of a man who sought to release his need for women in displays of adulation for them."

The egoism and ruthlessness marring his relationships with women extended also to his business life. He hated settling bills, he refused to pay royalties to his composers, he was arrogant with inferiors and he fawned on the important. Unable to tolerate differences of opinion, he quarreled with Abe Erlanger and Marc Klaw, the men who had put up the money for the *Follies*. He quarreled with the Schuberts and he quarreled with Oscar Hammerstein. Few of the many profiles written about him contrive to present a character any less objectionable than that of Albee or Keith.

Yet such was this man's charisma, so much charm could he bring to his fulsome appreciation of an artist, that stars as diverse as Mae West and Fanny Brice, Sophie Tucker and Will Rogers, Paul Robeson and W. C. Fields all worked for him and loved him. He bullied them and overworked them, he sent long rambling telegrams complaining about their performances, he betrayed them and frequently underpaid them – but they kept on coming back for more. And at first Ziegfeld was able to supply it. Apart from the *Follies* – and a boozy and short-lived sister show called *Midnight Frolics*, which was killed by Prohibition – he produced some of the biggest musical comedy hits in Broadway history. These included *Kid Boots*, *Whoopee!*, *Rosalie*, *Show Boat*, and Noel Coward's *Bitter Sweet*.

But as he grew older, the pettiness increased along with the extravagance. The diamond wristwatches and jeweled bracelets showered on his women increased in number. So did the unpaid bills on his office desk. It was this mean streak in his nature that led ultimately to his downfall. When the stock market crashed in October of 1929, Ziegfeld's brokers tried frantically all day long to contact him, to advise him to sell out and cut his losses. Ziegfeld was in court all day, countersuing on a trivial claim concerning an electric sign which he alleged was defective, so he lost everything. Three years later he died, leaving a million dollars' worth of debts.

But in the years immediately after the First World War, he was on the crest of the wave, America's greatest showman, the most dazzling star along the Great White Way. In his own desire to escape reality, he became a trailblazer in the supply of fantasy, and it was he as much as Cochran or Jacques-Charles who brought *pace* to the revue format – and he who shared with those European directors the credit for introducing a "cinematic" approach to theater presentation.

Meanwhile, back at the music hall ranch in Paris, all the horses were changing riders. As befitted a man of the turf, Volterra and his associates had previously acquired the best runners. Between them they controlled the Folies (for which Erté had been designing since 1915), the Alcazar, Les Ambassadeurs and the Casino de Paris – that is to say, all the "international" houses except Ba-ta-clan and the Olympia, which they had leased to Paul Franck. Now Dufrenne and Varna, who were already directing the Concert Mayol, took over Les Ambassadeurs and the Alcazar, and Derval, artistic director of the Folies, also became its administrator – a post he held with conspicuous success until his death in 1966, when he was succeeded by his widow and Michael Gyarmathy, who had followed him as artistic director.

At the end of the war, Chevalier and Mistinguett were rehearsing *Pari-Kiri* at the Casino for Volterra and Jacques-Charles – and it was at this time that the first rift in their real-life love affair appeared, although it continued ostensibly on stage for the benefit of their public. The reason for the private breakup was a professional one. It was in fact the old, old story: Maurice wanted to find his own feet, to be known as a star in his own right and not just as the partner of "La Miss." To put it more practically, he asked for equal billing.

Mistinguett was unwilling – not (according to the fine distinction Jacques-Charles drew later) because she wished to stop Maurice getting bigger; no, no – it was to prevent herself getting smaller. Whatever the reasons, rift there was. The two stars now left the theater separately each night, Mistinguett customarily on the arm of seventeen-year-old Charles Gesmar, the brilliant young designer who was to produce the star's most imaginative posters and costumes rivaling those of Poiret and Erté in their magnificence. Maurice and "Miss" appeared together in several more revues, including *Paris Qui Dance* and *Paris Qui Jazze* at the Casino. But Chevalier went on to capture the hearts of London's matinee ladies in a revue with the American vaudeville star Elsie Janis, before returning to France to star on his own in *Avec Le Sourire*. Mistinguett had in the meantime gone to New York with Jacques-Charles, where the director cemented a mutually profitable relationship with Ziegfeld and

George White which had originated before the war.

In 1912, Charles had hired George White, then working as a solo tap dancer, for one of his early revues at the Olympia. The American was not a success. But what he saw of the *revue à grand spectacle* during his stay in Paris inspired him to become a showman himself – and from this developed the series of *George White's Scandals* that were to rival the Ziegfeld *Follies* and Earl Carroll *Vanities* as the hit of Broadway. In the same prewar season Jacques-Charles had signed Vernon and Irene Castle. Vernon was making a name for himself as an old-time slapstick comic in a barbershop sketch complete with pratfalls and acres of property lather. It was only to give him the excuse to bring his girlfriend on the trip that their dancing act was formed. Both the sketch and the dance number flopped at the Olympia; but when the couple transferred to cabaret at the Café de Paris, they were a riot. French socialites waited for two weeks to book tables from which they could watch the Castles' graceful exhibitions of the fox trot, the shimmy, the one-step, and other transatlantic specialties (although Charles insists that Vernon Castle never came anywhere near the matchless artistry of Fred Astaire, who played the title role in the film version of the Castles' life). The dancers returned to New York not long before the war with ready-made reputations – although, ironically, their subsequent American success was due to their introduction of the tango and the maxixe, which they had learned from a Brazilian dance instructor in Paris.

When the war was over, such "cross-fertilizations" increased. In 1919, Poiret designed the famous London musical *Afgar*, starring Alice Delysia, and his "orientalism," allied to that of Diaghilev, Bakst and their colleagues, greatly influenced music hall and revue all over the world. It was later to make its mark, too, in the silent movie via Valentino, Novarro, Griffiths and de Mille. In the same way the lavishness of French stage productions was reflected, via Broadway, in the early film musicals masterminded by Busby Berkeley. Ziegfeld bought the right to stage a selection of Jacques-Charles's tableaux in his New Amsterdam Theater *Follies*; the French director took back "Tulip Time" and Irving Berlin's "A Pretty Girl Is Like a Melody" for the revue *Paris Qui Dance*. The latter song is usually associated with Ziegfeld's great production number – a spiral set mounted in wedding-cake tiers on a revolve, above which hundreds of showgirls and dress-suited beaux swing slowly one after the other into view, singing the melody. Charles's tableau – one

of his most famous – was entirely different. From a giant grand piano, there arose in succession the heroines of the world's most famous light operas – Mimi, Madame Butterfly, Carmen, the Merry Widow, Lakme, La Belle Hélène, each in an appropriately sumptuous costume. But the last of all was Venus, complete, *à la* Botticelli, with comb, mirror and shell – but minus costume or even G-string. This was the first time that a genuine "full-frontal" nude had been exhibited on a European stage.

During the postwar visit to the United States, Jacques-Charles also contracted Pearl White, the soap opera queen, to appear in one of his revues, and collaborated with the then unknown George Gershwin on "Swanee" and "Somebody Loves Me," which became the biggest hit of *George White's Scandals*. Gershwin himself always said that his European colleague's setting for "Rhapsody in Blue" was the

Rebuilt after the fire, the Moulin-Rouge advertises a "grand revue" that is "better than naked." The photo, taken in 1925, shows the separate entrances to the dance hall and the theater. Behind the latter, there is a glimpse of the garden, still in existence at that time.

199

only one to capture the true spirit of the composition, where the final section portrays the end of the night and presages the dawn. The designer's own words put it this way:

> Behind night-blue gauzes scattered with stars, girls with starshaped diamond headdresses appeared crossing and recrossing on invisible ramps, only their heads being illuminated. One by one, the gauzes melted away, until at last only the backcloth, which represented the Milky Way, remained. And then this, too, was flown to reveal Phoebus, splendid in gold, driving his four-horse chariot.

It was during the revue *Paris Qui Jazze* that Mistinguett launched her all-time hit, "*Mon Homme*" ("My Man"). The song was written by Maurice Yvain, who had also composed the music for a "fashion through the ages" tableau dressed by Poiret and Erte. In this particular scene, Mistinguett was to represent, as part of "the Armory of Women," the then fashionable Coty perfume named simply "Rose." Poiret and Erte had created for her a magnificent costume made from thousands of rose petals whose subtle colors varied from full-blown to faded. When the star saw it at one of the final rehearsals, she stamped her foot with rage. "I won't be a silly old faded rose!" she stormed. (Mistinguett always put on a little girl act when she was mad.) "Me, I have to be a rose that's freshly picked . . . with dewdrops still on it." She paused a moment and then added: "Dewdrops made of diamonds."

Swallowing their rage (for the star was also an important private client for whom they made not only costumes but street clothes, accessories and jewelry to match), the costumier and his artist were obliged to abandon their subtly shaded creation and do as she wished. It was thus with some diffidence that Volterra and Jacques-Charles approached the subject of Yvain's new song. They knew it was right for Mistinguett, but they also knew their star. The possessor of the world's most beautiful legs also possessed, along with many of her music hall contemporaries, one of the world's most exasperating temperaments. An aspect of the latter infuriating to a director was that she would always prefer to copy, amend or improve something she had seen another artist do, rather than try out an original idea. There had already been trouble over a comic sketch she was to play with Chevalier – mainly because she was scared that

Chevalier, with whom she had already broken in private life, might upstage her and get more laughs. Charles and his co-author, Willemetz, only obtained her approval of the final version by pretending they had not revised it themselves, but contracted the job out to Rip. How, then, were they to get her to consent to the inclusion of a song she'd never heard?

They decided to row Chevalier in on the deal. Yvain played through "*Mon Homme*" at the piano. As they had expected, "Miss" trotted out the little girl act. "Not bad," she said. "But not quite *quite*. That's not the song for little me." The authors protested, argued, extolled the virtues of the lyric, the merits of the tune. She shook her pretty head more firmly, astonished that they were not giving way as usual. They continued to insist. Voices were raised. And then, dead on cue, Chevalier entered.

"Look," Mistinguett burst out, casting desperately around for an ally, "here's Maurice. Ask him what *he* thinks!"

The composer played the song through once more. Said Chevalier, according to his script: "Miss, if you don't sing that song, I'll sing it myself!"

"I'll sing it," Mistinguett said.★

It was in this revue that the blond American dancer Earl Leslie made his French debut, following a successful season in London with the Dolly Sisters. Mistinguett had already imported Carl Randall from the United States in a previous show – perhaps with the idea of making Chevalier jealous. But by now Maurice was in love with Jane Myro, the Casino "house" singer – and this time it was Mistinguett herself who fell. Earl Leslie became her regular partner, and the two were inseparable for many years.

By 1923, the Folies, the Casino de Paris, Ba-ta-clan, the Olympia and Les Ambassadeurs were leading the lavish revue field. The Scala had switched to a policy of fashionable farces in 1920 and was only to feature music hall again for a short period in the mid-1930s. The Cigale – following a successful revue called *Batignolles-Clichy-Odéon*, after stations on the Paris Métro – had become an experimental theater. The Moulin-Rouge, rebuilt after the 1914 fire, had reopened, but was confining itself, like the Bal Tabarin, to programs of ballet and cancan dancing repeated several times each evening while the patrons dined. Then, twelve days after *La Revue aux Etoiles* had opened, the Casino itself was burned. Were those same anonymous forces which had attempted to impede the opening at work again? Nobody knew. But although the iron safety

★ In fact Chevalier really did like the song "Mon Homme." He liked it so much that he commissioned the author to write a parody, "C'est ma Bonne," which he sang in Avec le Sourire the following year.

*Barbette – fifty pounds of
ostrich feathers and a high wire.*

curtain preserved most of the auditorium, the whole
of the stage and backstage area was gutted. The show –
it was the revue for which Pearl White had been
booked – was abandoned (but the title was later revived
by Jacques–Charles for a production at the Moulin-
Rouge).

Six months later, Volterra reopened – having spent
a fortune on the latest stage machinery and effects.
The latter included a glass tank holding 100,000 liters
of water, which rose, *ready-filled*, from the depths to
take up the whole width of the new stage and receive
the entire cast in a mass dive at the end of the second-
act finale. The revue, which was titled *En Douce*,
starred Mistinguett and Dorville. Among other innovations it featured a product "Miss" herself had discovered and brought back from her New York visit:
a luminous paint to color flesh, with which Jacques-
Charles created a tableau of nude ebony, jade, purple
onyx and marble "statues" presented on a revolve.
In a theater plunged into total blackness, the effect was
remarkable. The show as a whole was such a success
that Volterra copied the example of C. B. Cochran –
whose "young ladies" were the hit of the London revue

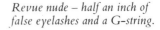
Revue nude – half an inch of false eyelashes and a G-string.

stage dominated by Tilly Losch – and presented a second edition immediately afterward.

This time, despite the sensational aquashow, despite the nudes and the additional presence of Yvonne Georges and the Japanese star Sessue Hayakawa, despite the ingenuity of the Casino's stage manager, Charles Plombin,★ the hit of the show was one of the specialties – a flying trapeze and high-wire act performing under the name of Barbette. Against a sky-blue backdrop, Barbette executed a series of graceful but breath-taking maneuvers in a diaphanous white ball gown loaded with fifty pounds of ostrich feathers. The act concluded with a dizzy *chute d'ange* (the famous angel's dive) onto a white carpet while the orchestra played music from *Scheherezade*. But instead of taking the customary curtsey-cum-bow, the artist then snatched off a blonde wig to reveal the near-bald head and engaging grin of a young Texan named Van der Clyde, hands clenched above his head in a wrestler's salute.

At the premiere there was a moment of stunned silence. It was always exciting to watch a daredevil aerialist work without a net; it was more spectacular

★ **Charles Plombin invented an electrical cue machine which, although it "resembled nothing as much as an iron bedstead recuperated from a garbage dump," enabled him from beside the orchestra conductor to control all the lights, all the artists' entrances and exits, and even raise musicians from the pit for featured solos.**

still when the performer was encumbered with a costume as ornate as one of Mistinguett's in a production number. But to find at the end that they had been deluded by a brilliant female impersonator as well . . . the audience broke into a storm of applause.

Successor to Julian Eltinge and forerunner of Arthur Blake, Danny Larue and Coccinelle, Barbette was one of the most tasteful and convincing drag acts ever to take the stage. He became one of the most sought-after – and most highly paid – performers in Paris throughout the twenties.

There was plenty of competition. A natural swing back to extravagance after the austerity of wartime was reflected in ever more exotic productions. And, paradoxically, the more sumptuous the décors, the less the performers actually wore. There was therefore a proportionally greater interest in such few items as did save them from total nudity – bizarre ornaments, costume jewelry and accessories, and especially the magnificent headdresses which were a feature of the period. Such art-déco pioneers as Ruhlmann, Lalique and Dufresne therefore added their design talents to those of the artists already working for the music hall. Of these, Erte was the acknowledged master, but José de Zamora, Ranson, Brunelleschi, George Barbier, Drian, Dulac, Freddy Wittop and Mistinguett's friend Gesmar were creating sets and costumes of almost equal brilliance. At a time when music hall stars still formed part of a social tradition that shaped the pattern of life in the capital, Mistinguett herself – gowned, hatted, furred, gloved, jeweled and even perfumed by Erte and Poiret – was the epitome of glamor for Parisians. She was at the center of the universe of talent brightening the lives of France's Bright Young People.

Around her, other highlights of the music hall firmament revolved – stars like Loie Fuller and Gaby Montbreuse, Damia and the Dolly Sisters, Vivian Romance and Yvonne Printemps; satellites such as Raimu and Fernandel and Arletty. There was, too, a talented newcomer named Jean Gabin, originally hired by Mistinguett as a master of ceremonies and sketch actor because of an imagined resemblance to Chevalier.

It was Maurice himself who headed the revue which electrified Paris at the Empire in 1924. After a series of popular operettas, the theater had been demolished and the architect Farge built for Dufrenne and Varna an immense auditorium with a stage so big that it could be turned into a circus ring (it was one hundred feet wide and seventy feet deep) and seating for an audience of three thousand. With *La Revue Olympique* running at the Casino, the Empire curtain rose for the first time on February 29 (it was leap year as well as Olympic year), and the initial productions dazzled even Paris with their richness and variety. Chevalier was surrounded by a huge ballet and forty horses; Little Tich crossed the Channel for his last memorable appearance; Jack Hylton's band came from London and Sophie Tucker from New York; Jenny Golder and the Fratellinis were followed by Powers' Musical Elephants and Captain Winstone's Mermaids and Seals. And after them came Barbette, Bagesson, Damia, Grock, the return of Yvette Guilbert, Layton and Johnston, Raquel Meller, Gaby Morlay and a host of others. Nobody had ever seen anything like it.

They were, however, soon to do so. The older music halls countered the offensive with talent and with magnificence. Les Ambassadeurs imported Florence Mills and *Blackbirds*, followed by Cole Porter's first musical and George Gershwin playing "Rhapsody In Blue" in front of the décor he liked so much. After a South American tour with his Casino productions,★ Jacques-Charles took Mistinguett to the Moulin-Rouge and staged another series of fabulous revues there. Erte and his contemporaries garnished the shows at the Folies and the Casino de Paris even more audaciously. Revitalizing such standard tableaux as the Seven Deadly Sins, the Four Seasons, Hours of the Day and, perhaps, Flowers in a Bouquet or the alcoholic components of Cocktail, Erte created the "Multiple Costume" and the "Living Curtain." The first of these was a huge single "garment" which might spread across a quarter of the stage, "worn" by anything up to a dozen girls; it was, in effect, a piece of décor animated by performers. And that effect, heightened by complementary costumes on single artists, was poetic rather than grotesque. At its simplest, the "Living Curtain" was a means of hiding the stage with people instead of drapes or gauzes. Sometimes they were lowered like a real curtain; sometimes, in acrobatic pyramids and diamonds, they rose from podiums and blocks; sometimes, arms and legs extending like trellises, they moved out in several tiers from each side of the stage. But the end product was always the same: the whole proscenium arch was filled, in an agreeable pattern, with a phalanx of gorgeously dressed beauties.

Other designers added to the antique, tropical and mythical set pieces typical of revue comments, visual rather than truly satiric, on the modern world. In a technique borrowed from the ballet, showgirls imper-

★ Mistinguett did not make Jacques-Charles's South American trip. She had previously been contracted by Mme. Rasimi of Ba-ta-clan to make a similar tour, following the same route, three weeks after Charles's company. Volterra had given her permission to play the sketches that she had made famous at the Casino, but he made no promise that the same material would not be used by his own company, played by Mistinguett's replacement. In fact, the replacement in the touring company was the young and beautiful Florelle. To her chagrin and rage, Mistinguett discovered, arriving in South America with a scratch team, that audiences had already seen all her best material, played by a younger and prettier rival with a highly organized supporting group, only a short time before. The Rasimi tour was not an unqualified success, which doubtless contributed to the bankruptcy of Ba-ta-clan in 1926.

sonated telephones, typewriters, roulette wheels, spirits
of jazz, subway trains and even cushions. This literal
anthropomorphism, allied to the directors' demands
for eroticism and nudity, inevitably resulted in costumes that were at times fetishist in the extreme.
While Erte remained faithful to splendid orientalism,
José de Zamora, Umberto Brunelleschi, Michael
Gyamarthy, Zig, Revolg and Paul Seltenhammer
experimented with shapes and materials as up-to-date
as the avant-garde art schools producing them.

Typical were Revolg's Casino de Paris costumes for
Yvonne Robinson as a soldier in a park, and for Kitty
Glen as a policewoman. The former comprised
extravagant cavalry thigh boots, a kepi, and very little
else; the latter, based loosely (if the term may be permitted) on a London policeman's uniform, employed
a close-fitting, buckled, neck-to-crotch tunic teamed
with spike-heeled shoes, long black gloves, a truncheon
and the regulation helmet. Doubtless, as Jacques-
Charles has pointed out, these were designed to make
the best of the physical attributes most pronounced
in those two particular girls. But it is interesting to
note that hints, discreet and not so discreet, of trans-
vestism, sadomasochism and transexualism were considered salable commodities back in the twenties.

One of Seltenhammer's creations consisted of laced
knee boots, a thigh bangle, and a tight, shiny black
tunic unflapped to bare the breasts. It was called
l'aiguicheuse – which means a flirt, a coquette, a whetter
of sexual appetites.

Zig designed some very elaborate costumes for
Mistinguett (one swathed the star's body in Grecian
pleats and then swept back in an immense train of
feathers to reveal the famous legs, the whole being
crowned by an absurd parody of a cocked hat with a
mountain of plumes over five feet high). But the
artist's most striking creation was again for a Casino
showgirl – the original drawing would go straight
under the counter in a Soho bookshop or a San
Francisco sex bazaar today. Cascades of lace foamed
around the shoulders and fell from the whole length of
the arms and from the knees. The rest of the body was
tightly encased in black, with a cutout that exposed
the entire front of the torso from the top of the thighs
to the neck. A deep leather belt was fastened around
the waist, and from its butch buckle five thin chains
fanned down to secure a female codpiece sheathing the
pubis. A Homberg hat in black velour completed the
ensemble.

Gyarmathy put Marlene Dietrich into skirts slit to

Mistinguett at her most kittenish, photographed in her dressing room in 1922. Collectors of period detail will relish the décor.

the hip. Palo, perhaps overimpressed by the Blue Angel's legs, designed costumes for the same lady as all seven of the deadly sins. In a style exquisitely reminiscent of Arthur Rackham, George Barbier★ drew chorus costumes that would have made the decadents swoon with ecstasy. More modern was Endré's vorticist design for *l'Esclave* (the Slave) – a black masochist with a saxophone. Zinoviev made girls look sexy as hatboxes, cameras, inkwells or coffee grinders. (Salvador Dali, after all, had done it on canvas with a chest of drawers.) Ranson's curiously suggestive *Mots Croisés* (Crossword Puzzle) could be accepted today as an exhibit at any contemporary op-art gallery, and Mia May played a sketch dressed in rubber – a black mackintosh gown, cape and helmet, with black boots, fringed leather gloves and goggles. Even Josephine Baker appeared in an early specialty wearing a skin-tight red latex catsuit studded with jewels – a garment which, as one reviewer put it, "made her look somewhat more than naked."

Naked she was, nevertheless, when Paris first saw her. Unknown and almost unannounced, she made her European bow in a Louis Douglas revue booked "blind" for the moribund Champs Elysées Music Hall in the Avenue Montaigne – whose sole claim to fame until then was that it was the first theater to be constructed of reinforced concrete. Designed and built in 1912 by the brothers Perret, this triumph of art déco

★ **Like Iribe and Lepape, George Barbier was a frequent contributor of fashion illustrations to such expensive periodicals as the Gazette du Bon Ton, Modes et Manières d'Aujourd'hui, the newly published Vogue, and Art, Goût, Beauté. These paintings, like his costume designs, were works of art in themselves – each a miracle of decorative composition, exquisitely conceived and executed.**

LEFT:
Roaring Twenties ballyhoo was not confined to the United States. When Mistinguett traveled to Brussells in the summer of 1922, she took her personal hairdresser with her "to administer a final touch of the comb before she was ready to face her fans."

RIGHT:
Mistinguett at the Casino de Paris – "I won't be a silly old faded rose!"

boasted frescoes by Maurice Denis and other decorations by Bourdelle, Marval and Vuillard. But despite the admirable acoustics and comfortable auditorium, despite seasons by Loie Fuller and, more recently, a Swedish ballet company uniting all the best talents in Scandinavia, despite appearances by Dranem, Harry Pilcer, a band of Chinese gladiators and an attempt at "chic" music hall starring Pavlova, the place had never quite made its mark with the public. It was the painter Fernand Léger, after the failure of a "Negro" ballet symbolizing the creation of the universe, for which he had designed the décor, who suggested that a cast of genuine blacks from the United States might inject some life into the theater. He had a friend, the Mexican painter Covarrubias, who lived in Harlem and could put them in touch with the right people, he said.

Rolf de Maré, the "angel" who had been financing the Swedish ballet, and André Daven, his director, agreed to give the idea a whirl. After all, Florence Mills had not done too badly at Les Ambassadeurs, just up the road. The show was booked by an American woman named Caroline Dudley and put together by Louis Douglas, who had already appeared in Paris as a dancer at Ba-ta-clan. But when Daven and de Maré attended the first rehearsals, they discovered that the "revue" was no more than an unrelated series of cross-talk acts and tap-dance routines, punctuated by spiritual songs rendered by a large lady named Maud de Forest.

"Catastrophic!" exploded de Maré. "We will pay them off and send them home at once!"

Daven was not so sure. Gémier, the director of the Odéon, had seen them in New York and said they were terrific. The music was lively. And the dancing, especially this novelty called "the Charleston," had a certain life. Before deciding, why not call in Jacques-Charles and ask if he could not turn this medley of disparate elements into a revue suitable for Parisian tastes? De Maré sighed. "Very well," he agreed. "What else can we lose?"

Charles at once saw the latent talent in the cast. There was, moreover, a remarkable jazz group with the show which included the great New Orleans clarinet and soprano saxophone star Sidney Bechet. Rhythm was their business; staging revues was Jacques-Charles's. Between them, they should be able to make something of it. He rehearsed them day and night, and the curtain rose on *La Revue Nègre* on October 23, 1925.

Its subsequent success is legendary. A number of misconceptions have, however, crept into the legend. To begin with, *La Revue Nègre* was not the whole show; it was only the second half. Reports as to its length vary from forty-five minutes to two hours, but in each of its two editions it was preceded by a program of French variety. The first of these included the singer-impressionist Saint-Granier and the Allison Girls; the second comprised the comic singer Gaba-roche, another impressionist named Pierre Pradier, and Damia. Curiously, Jacques-Charles's contribution escapes mention almost everywhere except in his own books. *Comoedia*, in its edition of September 26, 1925, even reported that the show was being rehearsed by Gémier. In her posthumous "autobiography" (compiled by her last husband, Jo Bouillon, from notes she left and the reminiscences of friends),[62] Josephine Baker herself says she never met Gémier – but of Charles she too makes no mention at all. Yet in the director's own autobiography it is clearly stated that, through the vagaries of touring, the couple didn't meet *again* for twenty five years – but that, on that second occasion, Miss Baker reproached herself for being an ingrate, "because I never thanked you, and yet I owe my entire career to you." Another mystery concerns the advertised "star" of *La Revue Nègre*, the overweight

PHOTO: HARLINGUE-VIOLLET

One of the more elaborate costumes dreamed up for Mistinguett . . .

. . . and a simpler design, featuring a hat with a huge transparent brim.

★ **Although the costumes for La Revue Nègre were un- important, there were some designs in the Maya-Aztec style by Alec Shanks – whose name, along with those of Brunskill and Loveday, has been familiar to readers of London theater programs as England's chief builder of stage sets for the past forty years.**

Maud de Forest. Apart from a report that the spotlight operators were discreetly ordered to leave her in shadow and concentrate their beams on the chorus, she seemed to vanish without trace. None of the reviews mentioned her; none of the innumerable memoirs of the period display her name in their indexes. Only Paul Colin, the man who designed the posters and playbills, recalled that, unfortunately, she "looked like an oriental carpet seller" among this lively company "with its cries and contortions, its flock of shaking backsides, it pairs of breasts, provocative, resilient, sporty or diverting, its wooly wigs, its ginghams and its boaters."[63]

The sets, dismissed by one columnist as "pink drapes with hams and watermelons," were in fact designed for the most part by Miguel Covarrubias himself. Extra décors, added to frame supplementary routines inserted by Jacques-Charles, were executed skyscraper-style by Colin. The costumes, unusually for Paris, were unimportant★ – although another legend, frequently repeated in press stories, has it that Josephine Baker wore a belt of bananas around her waist. In fact, Paul Derval was responsible for this when she appeared in a Folies revue some time later. Janet Flanner recalled

what really happened on that first night in the preface to *Paris Was Yesterday*.

The slender, supple, unknown black girl made her entrance nude except for a pink flamingo feather between her thighs (Miss Flanner remembered). She was doing the splits upside down on the back of a black giant.† "Mid-stage he paused, and with his long fingers holding her basketwise around the waist, swung her in a slow cartwheel to the floor, where she stood, like his magnificent discarded burden, in an instant of complete silence. She was an unforgettable female ebony statue. A scream of salutation spread through the theater. Whatever happened next was unimportant."

What happened next was that Miss Baker's performance proved to the French, long before anyone else, that black could be beautiful. And the effects of this, both in the long and the short term, were very important indeed.

Within a half hour of the final curtain on that unforgettable night, the news that a star had been born had spread to the sidewalk cafés of Montparnasse, Montmartre and the Champs Elysées. Large numbers of people who had been at the premiere booked again for the second, third and fourth nights. Such famous

"La Miss" on the traditional golden staircase in the finale of a Jacques-Charles revue. "Gowned, hatted, furred, gloved, jeweled and even scented by Erte and Poiret," she was the epitome of glamor for Paris's bright young people.

† **Miss Baker's partner was in fact Joe Alex, who was to partner her again at the Folies.**

211

*Fading but still a star –
Mistinguett at a Rue St.-
Honoré carnival with Josephine
Baker, the girl who was
destined to displace her. The
year was 1925. The man on the
right is Josephine's first
husband, the spurious "Count"
Pepito Abatino.*

names as Picabia, Van Dongen, Cocteau, René Clair, Léger and Blaize Cendrars – already switched on to African art by Nancy Cunard and her coterie – formed a claque in praise of black performers. The box office and the agencies were besieged. "So tremendous was the public acclaim," reported *The New Yorker*, "that for the first week's run the cast were completely disorganized. Drunken on the appreciation they had received, and on champagne . . . the Negro choruses split up into single acts consisting of whichever males or females could still keep their feet, or had not lost their voices from the fatigues of pleasure, all of them nevertheless alive and creative with the integral talent of their race and training."

Not every press review was ecstatic. René Bizet, the critic of *Candide*, wrote: "After this, don't let anyone tell us that the Americans are prudish. These blacks know how to make their caricatures grotesque . . . there is no finesse – or very little – in their irony. As for their actions, these are so disjointed that their frolics could be mistaken for St. Vitus's dance." Montboron, in *l'Intransigeant*, compared the dancers (more politely but in similar vein) to "hemi-demi-semiquavers making arpeggios with their legs." But only two notices were 100 percent critical. Robert de Flers saw the revue as "an offense against French good taste" and warned that if we were descended from the apes, Miss Baker's performance proved "that we are in

Poiret's love of extravagance extended also to the ridiculous. Josephine Baker first drew the attention of the critics because she made people laugh by squinting, pulling funny faces, and clowning around. What more natural, then, that they should get together for the famous designer's St. Catherine's Day ball on November 25, 1925?

danger of climbing back up more quickly than we came down." *La Rumeur* accused her of "dishonoring the French music hall by the indecence of [her] body."

More typical was Yvon Novy, the palindromatic critic of the show business daily, *Comoedia*, who enthused: "Astonishing Josephine – at once dancer, singer and mime, amazing us at every appearance yet contriving to show us a different person each time!" André Levinson, most influential of critics, complained that the revue provided "everything to please but not enough to astonish." But of the new star, he wrote:

Certain of Miss Baker's poses, back curved, buttocks out-thrust, arms interlaced and raised in phallic imagery, evoke the highest forms of Negro art. We are transfixed by the plastic sensuality of a race of sculptors, the transports of the African Eros. This is no longer the comic dancing girl: it is the Black Venus which haunted Baudelaire.

What was there about this performance that was so different? Why should an unknown American provoke such widely differing reactions? What did she actually do on the stage of the Champs Elysées Music Hall that night? Paul Colin saw it this way. "She bounced about," he wrote, "like a kangaroo boxer, a rubber woman, a Tarzan's mate. She contorted herself, squinted, blew out her cheeks as she pranced around on all-fours. Naked except for the feathers at her waist, her head lacquered black, she stirred the audience to anger or wild enthusiasm."

The accuracy of this description seems confirmed by a later issue of *Candide*, in which Pierre de Régnier spoke of some people who had seen the show six times, and others who had stormed out after two scenes, slamming doors and crying scandal. His report on Miss Baker was in almost the same terms as Colin's: "A strange character walking with bent knees, a kangaroo boxer in a ragged loincloth, she grimaces and contorts herself, squinting and blowing out her cheeks, disjointing her limbs and doing the splits, to exit finally on all-fours, the rump higher than the head, the legs stiff like a baby giraffe." De Régnier added that the dancer's lips were painted black, her skin was banana-colored, and "her short hair was plastered to her head as if she was wearing a wig of caviar." "Her voice is shrill," he said. "Her body perpetually shivers and shakes, she writhes like a snake, or rather like a saxophone in movement, so that the sounds of the orchestra actually seem to proceed from her."

Several other reviewers made the point that Josephine Baker's performance was such that *she* seemed to be playing (or stimulating) the musicians, rather than the reverse. This, no doubt, is literally true: it was after all an improvising jazz band. And, for the first few performances, an improvising artist too, Josephine herself admitted that she forgot all about the choreography and danced like a madwoman, "transformed by who knows what devil, at the mercy of the music, inflamed by the full house and the spotlights. I heard the band behind a wall of cottonwool. It seemed to me that when I leaped, I leaped as high as the sky; and when I came back to earth, the whole place belonged to me. I felt as tipsy as I did on the day of our arrival, when Louis Douglas, for a joke, made me drink an anisette. Whoopla!"[64]

There was a precedent for all this cavorting – and especially for the squint. Josephine Baker was born in St. Louis, Missouri, on June 3, 1906, experiencing

"The jungle image was fading and that of a sophisticated star, luxuriously gowned and sparkling with jewels, was taking its place" – Josephine at the Folies-Bergère.

At the Folies again, the magnificence of the Baker costumes rivaled the most splendid of Mistinguett's.

prejudice from an early age because she was the child of Eddie Moreno, a white Spanish-American dancer, and Carrie Smith Baker, a black woman. As a light-skinned Creole she was rejected both by black and by white communities. Leaving home at the age of thirteen because the family was too poor to support her, she finally talked herself into a job with a road show touring the South – as wardrobe mistress and odd-job girl. Stage-crazy already, she learned the chorus routines in the hope that they would try her out as a dancer. But she was turned down because she would spoil the homogeneity of the black chorus line: she was "too small, too skinny – and too pale." When finally she did get a chance because one of the girls fell ill, she was obliged to black-up like a minstrel before they would let her on stage. Then she was fired because, being a natural clown, her squinting and grimaces drew laughs – and the rest of the cast were jealous.

In Philadelphia, the all-black revue *Shuffle Along* – which had started Paul Robeson, Katharine Yarborough, Freddie Washington and Florence Mills on the road to success – was auditioning. This time Josephine was rejected because she was "too small, too skinny – and too *dark*." The show was due to open on

"In the flesh, she disseminated a personal magnetism that was unbelievable" – Josephine back at the Casino de Paris.

Broadway and the impresarios, Noble Sissle and Eubie Blake, wanted the chorus line to resemble the white Tiller Girls as much as possible (because it was, after all, the first time a Negro production had been booked for the Great White Way). Later, when *Shuffle Along* had drawn rave notices from the critics, a second company was formed to go on tour. This time, Josephine found herself a place with the show – as wardrobe mistress.

Once again she studied the routines; once more she was given a chance when a chorus girl pulled out because she was pregnant. This time it was the star, Eva Spencer, who complained bitterly that she had been upstaged by Josephine's squinting antics and demanded that she be fired. But the critic Langston Hughes had discovered "something in her rhythm, her warmth, her smile and a certain impertinent grace which makes you notice her and applaud." A small part was written for her in the next edition of the revue, allowing her to use her talent as a clown. This made her unpopular with the rest of the chorus. Once, one of the girls deliberately tripped her as she made her entrance. Josephine turned the stumble into a comedy routine and kept it in the act.

It was the same kind of story when she worked

finally in New York with the next Sissle–Blake show, *Chocolate Dandies*. The revue was considered "pretentious" and flopped – but Josephine was offered a spot at the Plantation, the Broadway cabaret where Florence Mills had starred. With other girls, she danced a Charleston while Ethel Waters, the current star, sang. The day came when Miss Waters fell ill. Josephine, it seemed, knew all her numbers: could she go on in the star's place? The distraught manager agreed.

She sang "Dinah," the big Waters hit – and then added a few numbers of her own, including "Ukelele Lady," and danced her own comic version of the Charleston. The unknown's sinuous, rubbery dancing, her high, fluting, mellifluous voice, took the audience by storm. The applause was deafening. Before the show the following night, Ethel Waters, who was supposed to have been away for two weeks, was back in her dressing room. Josephine Baker herself wrote up the sequel:[65]

" 'You can't do this to me!' I said to the director. 'You promised –'

" 'Nothing! I promised you nothing!'

" 'You told me when I came offstage that I'd had more success than her because I made them laugh!'

" 'Not more success. As much. But she's paler than you – and prettier.'

"So there I am back in the chorus. In the wings, I run across our star. She slings me a furious glance. Then I feel my impertinence urge me to say: 'That was a quick cure! Too bad for the show!' She is so enraged by so much audacity that an insult escapes her, something like 'Dirty nigger!,' and she would have grabbed me by the hair if it hadn't been so short. I was sickened."

It was soon after this incident that Josephine Baker received the offer from Louis Douglas. It can be seen, therefore, that she came to Paris with a sizable chip on her shoulder: she was too black, or she wasn't black enough; she wasn't good enough, or she was much too clever; whatever she did it seemed to be wrong – except with the audience. The resulting hatred of all forms of racism, allied to her inflexible determination to succeed at all costs, explains much of her subsequent behavior.★

In Paris, she was again unpopular with the cast of the show; she had after all eclipsed the star and pushed everyone else into the background. But she wasn't too worried about that. If folks wanted her to play funny girl and clown around, that was exactly what she would do. ("Just a little more effort and you can use your tongue as a scarf!" one of the chorus girls said acidly soon after they opened.)

★ Josephine Baker's class- and race-conscious bitterness cannot but have been exacerbated by a contemporary love affair. "Is it because I'm black or because I'm a dancer that you don't want to marry me?" she asked icily when the gentleman failed to propose to her. "Because you're black <u>and</u> because you're a dancer," he corrected.

So far as the customers were concerned, she was instant success. Nancy Cunard (who had herself outraged her mother and George Moore by taking a black lover) approved. Colette found her "the most beautiful panther of all"; Cocteau "a living poem in her magnificent plumage of light"; Paul Derval "someone who set the stage alight." And it was Derval who signed her – after *La Revue Nègre* had played a short season in Berlin – to star in his next Folies revue.

With the benefit of hindsight, two points need to be made about the impact of *La Revue Nègre*. The first is that, although Josephine Baker was in no sense a *meneuse de revue*, her personal triumph was due to a combination of natural talent, so far unexploited, with an atmosphere (created by Jacques-Charles, Paul Colin and the theater directors) in which it could blossom to the delight of a Parisian audience. The second point is that the "barbarism" and "jungle" quality of the whole cast's performance, of which so much was made by contemporary critics and later show business historians, was in fact no more than the natural exuberance and rhythmic brilliance of black American artists. What would have passed unremarked in Harlem had, because of its unfamiliarity, an explosive effect in Paris. It must be remembered too that the *revue à grand spectacle*, already galvanized by the cinema, by the influence of Ziegfeld, White and Carroll in the United States, and by Cochran and Charlot in England, visually spiced by the aggressivity of "the new modernism" in art, was wide open to anything original. Theatrical "barbarism" and the black influence thus took their places alongside Dadaism, surrealism, art déco and cubism with an effect that proved as electric and controversial as that of Diaghilev and the Russians fifteen years before.

The news spread quickly across the Atlantic, and a flood of black entertainers surged toward the new show business Mecca. Musicians such as Coleman Hawkins, Garland Wilson and the trumpeter Bill Coleman, cabaret stars like Elizabeth Welch and Adelaide Hall, specialties like Peg-Leg Bates, the astonishing one-legged dancer, homed on Paris and opened their own *boîtes* or found employment that was better paid – and more appreciated – than that they'd been used to back home.

Before this new influence was digested, the larger revues had settled into an approach that was in danger of becoming routine – costly and well designed though each might be in itself. It is instructive to analyze the content of a typical – one is tempted to say stereotyped –

The demands of revue writers in the 1920s resulted at times in costumes that were fetishist in the extreme. Left, Mia May, "the Mackintosh girl"; right, two Erté designs labeled "Charades" and "Migraine".

★ Paul Derval, the Folies administrator, was, like many people in the theater, superstitious. Because of an initial success with that number, he was convinced that the titles of all his shows must consist of thirteen letters. He once told Josephine Baker that he had taken the trouble to register 150 titles with the Society of Authors, all including the word "Folies" and each containing thirteen letters.

production of this kind which was running when the Louis Douglas show opened: Louis Lemarchand's *Un Soir de Folie* at the Folies-Bergère.★

Gaby Montbreuse was the *meneuse*; Dorly, the comic. Specialties included Benglia, Tera-Guinoh and Suzy Beryl. In addition to the star's *tour de chant*, there was a parody of an English pantomime, complete with a ten-foot-high stage goose, followed by *Les John Tiller's Folies Stars* in a tableau entitled "The Enchanted Lagoon" – forty-four dancers in leaf-green

costumes, only their legs, shoulders and faces showing up against the forest décor. The next tableau was designed on a wintry theme – Tirmont and Smolinska in "The Conquest of the Pole," set against a backdrop of icebergs and a boat with frozen rigging. This was succeeded by "Polar Nights," featuring a number of Junoesque ladies with bare, flattish breasts and fashionably shingled hair, and then a big production number with Suzy Beryl as the aurora borealis. The costume for this was spectacular – black tights arrowing up to a point between naked breasts, a headdress winged with the two halves of a crescent moon, and a diaphanous train spangled with stars which dropped from the artist's widespread arms and then rose behind her to fan out and disappear behind the proscenium arch twenty feet above in a shimmering representation of the northern lights.

There was a "Good-time Girls" scene with chorines brandishing top hats, ostrich plumes and long cigarette holders, and another set in Hades with angels, devils, Tera-Guinoh, and Benglia as an erotic black Satan. Dorly's sketch was "An Evening in Luna Park," complete with fairground décor; Gaby Montbreuse's an altercation with a harrassed cop in "The Traffic

Jam" – this one in front of a backdrop crammed with buses, cars and taxis. Three English dancers, Veronica and Adele Foote with Margaret Halsey, performed a chastity belt number in which the chorus teamed variations on this practical device with elaborate and impractical headdresses. And in "Behind Bars in Bordighera," showgirls representing Asti, Chianti, Barolo and other Italian wines posed before a vine-and-grape décor.

The finale was an Erte creation in gold, green, citron and mauve. It was called "Adoration" and it grouped the chorus, a number of whom were black, around a profusion of huge golden cubes which led up in gigantic steps to a gold bull in front of a façade of Greek columns. There was a nude astride the bull. The Grecian-style costumes were furnished with arrow quivers, bouzoukis, devil masks and, in some cases, purple togas as accessories.

The whole production, as was evident from the "souvenir program," the banality of the concepts and the *déjà-vu* quality of several tableaux, was geared to an international audience expecting to see a staged exaggeration of its own idea of an "ooh-la-la!" Paris that never existed. The program's embossed, gold-lettered, scarlet cover sported a cutout in the shape of a diamond framing a color photo of a showgirl – gold-leaves-and-pink-roses headdress framing blonde hair and a tiny cupid's bow mouth; one bare arm raised to display an elbow bangle and a single coy nipple. Its rosy sibling could be discovered by opening the booklet, when the whole picture was revealed. It was also revealed in an advertisement at the end of the program that similar "souvenirs" of the Moulin-Rouge, the Casino de Paris and the Palace could be obtained without the formality of actually going there. That for the Moulin-Rouge, the ad enthused, "*contient plus de 70 photos et dessins en couleur avec l'historique de l'ancien Bal at le tableau complet du Bal actuel.*" Like the present-day Paris chef who translated his *Gigot de Lotte Roti aux Herbes de Provence* as "roast leg of fish with provincial herbs," the copywriter was enthusiastic rather than accurate in his rendering for English and American clients. This read: "Contains more than 70 photos and colored designs of the nicest danceuses with the history of the old first Ball and the complete panorama of the actual one. Nearly sold out . . . Sent post-free with English translation on receipt of 3s. 6d or $1.00." And to strengthen the image of "sinful" Paris, there followed in parentheses: "Carefully packed in plain wrapper."

The program cited related, of course, to the Bal du Moulin-Rouge (which provided what was really a floorshow featuring the cancan) and not to the music hall next door. That was yet again being rebuilt – this time under the direction of the music publisher Francis Salabert, and Pierre Foucret, one-time legal adviser to the Isolas. Jacques-Charles, who had just produced *On Dit Ça* at the Casino with Jane Marnac, Lily Damita and Saint-Granier, was tempted away from Volterra to join them. In four years at the Moulin-Rouge he created eight sumptuous and splendid revues that were anything but banal and lacked a *déjà-vu* quality altogether.

The first, *New York-Montmartre*, was designed around the Hoffman Girls – a superb troupe of eighteen American dancer-acrobats who had already made two appearances in Paris and had just completed a successful run in London. The reopening was not without its dramas. First of all, the reconstruction was delayed (a chronic vexation which seemed to haunt the director). Despite huge payments for overtime, the curtain did not rise until a full month later than planned. Then there was a strike of stagehands during the final dress rehearsal. Charles refused to be held to ransom. He let the whole lot go. Suspecting that there might be trouble brewing, he had prudently staked out his faithful old team from the Olympia in a nearby bistro. Even so, there were twenty-four hours of agonizing work familiarizing the newcomers with every scene and cue in the show. Worse still was the embarrassing incident on the first night itself. The American members of the cast, fresh from Prohibition-ridden New York, had taken kindly to the drinking habits of Paris – especially a dozen showgirls "borrowed" from Ziegfeld, who had already caused trouble by refusing to appear in the same tableaux as eight black dancers. For the premiere, these beauties arrived at the theater in an unfit state to go on.

Charles paid them off on the spot and sent them back to New York. Gertrude Hoffman, trouper and ex-dancer, deputed a dozen of her own girls to replace them in the relevant scenes, just as she had insisted that they should appear with the black dancers "to avoid dishonoring the name of the United States."

The Hoffman Girls themselves had been far too rigidly supervised to allow them to fall for the blandishments of Parisian stagedoor johnnies armed with bottles of champagne. Every time Mme. Hoffman saw that one or more of the girls had arrived in her dressing room carrying what looked as if it might be a party dress, she called an impromptu and unexpected rehearsal after the final curtain. History does not record how many carefully planned suppers and seductions were ruined in this way – but it is known that when, on one occasion, she kept her troupe at the theater until 6:00 A.M., Henri Letellier, the editor-in-chief of *Le Journal*, spent the night alone with eighteen dinners and a fleet of empty rented cars.

Despite the dramas, *New York-Montmartre* was a huge success, in particular a "Queen of Sheba" tableau in which one of the girls, Florence, scored an immense personal triumph as the temptress of St. Anthony much as Flaubert must have imagined her. A great deal of the show's impact was due to its immense pace. Riding his old hobby-horse, Charles had borrowed a technique from the motion picture and presented the whole production as one continuous montage which moved much faster than the old Casino or Folies revues. The sketches, which had always been played in elaborate sets, were reduced to one- or two-minute blackout scenes in front of a drop curtain; none of the artists returned to take bows after their numbers; and tableau succeeded tableau with breathtaking speed by the adroit use of gauzes, revolves and all the latest devices of stage machinery and lighting.

Mistinguett, who was at the premiere, saw at once that the future of music hall revue must lie in this dynamic presentation. Life in the modern world was itself speeding up, and that acceleration must be reflected in the techniques of entertainment. The following day she called on Foucret and begged him to book her for his next production. The impresario was delighted. Despite the fact that he had already signed the Dolly Sisters, and guaranteed them star billing, he agreed, and drew up a contract for "Miss" on similar terms.

Foucret hoped to fulfill both contracts simply by titling the show *La Revue Mistinguett*. In this way, he reasoned, the Dolly Sisters, as per contract, would get their star billing immediately under the title – but, Mistinguett, whose name *as an artist* was at the foot of the bills as in America, also appeared in even larger letters as *part* of the title. The stratagem was unsuccessful. The Dolly Sisters sued, won their case, and donated the money to an artists' benevolent fund. Nevertheless, the revue was another triumph. It featured Jean Gabin and Henri Garat; it was notable for Charles's famous "Forest In Flames" tableau; and Mistinguett's big number, "Valencia," became a world-wide hit. By an odd coincidence, Chevalier launched "Valentin" at

* Like Polaire before her, Fréhel "borrowed" her stage name from a natural phenomenon – in her case a stormbound, rocky cape in her native Brittany. Red-haired and lusty of voice, Fréhel lived two separate and equally successful theater lives: young, slender and sensitive, as a singer of romantic songs; older and heavier, as an acid comedienne who could have been a character from a Lautrec painting. Described by admiring critics as une force de la nature (an elemental force), Fréhel was particularly praised for her handling of the "realist" songs written by chansonnier Jean Richepin. Widely criticized as a collaborator because she twice toured Germany entertaining French troops in World War II prison camps, she nevertheless retained a faithful following well into a bibulous old age.

The Dolly Sisters – Ziegfeld stars who made a hit in London and Paris.

the Casino at the same time – the year's two big songs, sharing the same two opening syllables, simultaneously created by the two ex-partners who were the biggest names in the business.

In those breathless jazz-age years between 1925 and 1929, the music hall in France reached the peak of its brilliance. Pierre Sandrini of the Bal Tabarin took over the Apollo and reinstated the lavish revue with productions starring Yvonne Georges, Lucienne Boyer, Maria Valente and Fréhel, surrounded by famous actors and actresses and such renowned specialties as Inaudi the "memory man," Henriette Lefèvre, the diabolo queen, and the magicians de Roze and de Rocroy.★ Les Ambassadeurs inaugurated a series of imported American shows including Johnny Hudgins in *Broadway à*

Paris, the *Show of 1928*, and a revue for the disappointed Dolly Sisters. Dufrenne and Varna acquired Ba-ta-clan and made Damia a *meneuse de revue*. Then they took over the Casino from Volterra and speeded up its tradition of beautifully dressed spectacles in keeping with the modern trend.

At the Folies-Bergère, Derval hired Irving Berlin and the blues' composer Spencer Williams to write music for the 1926 revue for which he had signed Josephine Baker. Louis Lemarchand again wrote the book. The costumes and décors were by Erte and José de Zamora. The title of the show – thirteen letters as usual – was *La Folie du Jour*. Baker made her entrance in an enormous metal ball which was lowered slowly from the flies, to ground gently in the middle of the orchestra, open like a flower, reveal a profusion of flowers themselves opening, and then finally the black girl unfolding to dance on a mirror. Later in the program came the famous "belt-of-bananas" number – sixteen yellow crescents surrounding her waist, points upward, to accentuate the bumps and grinds of the Charleston. But it wasn't just the dancing that inflated the success she had won overnight in *La Revue Nègre*: at the Folies, Josephine sang as well. "Pretty Little Baby," her big number, became an immediate hit – and this time there was no jealous star to consign her back to the chorus. At last she was the star herself.

She opened her own cabaret, Chez-Josephine, and it developed into a rendezvous for *le tout-Paris*. She made films – *Princess Tam-Tam, Siren of the Tropics* (especially written for her by Maurice Dekobra, best-selling author of *Madonna of the Sleeping Cars*), and *Zou-Zou*, opposite Jean Gabin. There were tours of Scandinavia, Eastern Europe, Spain, South America. She studied ballet under Serge Lifar, went everywhere accompanied by a leopard on a leash, and concluded a publicity deal whereby she drove herself around in a Delage automobile with snakeskin upholstery. She had, as one journalist put it, "so many strings to her bow that she could have made a harp out of it." But by the time Henri Varna signed her to head a revue at the Casino de Paris in 1929, the "jungle" image was fading and that of a sophisticated star, luxuriously gowned and sparkling with jewels, adapted to the country which had adopted her, was taking its place. Jo Bouillon, who later became her third husband, recalled the first time he saw her, when he was leading a band at Ostend in Belgium:

I knew her, of course, from her photos. But in the

flesh, she disseminated a personal magnetism that was unbelievable. The way she made her entrances, the suppleness of her figure, the length and grace of her neck and the way she carried her head, the fascinating movement of her shoulders, the harmonious proportions of her body and the perfect sweep of her legs – all this gave the impression of total equilibrium, of beauty in its purest state. "An African goddess," I thought, "or an Egyptian queen . . . !" But, goddess or queen, she joined in with the rest of us mortals without the slightest ostentation, smiling warmly, happy to be there with a joy that was almost animal. And then my musician's ear was conquered by the sensitivity of that voice – an extraordinary, warbling voice, a kind of free coloratura with an innate sense of musicianship as natural to her as a trill to a bird. I was knocked out by such a mixture of spontaneity and professionalism.[66]

The Varna revue, which followed his *Paris-Miss* with Mistinguett, was titled *Paris Qui Remue* (thirteen letters again, and a mild pun into the bargain. The verb *remuer* means to stir.) It certainly stirred interest far beyond the confines of Lower Montmartre. George Barbier's sets and costumes were good. Josephine made her entrance as *l'Oiseau des Iles*, the bird of the islands, clothed in an enormous pair of white wings, down a Jacob's ladder leading from heaven to a virgin forest. Mistinguett's partner, Earl Leslie, had been coopted to help with the book. And the show produced two worldwide recording hits – Josephine's personal theme song, "*J'ai Deux Amours*" (the two loves were "Paris and my own country") and "*La Petite Tonkinoise.*" The first of these was composed by Vincent Scotto. The second had originally been created by the same writer – as a folksy song called "*Le Navigatore*," which was of interest only in his native Marseille. Christiné had rewritten it in its "Tonkinoise" form years before at the suggestion of Polin. Now, disinterred, its "oriental" melody was a perfect vehicle for the new star's high, fluting voice with its compelling "period" vibrato. And it made that voice as familiar as the more raucous, gamey tones of Mistinguett. Josephine Baker was in fact near to toppling the queen of music hall from her throne.

This was a situation of which Josephine herself seemed well aware. Like many big names in show business, once she had "arrived" she fell a victim to her own publicity and cherished an inflated idea of her own importance. She wasn't "difficult" in the manner of "La Miss," but her extreme generosity to the underprivileged was matched by a corresponding arrogance when dealing with the successful. As early as 1926, when she had fallen temporarily in love with Berlin and was considering a legitimate theater offer from Max Reinhardt, she held the Folies up to ransom, threatening to repudiate the contract she had signed with Derval unless he increased the agreed salary by 400 francs (about $160 or £40) a performance. Derval, who had already commissioned book, music, sets and costumes, was forced to agree.

Later a Parisian nobleman dining at Chez-Josephine admired her cabaret act and sent a message via the headwaiter asking if she would grant him a dance. Graciously, the star complied. When the bill came, the last item read: *To one dance with Josephine Baker: 1,000F* (the sum represented about a month's salary for a whitecollar worker at the time). The Frenchman unclipped his gold fountain pen and wrote beneath it: *To one dance with the Comte S – – – – de la R – – – –: 1,000F. We are quits.* And he paid the bill less that sum. The deduction was not questioned. But subsequently he became her lover, so, to paraphrase George Orwell, they were more quits than ever.

A similar egoism lay behind the split with her first husband, "Count" Pepito Abatino. Acting as her manager, Abatino had successfully negotiated all her appearances until she was signed by Billie Burke for the *Ziegfeld Follies of 1936*. Here he fell down on the job. First, he had not been clever enough: Josephine discovered that she was only a featured specialty with three spots – and all the good numbers were sung by the star, Fanny Brice. Secondly, Abatino had hired a claque to applaud his artist, and the New York critics were not amused. "You don't persuade a reviewer with noise," Walter Winchell reproved. Despite direction by Vicente Minnelli, choreography by Balanchine, music by Vernon Duke and Ira Gershwin, and star spots for Bob Hope and the Nicholas Brothers, one notice for the show read, in its entirety: "Some people like Miss Josephine Baker. I do not like Miss Josephine Baker." That was enough. Josephine hated flops, hated not being top of the class, loathed failure of any kind, in anyone. From then on, Abatino was out.

A year later she married the French industrialist Jean Lion. They were divorced in 1939, after she had lost the baby her husband wanted, "because she wasn't content to be Mme. Jean Lion; she wanted to be Josephine Baker as well."

Jo Bouillon helped her in her tireless fight against racism in all its forms. He was with her when she retired to a Dordogne château to raise twelve orphan children of different races as a living proof of her theories. He did his best to help when plans to make the place a kind of Disneyland failed to attract visitors. But he had left before her lack of business sense had provoked creditors into forcing the sale of the property. Although they were never divorced, he was in fact running a restaurant in South America when she started her final, money-making, triumphant jubilee tour. He flew back as soon as he heard the news of her collapse, but she was already on her death bed.

Back in those heady years at the end of the twenties, though, the future looked bright all the way; and if the music hall's royal succession was contested, the court circles surrounding the two pretenders sparkled more brilliantly than ever. The songs had never been better, the nudes never more nubile, the chorus routines never zippier or as dynamic. The comics were at their most hilarious. The sketches were witty, the leading men pulsing with charm, and the *meneuses de revue* more bewitching than they had ever been. But above all, it was the settings which lent the era its opulence, its panache – and that distinction that sets it apart from any other show business period. From derivatives of the "spatial apparatus" created by Sternberg and the Russian constructivists to the most naturalistic and romantic evocations of reality, they ran the gamut of exotica from alpha to omega. From windmills to waterspouts, from train wrecks to the Taj Mahal, from Sicilian orange groves to ski slopes covered in real snow, they brought to the music hall stage an Arabian Nights fantasy that was never equaled in the real world of Haroun al Raschid. And through this enchanted universe moved the highest paid and most professional entertainers of the era, furred and feathered and jeweled and frilled, in costumes as audacious as the décor.★

Here is "Genet" of *The New Yorker* (in real life Miss Janet Flanner again) describing *Paris Qui Remue*, the first Casino revue headlining Josephine Baker. It was, she wrote, "as full of staircases as a Freudian dream," with "excellent British imported dancing choruses of both sexes, a complete Russian ballet, trained pigeons, a live cheetah, roller skaters, the prettiest Venetian set of the century, a marvelous first-act finale, acres of fine costumes, the four best cancan dancers in captivity, a thriller in which Miss Baker is rescued from a typhoon by a gorilla, and an aerial ballet of heavy Italian ladies caroming about on wires."

★ Even sketches for costumes and set designs by Erte, Barbier and their contemporaries were lavish and sumptuous in the extreme, vivid with gouache and watercolor, glittering with metallic paint and spangled by fragments of gold and silver leaf. Like those of Bakst, Dérain and Picasso for the ballet, they soon became collectors' items worthy of a catalog at Sotheby's or Christie's, and the smallest of them changes hands for many hundreds of dollars today. Picasso was the only artist to translate his designs into reality (he personally painted the bullring set for Le Tricorne); the others had their décors manufactured by stage studios, their costumes made by Max Weldy, the genius in whose workshops these two-dimensional confections became three-dimensional garments that could actually be worn on a stage.

Alas, such exhilarating extravagance was soon to disappear. The American show business periodical *Variety*, noted for the succinctness of its headlines,★ told all with a banner announcing: *Wall Street Lays an Egg!*

The year 1929 brought with it the stock market crash.

And although the short-term repercussions were hardly felt in Paris (its only visible effect, one gossip columnist remarked sourly, was that the girls at the Ritz bar were now paying for their own cocktails), the long-term result was decisive. For the men who had been buying the cocktails were no longer able to splash out on boxes at the theater. The managements in turn were thus no longer able to afford such extravagant overheads. And this (more in the United States and Britain than in France) naturally affected the entertainment offered – not so much in quality as in kind.

So far as French music hall was concerned, there were four factors contributing to its demise, and for two of them, ironically enough, music hall itself was responsible. First, there was the economic factor, and it was to meet this threat that the second arose. It has already been pointed out that, in the lavish revues staged by the bigger halls, the production itself was as much the star as the performers whose names were in lights outside. Very well, said the directors – if shortage of cash forces us to cut something, we will cut the stars. And from then on they concentrated more and more on ensemble production, less and less on the big names. Instead of a team to provide a setting for the stars, they made the team itself the star.

The third factor affected the smaller halls. This was the increasing use of that nudity which had itself been pioneered by the spectacular revue. What had originally been one component, and largely a decorative one at that, designed to draw the male customers, became the show, the whole show, and nothing but the show. The big revues were partly to blame, with their "naughty" approach and peep-hole image fostered by the "souvenir program" routine, but from the 1930s on, nude shows and strippers effectively displaced the elegant programs of specialties which had previously enlivened these little theaters. If the customers would pay to see flesh, why cut the profits by hiring talent as well?

The fourth factor was the most important of all: the steadily encroaching assault of the motion picture.

It need scarcely be emphasized that although a film

★ **Variety's most famous headline, definitive of the style set by publisher Sime Silverman, was "Stix Nix Hix Pix," a prose translation of which reveals that rustic communities had turned thumbs down on motion pictures with a country theme.**

PHOTO : ROGER-VIOLLET

costs a great deal of money to make, an indefinite number of copies of it can be shown many hundreds of times to an audience that will finally number millions, whereas a live revue with a limited run, playing nightly to an audience of hundreds, will show a proportionately smaller return on the money invested. This single hard fact of economic life was to have a disastrous effect on the music hall, especially in Paris.

Fréhel on stage. First starred at the Apollo by Pierre Sandrini of the Bal Tabarin, she changed from a singer of romantic songs to "an acid comedienne who could have been a character from a Lautrec painting."

231

Between 1929 and 1931 the Alcazar closed down and was demolished; Les Ambassadeurs was split in two and reopened as a small theater with an adjacent cabaret; the Apollo, which had been starring Chevalier, Gracie Fields, Ted Lewis and other imported headliners, became a theater and then a cinema; the Concert Mayol switched to a policy of nude shows; the Eldorado, after a temporary success with the *théatre-chantant* of Georgius, was pulled down to make way for a bank; the Eden-Palace became a movie theater (although later it was to reopen with a different kind of live show); the Empire became a movie theater alternating with variety; the Fémina disappeared; the Gaieté-Rochechouart became a movie theater; the Olympia became a movie theater and remained one until Bruno Coquatrix reanimated it as a variety theater in 1954. The Alhambra, which had burned down in 1925, reopened in 1932 with a mixed program of films, variety, ballet and light opera.

Even the Moulin-Rouge was unable to escape entirely. Loie Fuller's ballet had played a ten-week season there in 1927 at a record fee of 25,000 francs (about $4,000 or £1,000) per week.* The last three revues – Jacques-Charles's triumphant *Ça C'est Paris!*, with Mistinguett, Carl Randall and music by Padilla; another *Revue aux Étoiles*; and *Paris Qui Tourne*, again with "Miss" and Earl Leslie† – had been enormous successes. But the director quarreled with the management over the responsibility for a deficit arising out of a South American tour by the company, and quit when his contract ended. Minus his star author-director, Foucret produced a few seasons of insipid variety and then turned the music hall auditorium into a movie theater. It has remained one ever since.

Jacques-Charles's next engagement was symptomatic of the times. He was hired to produce the first troupe of Blue Bell Girls in a program of continuous ciné-variety which ran from 9:00 A.M. until 2:30 A.M. at the new Paramount theater.

More symbolic still was the death of La Goulue, for it occurred in the critical year of 1929. Shortly before, the one-time star who had once lived in the Champs Elysées mansion of Paiva, the mistress of Napoleon III, had been seen on the screen – fat, old, and dancing drunkenly in a documentary about the rag-pickers of "the Zone," the wilderness between the inner and outer fortifications of Paris.

* Loie Fuller was always eager to look after the interests of her troupe. Each girl was guaranteed a salary of 3,000 francs (almost $500) a month, whether she worked or not, and there were bonds lodged in a London bank providing a legacy for them all in the case of Miss Fuller's death. Partially blinded by laboratory experiments in electrical effects for her productions, she did in fact die in 1928, the same year as Nora Bayes. "A butterfly has folded its wings," said Figaro.

† Carl Randall returned for Ça C'est Paris because, to Mistinguett's annoyance, Earl Leslie, her customary partner, had been "poached" for a short while by Varna – to act as foil to Josephine Baker in Paris Qui Remue at the Casino.

A Question of Numbers

THAT UNDERRATED AMERICAN COMEDIAN, Pat Henning, used to tell, somewhere in his act, a story about his father. "He was a drinkin' man, my fadder," Mr. Henning would confide. "One day he's standin' onna banks of a river, wonderin' what the hell folks can do with all that water, when suddenly he sees a great big sign on the other side – and on the sign it says like *Drink Canada Dry!*" The comedian pauses, and then adds matter-of-factly: "So he went up there."

Those who wish to relive the delights of the music hall in its glory will have to follow Henning Senior's example and set out on a similar voyage of discovery and fulfillment – but although they may find each of the components in one place or another, the final synthesis will have to be in their minds, for nowhere today can the sum of the parts be found which made up the splendid whole, let alone anything greater than it.

Fast-moving and lavishly dressed revue can be seen at the Folies-Bergère, cancan dancers at the Moulin-Rouge, spectacle at the Lido, and stars at Bobino and the Olympia. In Line Renaud there is even a permanent *meneuse* heading the glamorous shows at the Casino de Paris. ("There is only one revue star today," Josephine Baker said not long before her death, "and Line is the one. I look on her almost as a daughter – but we have the same father: Henri Varna.") As for performers in the grand music hall tradition, they have been around since the golden days: Edith Piaf, Yves Montand, Georges Brassens and Jacques Brel adding lustre to the *chanson réaliste* in France; W. C. Fields, Pearl Bailey, Danny Kaye, Jack Benny and Groucho Marx adding new dimensions to comedy in the United States; Sid Field, Max Miller, Tony Hancock and Frankie Howerd in England. Each of these (as distinct from those equally talented artists specializing

Jack Benny (right) *added a new dimension to comedy in the United States. He is seen here with singer Dennis Day* (left) *and the author during a London Palladium season in the 1950s.*

in radio, films or television) could have held their own with the great ones in their day. The international specialties have also been as brilliant – notably Victor Borge, almost a reincarnation of Fragson at his piano; the elegant Channing Pollock with his white doves; Les Frères Jacques; Denmark's Sven Asmussen and Switzerland's Hazy Osterwald with their original mixtures of fine comedy and good jazz. To these can be added the incomparable Spanish ventriloquist, Senor Wences, and a trio of "musical fantasists" billed as Jo, Jak and Joni.

Wences rivaled a famous French "vent act" between the wars who talked in several voices while eating and drinking. He used two dummies – an absurd, oversized cockerel glove puppet and a severed Moor's head in a box. Such was his skill that he could make the "voice" of the fearsome Moor, who was always threatening and blustering and yelling to be let out, become gradually more muffled as Wences remorselessly closed the lid of the box. When this was rapidly alternated, in a three-way argument, with his own voice and the shrill, cackling remarks of the bird, the effect was truly astonishing. Perhaps more astonishing still was the way the act had developed. Wences had once been a conjuror. The conjuring act had itself developed from an illusionist's routine relying on sleight-of-hand. And

Wences had in the first place been medically advised to practice card tricks in order to rehabilitate the muscles of his right hand – badly gored during the exercise of his original profession as a bullfighter.

The humor of Jo, Jak and Joni leaned more toward the surrealist. Three pale, thin young men in rusty tailcoats and stovepipe hats, they shambled on stage with a variety of musical instruments, including a double bass on a low trolley fitted with rollerskate wheels. The leader, who carried a violin, then delivered a short speech in fluent and sibilant Castilian (unless they were appearing in Spain, in which case it would be another language), after which they indulged in a succession of expert musical numbers interspersed with eccentric dancing. At one point, a small door in the bass was opened and a boiling electric kettle removed from which tea was brewed. At another, a telephone rang – and this too was produced through a second door in the instrument and answered. As a finale, they all climbed aboard the trolley, a whistle blew, smoke puffed from the neck of the bass, and they chugged offstage.

With all these ingredients of the classic music hall available, the form as a whole has nevertheless failed to reappear. Perhaps there is a clue in the words of novelist and playwright J. B. Priestley, written several decades ago in praise of British music hall in the 1920s:

> There were no microphones and nobody needed them. There were no stars who had arrived by way of amusing farmers' wives and invalids on the radio. There were no reputations that had been created by gramophone records for teenagers. The men and women who topped the bills had spent years getting there, learning how to perfect their acts and to handle their audiences . . . and the audiences, which laughed at jokes and did not solemnly applaud them as [radio and television] audiences do now, were an essential part of the show; they too had vitality, and were still close to the cockneys who helped to create, a generation earlier, the English music hall of the period.[67]

Once lack of money after the Depression had forced a swing away from the big-star system, those halls still producing revue concentrated on the ensemble production fusing singers, dancers, showgirls, chorus and specialties with the costumes, the décor and the music. Thus Pierre Sandrini's sophisticated choreographic extravaganzas at the Bal Tabarin in the 1930s, thus the fast-paced girlie shows which alternated – and

Cécile Sorel. To play the lead in a Sacha Guitry revue in 1933, she came out of retirement – and came down with a bang.

still do alternate – with dining and dancing at the modern successor to the old Bal du Moulin-Rouge, and thus the current Casino and Folies offerings.

There were of course lavish revues produced after 1929. Derval's 1936 *En Super Folies*, designed to run through the 1937 Paris Exposition, guaranteed Josephine Baker 42,000 francs (about $7,000) per month and furnished her with a first entrance on a plumed palanquin drawn by a jade-green elephant surrounded by ten rampant tigers; but for her next tableau, despite the skins of thirty white foxes in which she was draped, she was in fact surrounded by a rehash of the Lemarchand Aurora Borealis set from the previous decade. The tigers were made of papier-mâché.

Another attempt at artificial respiration – the Casino's *Vive, Paris!* in 1933 – had lured the aging Cécile Sorel, doyenne of the Comédie Française, out of retirement to star in a revue written by Sacha

Guitry and dressed by Drian. Mme. Sorel made her entrance, in a parody of Mistinguett, down a huge, Versailles-type staircase in gold, and Guitry's opening line for her was: "Did I come down good?"

She did – with a bang. And so did most of the other essays into recapturing the spirit of the golden years. Somehow they all lacked the touch, the fire, the imagination and the vitality of their predecessors. They lacked the daring of Jacques-Charles's famous "Forest in Flames" tableau, which filled the stage with half a hundred cowboys, Indians, outlaws and mounted cavalry, a half-sized Wild West locomotive, and dozens of property trees each of which was so electrically wired and doctored that it could apparently burst into flames, scorch and shrivel to a different shape. They lacked the initiative that had taken twelve revues and four operettas on a tour of South America complete with two hundred different décors, their staircases, scenery and effects, and twelve thousand separate costumes. In short, they lacked scale and charisma. If Charles had directed *En Super Folies*, the tigers would have been real.

Lack of value for money was not restricted to the spectacular. Of one mid-1930s production, a reviewer wrote tartly: "The show even contains long glimpses of the beautiful Josephine Baker – longer, certainly,

LEFT:
One of the factors distinguishing true music hall from all other forms of entertainment was the special relationship established between performer and audience. Pearl Bailey is among the most notable of the stars maintaining this tradition today – and, along with Josephine Premice, she's out on her own when it comes to subduing an unruly crowd.

RIGHT:
Josephine Premice was one of the black stars who came later to Paris and "found employment that was better paid – and more appreciated – than that they'd been used to back home."

237

Mistinguett soldiered on almost to the day of her death, at the age of eighty-one, in 1956. This picture was taken in 1954.

than when she appeared as a headliner at the Folies a few years ago, but all too brief compared to the hard-working tradition of the Casino set by her venerable predecessor, Mistinguett."★

As for the smaller music halls, those not forced to close down by the threat of movies and, later, television, inevitably turned toward the nude revue, the strip cabaret and the sex show. Flesh had taken the place of fantasy: at the time, it was the one thing they could provide that the screen couldn't.

But the absence of fantasy entailed also the loss of

the "big" personality – and here the show business tycoons themselves were at fault. Too many of them forgot Max Reinhardt's dictum that the only thing that "worked" on a stage was human nature; that no matter how gorgeous the décors or clever the lighting, they remained without interest until the artist lent the show a life and a heart. Albee started the rot back in the 1890s, with his celebrated verdicts on performers in terms of dollars-per-week ("Good at forty, fair at fifty, lousy at sixty"). A recently ennobled baron of British show business proved not long ago that the trend continued. "Frank Sinatra?" he said. "Judy Garland? Max Bygraves? To me, boy, they're just numbers in a book."

The whole sorry story was epitomized in the summer of 1975 when passers-by on the Boulevard Montmartre could see beyond the elegant classic façade of the Théâtre des Variétés a demolition gang at work on the auditorium. The red plush seats were in perfect condition, the gilt scrollwork on the balconies shone, around the painted cupids lining the cupola there were cartouches enshrining the titles of operettas which had played there to capacity: *La Belle Hélène, Tales of Hoffman, La Grande Duchesse*. There were even tables, chairs and part of a set still on the deserted stage where once Anna Judic and Paulette Darty, Dranem and Fréhel and Polaire had taken their bows. Yet between the four pillars supporting the Palladian pediment outside, wheelbarrows full of plaster rubble were trundling down a plank leading to a dump on the sidewalk. And next door, along the jazzy chrome front of a single-story concrete shack, crowds were forming a line, at eleven o'clock on a sunny morning, to see a "live nude" show and "the Sexiest Swedish Movie in Town." (In fact the theater was in the process of renovation. Today, side by side with its rival, it is one of the very few places offering seasons of unpretentious revue presented by a resident company. But, symbolically, the lesson to be learned was there for everyone to see.)

Throughout the years of decline Mistinguett soldiered on almost to the day of her death in 1956 at the age of eighty-one. So did Chevalier. And so, making as many farewell tours as an opera star to support her adopted family, did Josephine Baker. But each in his or her later years was an anachronism. Like Ethel Waters and Sophie Tucker in the United States, they had outlived their era. From the thirties on, parallel with the development of the strip show, the theater witnessed the emergence of the team as the dynamic

* Mistinguett's reputation as a trouper was well deserved. She dived into the Volterra water tank with the rest of the cast although she was a poor swimmer; she was often in actual danger – as in a train wreck tableau when she was menaced by property coaches catapulted across the stage on either side of her. Because of her dutiful example, a whole revue for Pearl White, the ill-fated Revue aux Étoiles, had to be rewritten: Jacques-Charles had naively imagined that, in common with his own star, the American soap opera queen herself performed the hair-raising acrobatic feats in fact filmed by doubles in The Perils of Pauline . . . and he had written scenes for her accordingly.

factor in revue – the beginning of the syndrome whose end product is *West Side Story*, which may be breathtaking, but it isn't music hall.

The New Yorker saw the writing on the wall as long ago as 1930 – two years before the Palace folded as a two-a-day. Reviewing an exhibition of ballet and music hall costumes and décor by Bakst, Braque, Brunelleschi, de Chirico, Gris, Erte, Marie Laurencin, Léger, Picasso, Rouault and Stenlein, "Genet" wrote: "From those brief seasons when the greatest artists of Europe were scene painters for the brightest theatrical flush Paris has known since the operatic ball days of Gavarni . . . a form of theatrical life is recalled which any mourning critic admits is definitely defunct but whose mummy, embalmed by memory, is still livelier than anything that has appeared since to take its place."

A trouper to the end, Polaire died in 1939.

PHOTO: ROGER-VIOLLET

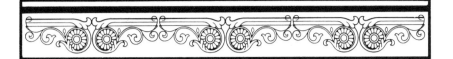

Music Hall's Top 100s

There were no hit parades and no charts in the golden days of music hall. No value judgments can therefore be made on the popularity – still less on the relative merits – of one performance against another. The following pages nevertheless list the hundred artists, the hundred theaters and the hundred songs which were, in the author's opinion, most influential in, or most typical of, the idiom. To these are added fifty contemporary supporting acts and fifty more recent stars whose work perpetuates the particular kind of professionalism, zest and communication characterizing music hall during the brief span of its existence.

Such a selection cannot of course pretend to be definitive; it must remain personal and idiosyncratic. The names of many brilliant performers in the fields of variety, vaudeville, recording and musical comedy will thus be absent simply because their talents, however scintillating, do not come within the author's personal definition of music hall.

The top one hundred artists are presented roughly in chronological order of their appearance in the world of show business; the other lists are alphabetical. Even in this form, a glance through the song titles emphasizes the close links between performance and people . . . on both sides of the footlights. From Grimaldi's "Hot Codlins" to the Ziegfeld-inspired "Bicycle Built for Two," they reflect – satirically, dramatically, ruefully, or just humorously – the ups and downs of life as it was lived in "the good old days."

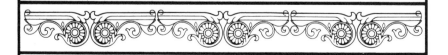

CHARACTERS
In Order of Their Appearance

One hundred of the top stars whose personality or performance left an indelible mark on music hall:

Joseph Grimaldi
Charles Dibdin
Elizaveta Sandurova
Buleschov
Lazarev
Ivan Rujsin
Sam Cowell
Ada Isaacs Mencken
Lydia Thompson
Pauline Markham
Mabel Santley
May Howard
Thérésa
George Leybourne
The Great Vance
Gus Elen
Blanche d'Antigny
Thérèse Rentz
Harry Champion
Bessie Bellwood
Albert Chevalier
George Formby, Sr.
Frederick Robson
Nellie Wallace
Dan Leno
Herbert Campbell
Vesta Victoria
Otto Reuter
George Robey
Vesta Tilley
Marie Lloyd
Little Tich
Anna Judic
Pacra

Aristide Bruant
Eugénie Buffet
Yvette Guilbert
Jane Avril
La Goulue
Paulus
Cora Laparcerie
Cléo de Mérode
Loïe Fuller
Liane de Lancy
Emilienne d'Alençon
Liane de Pougy
Anna Held
Max Déarly
Claudius
Baldy
Paulette Darty
Fragson
Polaire
La Belle Otéro
Polin
Dranem
Félix Mayol
The Barrison Sisters
Georgius
Sulbac
Vilbert
Little Egypt
Lillie Langtry
Max Linder
Lillian Russell
Pasto Imperia
Argentina
Isadora Duncan

Harry Pilcer
Gaby Deslys
Alice Delysia
Louise Balthy
Lise Fleuron
Mistinguett
Cécile Sorel
Yvonne Printemps
Grock
Bagesson
Podrecca and his Piccoli
Suzanne Lagier
Anna Thibaud
Jane Aubert
Maurice Chevalier
Lucienne Boyer
Florelle
Fernandel
Yvonne Georges
Raquel Meller
The Dolly Sisters
Eva Tanguay
W. C. Fields
Nora Bayes
Fanny Brice
Jack Benny
Jimmy Durante
Marie Dubas
George Jessel
Damia
Fréhel
Josephine Baker

THE SUPPORTING CAST

Half a hundred of the artists – many of them stars in their own right later – who contributed to the success enjoyed by the headliners in the golden years of music hall:

Germain Aéros
Barbette
Boulicot
Cinquevalli
Beau Colléano
Colette
Gilda Darthy
Valentin le Désossé
El Did
Dorville
Grille d'Egoût
Edmée Favart
Fortugé
Frégoli
Roger Fursy
Jean Gabin
Vinnie Henshaw

The Hoffman Girls
Houdini
Inaudi
Joe Jackson
Elsie Janis
Jules Jouy
The Fred Karno Troupe
    with Charles Chaplin
Henriette Lefèvre
Millie de Leon
Earl Leslie
Cissie Loftus
Jane Marnac
Maskelyne and Devant
Florence Mills
Moncharev
Gaby Montbreuse

Angèle Moreau
Moricey
Gaby Morlay
Morton
Nikitin
Nunès
Nini Patte-en-l'Air
Raimu
Carl Randall
Enrico Rastelli
Charles Rivels
Viviane Romance
Ryss
Saint-Granier
Serverus Scheffer
Steens
Zelaska

IN THE GREAT TRADITION

. . . and another fifty big names: those of the performers whose work – even in different media – has kept alive and glowing the fire that sparked off music hall at its brilliant best:

The Hassan Ben Ali Troupe
Fred Allen
Sven Asmussen
Fred Astaire
Pearl Bailey
Marie-Paul Belle
Shelley Berman
Victor Borge
Georges Brassens
Jacques Brel
Lennie Bruce
Collins and Hart
Tommy Cooper
Professor Irwin Corey
Bing Crosby
Dalida
Leon Errol

Sid Field
Judy Garland
Juliette Greco
Tony Hancock
Arthur Haynes
Pat Henning
Hickey and Nelson
Benny Hill
Stanley Holloway
Bob Hope
Frankie Howerd
Zizi Jeanmaire
Jo, Jak and Joni
Danny Kaye
Buster Keaton
Laurel and Hardy
The Marx Brothers

Max Miller
Yves Montand
Morecambe and Wise
Bob Newhart
Edith Piaf
Line Renaud
Mort Sahl
The Salici Puppets
Red Skelton
Jacques Tati
Sophie Tucker
The Seven Volants
The Wazzan Troupe
Senor Wences
Herb Williams
Wilson, Keppel and Betty

WHERE THEY PLAYED...

A hundred of the café concerts, theaters and true music halls on whose stages the form first blossomed and then flowered:

A.B.C., 11 Bvd. Poissonnière, Paris (formerly Plaza).

Alcazar d'Eté, Champs-Elysées, Paris (formerly Café Morel).

Alcazar d'Hiver, 10 Faubourg Poissonnière, Paris.

Alhambra, Leicester Square, London (formerly Royal Panopticon of Science & Art).

Alhambra, 95 Rue de Richelieu, Paris (later moved to old Château d'Eau, near Pl. de la République).

Les Ambassadeurs, Champs-Elysées, Paris.

American Theater, Eighth Avenue between 41st and 42nd Streets, New York (later named American Music Hall).

Apollo, Rue de Clichy, Paris.

Barnum's American Museum and Lecture Room, Broadway and Ann Street, New York (later *N.Y. Herald* building).

Ba-ta-clan, 50 Bvd. du Prince Eugène (now Bvd. Voltaire), Paris (formerly Palais Chinois).

Bobino, 20 Rue de la Gaîté, Paris (formerly in Rue de Fleurus).

Bouffes-Parisiens, Passage Choiseul, Paris.

Café-concerts in Paris:
  des Aveugles,
  du Cadran Bleu,
  du Géant,
  de la Grand' Pinte,
  de la Nouvelle Athènes,
  des Sauvages.

Café des Beaux Arts, W.40th Street, New York.

New Canterbury, adjoining Canterbury Arms, Lambeth, London.

Casino de Paris, 16 Rue de Clichy, Paris (formerly in Rue de Lyon).

Champs-Elysées Music Hall, Avenue Montaigne, Paris.

Cigale, 122 Bvd. Rochechouart, Paris.

Chat Noir, Rue Victor Massé, Paris (formerly in Bvd. Rochechouart).

City Palace of Varieties, Leeds, Yorkshire.

Coal Hole, Strand, London.

Coliseum, St. Martin's Lane, London.

Collins', Upper Street, Islington, London.

Concert de l'Époque, Bvd. Beaumarchais, Paris.

Concert Mayol, 10 Rue de l'Échiquier, Paris (formerly Concert Parisien).

Concerto della Variete, Rome.

Cyder Cellars, Maiden Lane, London.

Daly's, Leicester Square, London.

Daly's, 1221 Broadway, New York (formerly Wood's Museum and Menagerie, and the Broadway Theater).

Divan Feyouac, Rue des Martyrs, Paris.

Divan Japonais, 75 Rue des Martyrs, Paris (subsequently Madame Arthur's).

Eden-Palace, 8 Rue du Faubourg-Montmartre, Paris (formerly in Bvd. de Sébastopol).

Eldorado, Bvd. de Strasbourg, Paris (formerly in Faubourg St.-Martin).

Elysée-Montmartre, Bvd. Rochechouart, Paris.

Empire, Leicester Square, London (formerly Leicester Music Hall, and Walhalla).

Empire, 39–41 Avenue de Wagram, Paris (formerly Étoile-Palace).

Européen, 5 Rue Biot, Paris.

Evans's Song and Supper Rooms, Covent Garden, London.

Fantaisies Oller, 27 Bvd. des Italiens, Paris (later Les Nouveautés).

Fémina, Rond Point des Champs-Elysées, Paris.

Folies-Bergère, Rue Richer, Paris.

Folies-Marigny, Champs-Elysées, Paris (formerly Bouffes-Parisiens, subsequently Le Panorama and finally Théâtre Marigny).

Fulton, 210 W.46th Street, New York (formerly Folies-Bergère, subsequently the Helen Hayes Theater).

Gaîté-Rochechouart, 15 Bvd. Malesherbes, Paris

Gaiety, Strand at Aldwych, London (formerly between Catherine Street and Wellington Street; formerly Strand Musick Hall).

Gatti's, Westminster Bridge Road, London (also in Villiers Street, Strand).

Grecian, adjoining Eagle tavern, Elephant and Castle, London.

Hermitage, Garden of Marvels, Moscow.
Hippodrome, Charing Cross Road, London.

Jardin de Paris, Champs-Elysées, Paris (formerly Pavillon de l'Horloge).
Jovincelli's, Rome.

Laura Keene's Varieties, 622 Broadway, New York (formerly home of the Rentz-Santley Female Minstrels, subsequently the Olympic Theater).
Koster and Bial's, W.23rd Street and Sixth Avenue, New York (later moved to former Manhattan Opera House on 34th Street between Broadway and Seventh Avenue; now Macy's department store).

London Pavilion, Leicester Square, London.
Lido, 78 Champs-Elysées, Paris.

Marisetti, Milan.
Maskelyne's Theater of Mystery, Langham Place, London (previously St. George's Theater, later the BBC Music Hall).
Les Montagnes Russes, Rue Basse-du-Rempart, Paris.
Metropolitan, Edgware Road, London.
Mirliton, Bvd. Rochechouart, Paris (previously the original Chat Noir).
Moulin de la Galette, Butte de Montmartre, Paris.
Moulin-Rouge, Place Blanche, Paris.

New Amsterdam, 214 W.42nd Street, New York.
Niblo's Garden, 568–74 Broadway, New York (previously the Stadium, and the Sans Souci).
Nouveau Cirque, Rue St.-Honoré, Paris.

Olympia, Bvd. des Italiens, Paris.
Olympic, Newcastle Street, London.
Oxford, Tottenham Court Road and Oxford Street, London (later the Oxford Corner House).

Pacra, 10 Bvd. Beaumarchais, Paris (formerly Grand Concert de l'Époque).

Palace, Broadway and 47th Street, New York.
Palace, Cambridge Circus, London (formerly The Old Mogul).
Palladium, Argyll Street, London.
Paragon, Whitechapel, London.
Parisiana, 27 Bvd. Poissonnière, Paris.
Tony Pastor's, 14th Street between Third Avenue and Irving Place, New York (formerly Bryant's Minstrel Theater).
Petit-Casino, 12 Bvd. Montmartre, Paris (formerly Théâtre des Seraphins).
Polygraphic Hall, King William Street (now William IV Street), London.

Royal Holborn, High Holborn, London.
Royal Music Hall, Strand, London (formerly Royal Adelaide Gallery).

Sans Souci, Leicester Place, London (later incorporated in Saville House complex housing Empire music hall).
Scala, 13 Bvd. de Strasbourg, Paris (formerly Concert du Cheval Blanc).
Scala, Charlotte Street, London.
Surrey, Blackfriars Road, London (formerly The Winchester).

Tivoli, Strand, London.
Trianon, 80 Bvd. Rochechouart, Paris (formerly Trianon-Lyrique).
Trianon, Milan.

Umberto, Naples.

Valhalla, Berlin.
Variétés, Grands Boulevards, Paris.
Victoria Palace, Victoria Street, London (formerly the Royal Standard).

Weber and Fields Imperial Music Hall, Broadway and 30th Street, New York.
Weston's, High Holborn, London (later the Holborn Empire).
Wilton's, Graces Alley, Wellclose Square, London.
Wintergarten, Berlin.

Ziegfeld, Sixth Avenue and 54th Street, New York.

...AND WHAT THEY SANG

The songs below have been selected from the hundreds existing because they most strikingly represent the links between music hall and the life it reflected. The titles read like a potted social history of the period, and even in alphabetical order some of the ironies and antitheses are evident.

Act on the Square
Always Put Your Shoulder to the Wheel
Any Old Iron?
À Saint Lazare

The Ballad of Sam Hall
Bang Went the Chance of a Lifetime!
A Bicycle Built for Two
Boiled Beef and Carrots
Boum!
The Boy I Love Is Up in the Gallery

Champagne Charlie
Come Where the Booze Is Cheaper

Daddy Wouldn't Buy Me a Bow-wow
The Daring Young Man on the Flying
  Trapeze
A Dark Girl Dressed in Blue
Dear, Kind Doctor
Dear Old Pals
Dinah
Do It No More
Don't Go Out Tonight, Dear Father
Down at the Old Bull and Bush

Every Little Movement

Le Fiacre (The Horse-drawn Cab)
Following in Father's Footsteps
The Future Mrs 'Awkins

Gilbert the Filbert, the Colonel of the Knuts
Go As Far As You Like

Have You Paid the Rent?
Heaven Will Protect an Honest Girl
Hot Codlins

If It Wasn't for the 'Ouses in Between
I'll Get My Own Back
I'm One of the Ruins Cromwell Knocked
  About a Bit
I'm Twenty-one Today
It Ain't All Lavender
It's All Been Done Before (but Not the Way
  I Do It)
It's a Long Way to Tipperary
It's a Marvel 'Ow 'E Does It but 'E Do!
I've Never Lost My Last Train Yet
I Want Someone to Go Wild with Me

J'ai Deux Amours (I Have Two Loves)
Jerusalem's Dead

Knees Up, Mother Brown!
Knocked 'Em in the Old Kent Road

Laissez-les Tomber! (Let 'Em Fall!)
The Lily of Laguna
Little Brown Jug, Don't I Love Thee!
A Little of What You Fancy Does You Good
Louise

The Man Was a Stranger to Me
The Man Who Broke the Bank at Monte
  Carlo
Married to a Mermaid
Ma Tête (My Head)
Me And 'Er
Mon Homme (My Man)
Mother Kelly's Doorstep
A Motto for Every Man
My Fiddle Is My Sweetheart
My Old Dutch
My Old Man Said Follow the Van

Nellie Dean
Never Introduce Your Donah to a Pal

Oh, Mr Porter!
One of Every Sort
One of the Deathless Army
On the Sands
Our Lodger's Such a Nice Young Man

Pack Up Your Troubles in Your Old Kitbag
Poor Old Horse
Pop! Goes the Weasel
A Pretty Girl Is Like a Melody
Pretty Polly Perkins of Paddington Green

The Ratcatcher's Daughter
El Relicario (The Memento)

Shelling Peas
She Was a Stranger in London
She Was Poor but She Was Honest
Since Poor Father Joined the Territorials
Somebody Loves Me
La Soularde (The Drunken Crone)
The Spaniard That Blighted My Life
Swanee

Song of the Flea

Ta-ra-ra-boom-de-ay!
Tipitywitchet
Tu Ne Sais Pas Aimer (You Don't Know
  How to Love)
Two Little Girls in Blue
Two Lovely Black Eyes

Ukelele Lady

Valencia
Valentin

Vilikens and His Dinah
La Violetera

Waiting at the Church
We Don't Want to Fight, but By Jingo If
  We Do . . .
What Cheer, 'Ria!
Where Did You Get That Hat?
Would You Be Surprised to Hear?

You'll Be Sorry Just Too Late
Young Men Taken In and Done For

Footnotes

1. Quoted by Diana Holman-Hunt in *My Grandfather, His Wives and Loves*, Hamish Hamilton, London, 1969.
2. See also Chapter 2, page 42.
3. Peter Davison, *Songs of the British Music Hall*, Oak Publications, New York, © 1971. Reprinted by permission of Oak Publications. All rights reserved.
4. Douglas Gilbert, *American Vaudeville, Its Life and Times*, Dover Publications, Inc., New York, 1940.
5. Quoted by Bernard Sobel in *Burleycue – An Underground History of Burlesque Days*, Farrar and Rinehart, New York, 1931. Reprinted by permission of Holt, Rinehart and Winston, Publishers.
6. Bernard Sobel, *ibid.*
7. Bernard Sobel, *A Pictorial History of Vaudeville*, Citadel Press, New York, © 1961 by Lorraine Sobel Lee. Published by arrangement with Lyle Stuart.
8. *Ibid.*
9. *Ibid.*
10. Joe Laurie, Jr., *Vaudeville, from the Honky-tonks to the Palace*, Henry Holt, New York, 1953. Reprinted by permission of Holt, Rinehart and Winston, Publishers.
11. Peter Davison, *op. cit.*
12. W. Macqueen-Pope, *The Curtain Rises*, Thomas Nelson, Edinburgh, 1961.
13. Peter Davison, *op. cit.*
14. Sung by Derek Lamb on the phonograph record *She Was Poor but She Was Honest*, Folkways FW-8707.
15. *Selected Essays by T. S. Eliot*, Faber and Faber, London, 1941.
16. Douglas Gilbert, *op. cit.*
17. Album note to the long-playing phonograph record *Champagne Charlie* by Stanley Holloway (World Record Club, Catalog No. T.325). Chilton, for many years a distinguished BBC radio producer, is a leading authority on tavern and music hall songs, but is perhaps best known to the public as the author of *Oh, What a Lovely War!*, first produced on stage by Joan Littlewood and later made into a successful movie.
18. It is not generally realized how recent the Sacré-Coeur is. Designed as a symbol of "national reconciliation," the basilica was far from complete in the early 1890s.
19. Raymond Rudorff, *Belle Epoque*, Hamish Hamilton, London, 1972.
20. *Ibid.*
21. This has always been one of the great strengths of the establishment in capitalist countries: the ability at least to affect pleasure in being held up to ridicule. The satirists thus become fashionable (i.e., ingested into the establishment) and their venom safely diluted – as occurred in England in the 1960s and 1970s.
22. Raymond Rudorff, *op. cit.*
23. As described in the popular ballad, *"La Guingette a Fermé Ses Volets."* The song, one of the earliest phonograph record hits, laments the fact that the shutters are going up because it is the end of the season, winter is coming and the place is about to close.
24. Jacques Feschotte, *Histoire du Music-Hall*, Presses Universitaires de France, Paris, 1965.
25. Italy and Germany are referred to here in the modern sense, but it must be remembered that the former was a collection of separate states, each with its own traditions, until Victor Emmanuel I became king of all Italy in 1861, a year after the victories of Garibaldi. Venice was not incorporated until 1866 and Rome in 1870. It was a year after that before Wilhelm I and Bismarck unified the Teutonic states into the German Empire.
26. Sacheverell Sitwell, *Theatrical Figures in Porcelain*, The Curtain Press, London, 1949.
27. Subsequently Boulanger fled to Brussels, where he lived in exile until 1893, when he committed suicide on the grave of his mistress, a Parisian hostess whose friends had done much to urge him to revolt against the establishment.
28. *Le tout-Paris*: roughly, a Victorian equivalent of "the top people," "the jet set."
29. Raymond Rudorff, *op. cit.*
30. Raymond Rudorff, *op. cit.*
31. Jacques Feschotte, *op. cit.*
32. Douglas Gilbert, *op. cit.*
33. The words *meneur* and *meneuse* simply mean "leader" – the one around whom the show is built.
34. Jacques Feschotte, *op. cit.*
35. Jacques-Charles, *La Revue de ma Vie*, Arthème Fayard, Paris, 1958.
36. Published in the London *Daily Telegraph* of May 26, 1975.
37. Jacques Feschotte, *op. cit.*
38. Abel Green and Joe Laurie, Jr., *Show Biz from Vaude to Video*, Henry Holt, New York, 1951.
39. Douglas Gilbert, *op. cit.*
40. The literal meaning of *poulailler* is hen roost.
41. Jacques Feschotte, *op. cit.*
42. Colette, *My Apprenticeships* (translated by Helen Beauclerk), Secker and Warburg, London, 1957.
43. *Ibid.*
44. *Ibid.*
45. Jacques-Charles, *op. cit.*
46. Peter Davison, *op. cit.*
47. Colette, *Envers du Music-Hall*, Flammarion, Paris, 1913.
48. *Ibid.*
49. *Les rôles à maillot* is a theatrical term, which could roughly be translated as "tights talent," used to designate those who had been hired for their visual and sexual attractiveness rather than for their histrionic skill. Showgirls, in fact.
50. Janet Flanner, *Paris Was Yesterday*, copyright 1925–1939 (inclusive), © 1972 by the New Yorker Magazine Inc. Some material first appeared in *The New Yorker*. Reprinted by permission of The Viking Press.
51. Jacques-Charles, *op. cit.*
52. Jacques-Charles's books include *La Revue de ma Vie, Cent Ans de Music-Hall, De Dranem à*

Maurice Chevalier, De Gaby Deslys à Mistinguett, La Vie Prodigieuse de Max Déarly, Le Music-Hall en France and Naissance du Music-Hall, Fayard, Bejiat and NRF.

53. Janet Flanner, op. cit.
54. Ibid.
55. Jacques Chastenet, La France de M. Fallières, Arthème Fayard, Paris, 1959.
56. Douglas Gilbert, op. cit.
57. Ibid.
58. Ibid.
59. Charles Higham, Ziegfeld, Henry Regnery Company, Chicago, 1972.
60. Ibid.
61. Ibid.
62. Josephine Baker and Jo Bouillon, Joséphine, Robert Laffont, Paris, 1976.
63. Ibid.
64. Ibid.
65. Ibid.
66. Ibid.
67. Quoted by John Montgomery in The Twenties, George Allen and Unwin, London, 1957.

Selected Bibliography

Josephine Baker, Maurice Chevalier, Colette, Yvette Guilbert, Mary Marquet, Felix Mayol, Mistinguett, Paulus, Liane de Pougy and Theresa have all published memoirs relating their experiences in music hall from a French point of view. Albert Chevalier, Charles Coborn, Dan Leno, Billy Merson and George Robey were among the British stars treading the same literary path. The books listed below are written from a more generalized, historical angle.

CHASTENET, Jacques, La France de Monsieur Fallières, Arthème Fayard, Paris, 1959.

DAMASE, Jacques, Les Folies du Music Hall, Spectacles, Paris, 1962.

DAVISON, Peter, Songs of the British Music Hall, Oak Publications, New York, 1971.

FESCHOTTE, Jacques, Histoire du Music Hall, Presses Universitaires de France, Paris, 1965.

FRÉJAVILLE, Gustave, Au Music Hall, Du Monde Nouveau, Paris, n.d.

FLANNER, Janet, Paris Was Yesterday, Viking Press, New York, 1972.

GILBERT, Douglas, American Vaudeville, Its Life and Times, Dover Publications, New York, 1940.

GREEN, Abel (with Joe LAURIE, Jr.), Show Biz from Vaude to Video, Henry Holt, New York, 1951.

HIGHAM, Charles, Ziegfeld, Henry Regnery, Chicago, 1972.

HUDD, Roy, Music Hall, Eyre Methuen, London, 1976.

JACQUES-CHARLES,
Cent Ans de Music Hall, Ichéber, Paris, n.d.
La Revue de ma Vie, Arthème Fayard, Paris, 1958.

LAURIE, Joe., Jr., Vaudeville, from the Honkytonks to the Palace, Henry Holt, New York, 1953.

MACQUEEN-POPE, W.,
The Curtain Rises, Thomas Nelson, Edinburgh, 1961.
The Melodies Linger On, Thomas Nelson, Edinburgh, 1950.

MANDER, Raymond and Joe MITCHENSON,
Lost Theaters of London, New English Library, London, 1976.
British Music Hall, Hart-Davis, London, 1968(?).

RIVOLLET, André, De Menilmontant au Casino de Paris, Grasset, Paris, n.d.

ROMI, Petite Histoire des Café-Concerts Parisiens, Chitry, Paris, n.d.

RUDORFF, Raymond, Belle Époque, Hamish Hamilton, London, 1972.

SOBEL, Bernard,
Burleycue - an Underground History of Burlesque Days, Farrar and Rinehart, New York, 1931.
A Pictorial History of Vaudeville, Citadel Press, New York, n.d.

Index

Page numbers in italics refer to the illustrations and their captions.

Abadas, Martinez, 185
Abatino, Pepito, 228; 212
ABC music hall, Paris, 161n.
acrobats, 17, 119–21
Adèle, Mademoiselle, 156
Ader, Clément, 111
Adrian, 116–17, 119
Aéros, Germain, 119
Agar, 70
Albee, E.F., 124–6, 187, 188, 190, 239
Albert, Prince Consort, 47–8
Alcazar d'Eté, 66–7, 77, 82, 104, 110, 118n., 155, 158, 197, 232
Alcazar d'Hiver, 66–7, 77, 82, 110
Alençon, Emilienne d', 14, 127, 153
Alex, Joe, 211n.
Alfonso XIII, King of Spain, 181
Alhambra, London, 23, 25n., 71,

77, 170, 192, 232; *70, 115*
Allais, Alphonse, 94
Allemand, M. and Mme., 78
Allen, Fred, 130, 140
Allison Girls, 209
Amati, Mme, 70
Les Ambassadeurs, 65, 102, 155,
  160, 197, 232; restaurant, 67,
  171; Eugènie Buffet at, 83n.;
  Yvette Guilbert at, 108; under
  Chauveau and Cornuché, 158;
  Mayol at, 170; *Blackbirds*,
  205; American shows, 225–6
American Civil War, 45, 72
American Music Hall, Chicago,
  52
American Music Hall, New
  York, 52n.
American Theater, New York,
  190
Ancelet, 66
Anderson, Eddie, 12
Anquetin, 94
Antigny, Blanche d', 70; *68*
Apollinaire, Guillaume, 152
Apollo, Berlin, 74
Apollo, Milan, 75
Apollo, Paris, 160, 170, 183,
  225, 232
The Arcadians, 170
Argentina, 123, 184
Arlecchino, 43
Arletty, 178, 204
Arnao theater, Barcelona, 185
art déco, 219
Asmussen, Sven, 234
Astaire, Fred, 198
Astley, 42
Aubert, Jane, 127, 176, 178
Autrey, Marion d', 141
Avec le Sourire, 182, 197, 201n.
Avril, Jane (Mélinite), 80,
  92–4, 99, 108, 116, 123; *93*

Bach, 141
Bacon, Francis, 16
Baez, Joan, 46
Bagessen, 120, 205
Bailey, Pearl, 51, 233; *237*
Baker, Carrie Smith, 216
Baker, Josephine, 127, 163n.,
  232n.; *13, 212–16*; costumes,
  207; success, 209–19, 226–9;
  on Line Renaud, 233; in *En
  Super Folies*, 236, 237–8;
  farewell tours, 239; death,
  10–11
Bakst, Léon, 171, 198, 229n., 240
Bal Bullier, 93
Bal des Quatz' Arts, 110
bal musette, 64, 65, 87
Bal Tabarin, 104, 171, 201, 235;
  172
Balaclava, 45
Balanchine, Georges, 228
Baldy, 107, 110
ballet, 124

Ballets Russes, 171–2
Balthy, Louise, 14, 127, 183
Balzac, Honoré de, 60
Bannel, Clément, 161, 177
Banville, Théodore de, 66
Baraque à Bobino, 77–8
Barber, John, 128–30
Barbette, 203–4, 205; *202*
Barbier, George, 204, 207, 227,
  229n.
Barcelona, 185
Barnum, P.T., 28, 31–2
Baron and Doorn, 74
Barrault, Jean-Louis, 77n, 87n.
Barret stage company, 110
Barrison Sisters, 147–8
Ba-ta-clan, 69, 106, 110, 113,
  166, 176, 181, 197, 205n., 226
Bates, Peg-Leg, 219
Batignolles-Clichy-Odéon, 201
Baudelaire, Charles, 213
Baumbarten, Captain Ludoc, 28
Bayes, Nora, 188–9, 194, 232n.;
  188
Beardsley, Aubrey, 80, 82,
  153n.; *84, 103*
Beau Colleano, 119
Bechet, Sidney, 209
Becker, Jacques, 60; *Casque
  d'Or*, 65n.
Beerbohm, Max, 46, 48; *49*
Belbeuf, Marquise de, 139
Belgium, 96
Belle, Marie-Paul, 243
Bellwood, Bessie, 38, 40–1; *39*
Benglia, 220–1
Benny, Jack, 12, 40, 41, 128,
  189, 190, 233; *234*
Benois, Alexandre, 171
Bépoix, Henriette, 178
Bérard, 139
Beraud, Henri, 184
Berkeley, Busby, 198
Berlin, 72, 74, 150
Berlin, Irving, 198, 226
Bernard, Tristan, 152
Bernhardt, Sarah, 114–15, 135,
  152
Beryl, Suzy, 220–1
Besselièvre, 65
Bizet René, 212
The Black Crook, 27–8, 31, 108
Blackbirds, 205
Blake, Arthur, 204
Blondin, *67*
Blue Bell Girls, 232
Bobino, 77–8, 233
Boer War, 111
Boîte à Fursy, 96
boîtes, 64, 155
Boldini, 152
'bone-crushers', 130–2
Bonnard, Pierre, 82, 172
bordels, 154
Borge, Victor, 234
Bosc, 107n.
Boston, 34, 125, 191

Boswell, James, *London Journal*,
  18
Boucheron, 161n., 162
Bouffes-du-Nord music hall, 95
Bougereau, 125n.
Bouillon, Jo, 209, 226–7, 229
Boulanger, General Georges, 83
Boulicot, 119
Boum!, 182
Bourdelle, Emile Antoine, 208
Bourgeois, Jeanne, *see*
  Mistinguett
Boyer, Lucienne, 176, 184, 225
Braque, Georges, 172, 240
Brassens, Georges, 60, 233
Brecht, Bertold, 41, 45
Brel, Jacques, 233
Brialy, Jean-Claude, 11
Brice, Fanny, 189, 196, 228
Brigliano, 107
Broadway à Paris, 225–6
Brown, Joe E., 189
Browne, Sir Thomas, 17–18
Bruant, Aristide, 62–4, 78,
  79–80, 82, 96, 97, 103, 108,
  111, 112; *62, 86*
Bruce, Carol, 53
Bruce, Lennie, 46, 64, 130
Brunelleschi, Umberto, 204,
  206, 240
Brunskill, 210n.
Bryant and Saville, 136–7
Buffet, Eugénie, 64, 83n.
Buleschov, 76
Burbage, 16; *17*
Burke, Billie, 195, 228
burly shows, 34
Burney, Fanny, 47; *Evelina*, 53
Bygraves, Max, 239
Byron, Lord, 27

Ça C'est Paris!, 232
Cach' Ton Piano, 182
Cadran Bleu, 65
Cadudja, 92
café chantants, 56–7, 60, 65–6, 74
café concerts, 66–70, 72, 76, 87,
  117, 124, 133
Café de Paris, 198
Café des Aveugles, 65
Café des Beaux Arts,
  New York, 191
Café des Sauvages, 65
Café Morel, 66
Cahill, Marie, 189
Camargo, Marianne de, 70–1
Campbell, Herbert, 51; *49*
cancan, 87, 91, 103–4, 123; *172*
Candide, 212, 214
Canterbury Hall, 22, 38, 120
Cantor, Eddie, 189
Caran d'Ache, 61, 152
Carco, Francis, 139
Carjol, 170
Carné, Marcel, 60; *Les Enfants
  du Paradis*, 77n.
Carpentier, Georges, 183

Carroll, Earl, 124, 219; *Vanities*, 198
Casino de Paris, Rue de Clichy, 12, 106, 113, 118n., 138, 160, 197, 205; *164*; 'Blackbirds' revue, *159*; decline of, 176–7; under Volterra, 182–3; fire, 201–2; rebuilt, 202–3; *On Dit Ça*, 223; under Dufrenne and Varna, 226; *Vive, Paris!*, 236–7
Casino de Paris, Rue de Lyon, 70, 106
Casino Theater, New York, 192
Castellane, Comte Boniface de, 155, 156, 173, 175
Castle, Vernon and Irene, 198
Caulfield, Miss, 20
Celey, Gabriel Tapie de, 78
Cendrars, Blaise, 212
Cézanne, Paul, 175n.
Chagall, Marc, 172
Chaliapin, Fedor, 75, 114
Champion, Harry, 38
Champs Elysées music hall, 207–15
chanson réaliste, 60, 99, 127, 233
chansonniers, 57–8, 60, 62, 74, 75, 76, 112
chansons sensuelles, 111
Chaplin, Charles, 171, 183–4
Charles II, King of England, 18
Charleston, 124
Charlot, 124, 219
Chastenet, Jacques, 174–5
Chat Noir, 60–2, 63, 87, 96, 99
Château d'Eau, 170
Chatelet, 171–2, 184
Chauveau, 158, 170
Chéret, 82, 99, 124, 172
Chevalier, Albert, 37–8, 50
Chevalier, Maurice, 14, 127, 170, 181–2, 204, 232, 239; *176*; partnership with Mistinguett, 177–8, 181, 183, 197, 200–1; 'Valentin', 224–5
Chez-Josephine, 226, 228
Chicago Times, 53
La Chilito, 185
Chilton, Charles, 56
Chirico, Giorgio de, 171, 240
Chocolate Dandies, 218
chorus lines, 124
Christiné, 227
Cigale, 83n., 107–8, 110, 160, 201
cinema, 190, 230–1
Cinquevalli, 108, 146
circus, 42, 72–4, 119
Clair, René, 212
Claudius, 107, 128, 170
Cleveland Palace, 125n.
clowns, 119
Coal Hole, 19, 20, 45, 61
Coccinelle, 204
Cochran, C.B., 124, 197, 202–3, 219; *144*

Cocquelin, 156
Cocteau, Jean, 152, 212, 219
Cohan, George M., 187
Coleman, Bill, 219
Colette, 139n., 143–4, 145, 148, 219; *174*; *La Vagabonde*, 175n.
Colin, Paul, 210, 214, 219
Coliseum, London, 24
Collins' music hall, 24, 25n.
Collins, Sam, 24, 45
Collins and Hart, 130; *129*
Colonial theater, Boston, 125
Columbia Amusement Company, 133
Comédie Française, 68, 236
commedia dell'arte, 43, 74
Comoedia, 209, 213
Concert du Cheval Blanc, 70
Concert Mayol, 118n., 160, 176, 197, 232; *237*
Concert Parisien, 83, 95, 107, 176
Concerto delle Variete, 75
The Convict's Return, 122
cooch, 135
Cooper, Tommy, 120
Coquatrix, Bruno, 232
Corey, 'Professor' Irwin, 130
Cornélie, Mme., 68–9, 114, 135
Cornuché, 153, 158, 170
Corot, Jean Baptiste Camille, 125n.
Corrard, Saint-Yves, 107
Cortot, Alfred, 170
Covarrubias, Miguel, 208, 210
Covent Garden, 17n., 45
Coward, Noel, *Bitter Sweet*, 196
Cowell, Sam, 38, 42; *21*
Cremorne Gardens, 19
Cri-Cri, 92
Crimean War, 45
Cromwell, Oliver, 17
Cross, Edward, 19, 45
Cruikshank, George, *19*
cubism, 172–3, 219
Cunard, Nancy, 212, 219
Cyder Cellars, 19, 20

Dadaism, 219
Dali, Salvador, 207
Daly's, 28, 40
Damia, 178, 184–5, 189, 204, 205, 209, 226; *184*
Damita, Lily, 223
Darthy, Gilda, 153; *154*
Darty, Paulette, 107, 114, 141, 142–3, 170, 239; *141*
Daven, André, 208–9
Davison, Peter, 46–7
Day, Dennis, *234*
Déarly, Max, 107, 127, 128, 141, 146, 170, 177, 183
Débans, Camille, 116
Deburau, Charles, 77
Deburau, Jean-Baptiste Gaspard, 77n.
Debussy, Claude Achille, 152

Dédé, 140
Dégas, Edgar, 79
De Gaulle, General, 10
Dekobra, Maurice, 226
Delinière, Angèle, 153
De Lorge, 67–9, 70
Delysia, Alice, 198; *144*
Demange, 106
De Max, 173
De Mille, Cecil B., 198
Denis, Maurice, 208
Dérain, André, 171, 229n.
De Roerby, 225
Derval, Mme, 197
Derval, Paul, 110, 158–60, 161, 163n., 197, 210, 219, 226, 228, 236
Deslys, Gaby, 14, 89, 118n., 127, 178, 182–3; *131*
Desmonde, Jerry, 51
Diaghilev, Serge, 75, 171–2, 173, 198, 219
Dibdin, Charles, 42, 43, 45; *20*
Dibdin, Tom, 42n., 44; *20*
Dietrich, Marlene, 206–7
Dion, Marquis de, 111, 156
Disher, M. Wilson, 147
Divan Feyouac, 157
Divan Japonais, 102, 110–11
D'Obigny Ferrières, Alexis Pitron, *see* Derval, Paul
Dolly Sisters, 14, 189, 201, 204, 224, 226; *225*
Domergue, Jean-Gabriel, 10
Dongen, Kees van, 212
Donne, John, 16
Dorgère, Arlette, *154*
Dorly, 220–1
Dorville, 202
Doucet, 173
Douglas, Louis, 207, 208, 215, 218, 220
Drake, Sir Francis, 15
Dranem, 14, 107, 110, 128, 139, 141, 170, 208, 239; *128*
Dressler, Marie, 189
Dreyfus, Captain, 111
Drian, 204, 237
Drury Lane, 17n., 18–19, 44, 45; *18, 22*
Dubas, Marie, 176, 184
Ducarre, Pierre, 67
Dudley, Caroline, 208
Dufour, 87
Dufrenne, Oscar, 118n., 158, 160, 176, 197, 204, 226
Dufy, Raoul, 175
Duke, Vernon, 228
Dulac, Edmund, 204
Duncan, Isadora, 124, 171, 175
Durante, Jimmy, 41, 189; *189*
Dutard, 170
Duval, Marguerite, 170

Eagle tavern, 42n.
Eden-Palace, 75, 95, 96, 160, 232; *169*

Edward VII, King of England, 135n., 153
Eiffel, Baron Gustave, 83n.
Eiffel Tower, 85
El Did, 120–1
Eldorado (Italy), 75
Eldorado, Paris, 68–9, 70, 95, 110, 128, 139–40, 232; *138*
Elen, Gus, 38
Eliot, T.S., 48
Elizabeth I, Queen of England, 16
Elliston, R.W., 42n.
Eltinge, Julian, 204
Elysée-Montmartre, 87, 88, 90, 91, 92, 93
Empire, Leicester Square, 24, 99
Empire, Paris, 114, 160, 204–5, 232
Endré, 207
Erlanger, Abe, 196
Ernst, Max, 171
Errol, Leon, 51, 189
Erte, 176, 180, 204, 206, 229n., 240; *221*; designs for Mistinguett, 175, 200; *175*, *178*; association with Poiret, 175; at the Folies-Bergère, 197, 205, 222; *La Folie du Jour*, 226
escapologists, 121
Evans, Charles Evan, 192
Evans and Hoey, 192
Evans's Song and Supper Rooms, 20; *21*
Exposition Universelle, (1900 and 1901), 156–7

Fabris, 118n.
Falguière, Jean Alexandre Joseph, 139; *140*
Les Fantaisies Oller, 106
Farbacher, 191
Farge, 204
Fauvists, 172–3
Favert, Edmée, 170
Fay, Elfie, 189
Féfé, 154
Fémina theater, 181–2, 232; *178*
La Feria, 156
Fernandel, 14, 127, 141, 176, 178, 204
Feschotte, Jacques, 98, 111, 117, 118, 127, 158, 184
Feydeau, 106, 152; *Le Dindon*, 176
Field, Sid, 51, 122, 128, 233
Fields, Gracie, 232
Fields, W.C., 51, 128, 189, 196, 233
Fifth Avenue Theater, New York, 189
Flanner, Janet ("Genet"), 153, 210–11, 229, 240
Flaubert, Gustave, 60, 224
Flers, P.L., 110, 158, 159, 162
Flers, Robert de, 212–13

Fleuron, Lise, 110, 141
Florelle, 178, 205n.
Flory, Régine, 118n.
La Folie du Jour, 226
Folies-Bergère, 108, 115, 116, 138, 146–8, 197, 205; *70, 76, 160, 165, 169*; modelled on the Alhambra, 23, 71, 77; Aristide Bruant at, 78, 79, 82; Toulouse-Lautrec's drawings of, 78–9; *80*; cancan, 89; under Derval, 110, 158–9; Loie Fuller at, 124; revues, 133; prostitutes, 154–5; under the Isola brothers, 161; lavishness of, 180; *Un Soir de Folie*, 220–2; *La Folie du Jour*, 226; Josephine Baker at, 228; in present day, 233
Folies-Bobino, 78
Folies-Marigny, 66, 160
Foote, Adele, 222
Foote, Veronica, 222
Forain, 152
Forest, Maud de, 209, 210
Formby, George Sr., 38
Fort, Paul, 94
Fortugé, 184
Forzane, 177
Foucret, Pierre, 223, 224, 232
Foujita, 10
Four Sophisticates, 54
Fragson, Harry, 107, 118n., 128, 140–1, 145–6, 170, 171, 177, 183, 234; *144*
Fragson, Senior, 107n.; *144*
Franck, Paul, 183–4, 197
Frascati's, 65
Fratellinis, 205
free-and-easies, 34
Fregoli, 122
Fréhel, 127, 178, 184, 224n., 225, 239; *231*
Les Frères Jacques, 234
Frohman, Charles, 190
Fuller, Loie, 80, 123–4, 157, 171, 204, 208, 232
Fulton Theater, New York, 190
Fursy, Roger, 111, 176
futurists, 172–3
Fyffe, Will, 50

Gabaroche, 209
Gabin, Jean, 127, 178, 204, 224, 226
Gaieté, Paris, 113
Gaité-Rochechouart, 83n., 232
Gaiety, London, 40
Gaiety Girls, 126
Gallois, Germaine, 150n.
Garat, Henri, 224
Garden of Marvels, Moscow, 76
Garibaldi, Giuseppe, 45
Garland, Judy, 51, 190, 239
Garrick, David, 44
Gaudet, 139, 143
Gaudieux, *82*

Gautier, 122–3
Gauzy, 94; *86*
Gavault, 110, 170
Gay, John, *The Beggar's Opera*, 31n.
Gémier, 209
"Genet" (Janet Flanner), 229, 240
George White's Scandals, 198, 199
Georges, Yvonne, 118n., 184, 203, 225
Georgius, 128, 232
Germany, 72–4
Gershwin, George, 199–200, 205
Gershwin, Ira, 228
Gesmar, Charles, 197, 204
Gibert, 189
Gil Blas, 97, 143, 162
Gil Blas Illustrée, 153
Gilbert, Douglas, 27, 32, 33, 100, 130, 131–2, 148, 187
Gilbert and Sullivan, 125
Glatigny, 66
glee clubs, 56
Glen, Kitty, 206
Globe Theater, London, 182
Godfrey, Charles, *57*
Golder, Jenny, 205
Golovin, 171
Goncourt, Edmond de, 98, 100
Goons, 128
Goubert, 66–7, 77, 82, 158
La Goulue (Louise Weber), 14, 81, 90–2, 94, 95, 103, 107, 108, 232; *79, 90*
Grace, Princess of Monaco, 11
Grand Concert de l'Époque, 111
Grand' Pinte, 60
Great Exhibition, (1851), 47
Grecian saloon, 24, 42n.
Greco, Juliette, 60
Griffith Clowns, 146
Griffiths, D.W., 198
Grille-d'Égout, 92; *103*
Grimaldi, Joseph, 43, 44–5; *19, 20, 43*
Gris, Juan, 240
Grock, 119, 205
Guilbert, Yvette, 14, 50, 74, 80, 105, 107, 127, 153, 193, 205; *86, 97, 98*; Toulouse-Lautrec paints, 80, 95; at the Concert Parisien, 83; success, 96–103; at Les Ambassadeurs, 108; rivalry with Otéro, 150; at the Scala, 170
guingettes, 64–5, 87, 155
Guitry, Sacha, 184, 236–7; *236*
Gyarmarthy, Michael, 197, 206–7

Habrekorn, Gaston, 110–11
Hall, Adelaide, 219
Halsey, Margaret, 222
Hamburg, 72, 74
Hamilton, Mary, 80; *81*
Hammerstein, Oscar, 52, 125, 193, 196

Hancock, Tony, 51, 233
Handley, Tommy, 128
Hardy, Oliver, 51
Hari, Mata, 124, 175; *174*
Harlem, 54
Harlem Opera House, 195
Harlequinade, 43–5
Harris, J.E., *138*
Hassan Ben Ali Troupe, 120
Haussmann, Baron, 63
Hawkins, Coleman, 219
Hawkins, Sir John, 15
Hayakawa, Sessue, 203
Haynes, Arthur, 41, 128
Heath, Ida, 80
Held, Anna, 80, 141, 193–5;
  151, 193
Henning, Pat, 233
Henshaw, Vinnie, 189
Hérard, Angèle, 185
Hermitage pleasure garden, 76
Héros, 110, 170
Hervé, 70
Hickey and Nelson, 130–2
Higham, Charles, 196
Hill, Benny, 243
Hippodrome, London, 24–5,
  182
Hippodrome, Paris, 85
Hoffman, Gertrude, 223–4
Hoffman Girls, 223–4
Holborn Empire, 24; *24*
Holliday, Billie, 102
Holloway, Stanley, 47
honky-tonks, 31, 33–4, 44, 151
hootchie-kootchie, 134–5
Hope, Bob, 128, 190, 228
Houdini, 121
Howard, May, *53*
Howerd, Frankie, 40, 128, 233
Huby, Roberta, 122
Hudgins, Johnny, 225–6
Hughes, Charles, 42
Hughes, Langston, 102, 217
Hylton, Jack, 205

illusionists, 121
Illustrated London News, 67
Imperio, Pastora, 123
Imported English Blondes, 28
Inaudi, 121–2, 225
Inkerman, 45
Iribe, 175, 207n.
Irving, Henry, 42n., 44
Isola, Emile, 158, 161, 162, 170
Isola, Vincent, 158, 161, 162, 170
Italy, 72, 74–5

Jackson, Joe, 121
Jacobi, *85*
Jacques-Charles, 117, 150, 158,
  159, 161–2, 202; *144, 161,
  211*; on Yvette Guilbert, 99;
  on Dranem, 128; *La Revue de
  ma Vie*, 152, 162; Liane de
  Pougy hates, 153n.; behind
  the scenes at a revue, 162–8;

and Mistinguett, 177, 197–9,
  200–1, 205; at the Casino de
  Paris, 182; at the Olympia,
  183; *La Revue Nègre*, 209–10,
  219; at the Moulin-Rouge,
  223–4; *Ça C'est Paris!*, 232;
  and the Blue Bell Girls, 232;
  'Forest in Flames', 237
Janis, Elsie, 189, 197
Jardin de Paris, 85, 88, 93, 94,
  104, 155, 176, 178
Javelot, 77
Jeanmaire, Zizi, 123
Jefferson, Joe, 34n.
Jessel, George, 189
Jeu de Paume gallery, *90*
Jo, Jak and Joni, 234, 235
Jo-Jo, 32–3
John Street Theater, New York,
  31n.
Johnson, Dr., 117
Jolson, Al, 189
Joséphine, 11
Jouy, Jules, 60–1, 69, 101
Jovincelli's, 75
Judic, Anna, 78, 114, 127, 146,
  239; *69, 134*

Karno, Fred, 171
Karsavina, 171n.
Kaye, Danny, 128, 130, 140,
  233
Kean Edmund, 43, 44
Keaton, Buster, 51, 128, 131,
  183–4
Keith, Benjamin F., 34, 124–6,
  187, 188, 189, 190
Kelly, Mme., 154
Kemp, William, 45
Kid Boots, 196
Klaw, Marc, 196
Koster & Bial's, 52–3, 100, 148,
  194; *50, 51*
Kyasht, Lydia, 171n.

Lacaze, 66
Lafourcade, Marie, 70
Lagier, Suzanne, 70, 127
Lalique, René, 204
Laloo, 32–3
Lancy, Liane de, 152, 153, 155
Landolff, 162, 172–3
Landolff, Mme., 144
Langtry, Lillie, 135, 189, 194
Laparcerie, Cora, 175
La Rousse, Tica, 154
Larue, Danny, 204
Las Vegas, 12
Lasky, Jesse, L., 190
Lauder, Harry, 50
Laurel, Stan, 51
Laurencin, Marie, 10, 240
Laurie, Joe Jr., 34
Layton and Johnson, 205
Lazarev, 76
Leavitt, Mike, 28, 31
Leeds, 72

Lefèvre, Henriette, 119, 225
Léger, Fernand, 208, 212, 240
Legrand-Chabrier, 12, 117
Léhar, Franz, *The Merry Widow*,
  170, 183
Lely, Sir Peter, 125n.
Lemaître, Jules, 63–4
Lemarchand, Louis, 220, 226,
  236
Lender, Marcelle, 80
Leno, Dan, 36, 37–8, 41, 42,
  46n., 48, 51, 147; *49*
Lentovsky, V., 76
Leon, Millie de, 111, 135
Leopold II, King of the
  Belgians, 105; *140*
Lepape, 175, 207n.
Leslie, Earl, 201, 227, 232
Letellier, Henri, 224
Levasseur, André, 11
Levinson, André, 213–14
Lewis, Hayter, *70*
Lewis, Jerry, 128
Lewis, Ted, 232
Leybourne, George, 36–7, 38;
  37
Lido, Paris, 12, 233
Lifar, Serge, 226
Linder, Max, 183–4
Lion, Jean, 228
lion comique, 36–7, 38, 83; *57*
Little Egypt, 135
Little Tich, 146–7, 171, 205; *146*
Lloyd, Marie, 38, 40, 48–9,
  50–1, 193; *39, 129*
Loeffler, Jean, 100
Loftus, Cissie, 189
Lointier, 106
London Echoes, 70–1
London Palladium, 12, 24, 112,
  118, 189
London Pavilion, 40
Loraine, Violet, 47
Loren, Sophia, 11
Lorrain, Jean, 98, 99, 153n., 156;
  84, 97
Lorraine, Lillian, 195
Losch, Tilly, 203
Loti, Manon, 153–4
Loti, Pierre, 98
Louisville, 27n.
Loveday, 210n.
Lyons, J., *26*

McCloy, Fred, 133–4
Madame Arthur's, 111n.
Mme. Rentz's Female
  Minstrels, 28, 31
Madame Sans-Gêne, 109
Maizeroy, René, 97
Mallarmé, Stéphane, 94
Manchester, 72
Manet, Edouard, 64, 79, 154
Marceau, Marcel, 77n.
Marchand, 110, 153n., 154–5,
  158, 161, 193
Marchand, Mme., 145

Marcke, van, 125n.
Marconi, Guglielmo, 111
Maré, Rolf de, 208–9
Marigny music hall, 77
marionettes, 121
Marisetti, San Martino, 75
Markham, Pauline, 53
Marks, Ted, 100
Marlowe, Christopher, 16
Marnac, Jane, 178, 223
Marseille (wrestler), 156
Marseilles, 72, 183
Martelli, La Belle, 153
Martin, Louis, 191
Marval, 208
Marx, Groucho, 233
Marx brothers, 51, 128
Maskelyne and Devant, 121
masques, 15
Mathias, 110
Matisse, Henri, 171, 172
Maupassant, Guy de, 96, 100
Maurel, 128
Maxim's, New York, 191
Maxim's, Paris, 151–3, 154n., 154
May, Mia, 207; 220
Mayol, Félix, 107, 128, 170, 176
Méaly, 170
medicine shows, 34
Mélinite, see Avril, Jane
Meller, Raquel, 184, 185–7, 205
Mencken, Adah Isaacs, 27
Mendès, Catulle, 98
Menessier, 162
meneur de revue, 127–8
Mérode, Cléo de, 74, 123, 139, 150; 123, 140
Metropolitan, 24, 25n.
Midnight Frolics, 196
Milan, 72, 75
Miller, Marilyn, 189, 195
Miller, Max, 40, 128, 233
Mills, Bertha, 32–3,
Mills, Florence, 189, 205, 208, 216, 218; 159
Milton, May, 80
Minnelli, Vicente, 228
minstrel shows, 25, 31, 34
Mirbeau, Octave, 98
Mirliton, 63, 82, 96; 62
Mistinguett, 11, 14, 114, 127, 204, 227, 238; 109, 175, 176, 207, 208, 210–12, 238; debut, 109; at the Eldorado, 139–40; Erte designs for, 175, 200; 175, 178; partnership with Chevalier, 177–8, 181, 183, 197, 200–1; and Jacques-Charles, 183, 197–8; 'Mon Homme', 200–1; En Douce, 202; at the Moulin-Rouge, 205; Zig's designs for, 206; La Revue Mistinguett, 224–5; Ça C'est Paris!, 232; death, 239
Mitchell, Adrian, 60

Modes et Manières d'Aujourdhui, 207n.
Le Môme Fromage, 92
Moncharov, 76
Monegasque Red Cross, 11
Monroe, Marilyn, 139
Les Montagnes Russes, 106–7
Montand, Yves, 233
Montboron, 212
Montbreuse, Gaby, 204, 220–2
Montel, 139
Montesquiou, Comte Robert de, 155n.
Montmartre, 58–62, 65, 85–95, 106
Montorgeuil, Georges, 91
Monty Python's Flying Circus, 128
Moore, George, 219
Moreau, Angèle, 139
Morecambe and Wise, 51, 128
Moreno, Eddie, 216
Moricey, 107, 128
Morlay, Gaby, 205
Morning Telegraph, 53
Morton (conjuror), 141, 146
Morton, Charles, 21–3, 38, 45; 23, 26
Morton, James J., 52n., 107, 190
Moscow, 75
Moss, Edward, 24
Moulin de la Galette, 59–60, 65, 87, 90, 94, 155; 58
Moulin Rouge, 103–5, 138, 222; 86, 89, 97, 101, 179; opening, 83, 85–95; Yvette Guilbert at, 96, 102–3; Zidler leaves, 108; variety acts, 116; Loie Fuller at, 124; Colette at, 139n.; new music hall, 170, 171; fire, 178; rebuilt, 201; 199 under Jacques-Charles, 223–4; decline of, 232; in present-day, 233
Mucha, Alphonse, 152
mummers, 17
Munich, 72
Murphy, Jack, 136–7
Murray, Rob, 118
museum shows, 31–3, 34, 44, 116
Mussleck, Auguste, 83, 158
Myral, Nina, 127
Myro, Jane, 201

Naples, 72, 74, 75
Napoleon III, Emperor of the French, 232
Neuilly, 155–6
New Amsterdam Theater, 194–5, 198
New Canterbury, 22–3, 45, 52; 23, 51
New Orleans, 100, 191
New York-Montmartre, 223–4
New York Palace, 27, 112, 124–5, 189
New York Theater, 191

The New Yorker, 212, 229, 240
Niblo's Garden, 28
Nicholas Brothers, 228
Nikitin, 76
Nini Patte en l'Air, 92
Nino, the Wonder Dog, 121–2
North American, 135
Norworth, Jack, 189, 194
Nottingham, 72
Nouveau Cirque, 106; 104
Les Nouveautés, 106
Nouvelle Athènes, 60
Novarro, Ramon, 198
Novy, Yvon, 213
Nunès, 107–8

Oakley, Annie, 191
Odell, 190
Offenbach, Jacques, 59, 65, 66, 70; Bouffes-Parisiens, 77; La Créole, 78; 69
Old Mogul theater, 23
Oliver, Vic, 41
Oller brothers, 85, 87, 95
Oller, Joseph, 106–7, 108, 155, 158, 161
Olson and Johnson, 128
Olympia, Paris, 12, 112, 123, 138, 160, 197; 13, 104; opening, 107; striptease, 157; under Isola brothers, 161; dance floor, 170; Mistinguett at, 177; under Jacques-Charles, 183–4; becomes cinema, 232; in present-day, 233
Olympic music hall, 24
Opéra, Paris, 71, 155, 161
Opéra-Comique, 161n.
opéras bouffes, 66
Orfeo, Rome, 75
L'Orient Merveilleux, 178
Original Dixieland Jazz Band, 183
Orpheum, San Francisco, 52
Orpheum chain, 124
Orton, Arthur, 46n.
Osterwald, Hazy, 234
Otéro, La Belle, 74, 148–9, 150, 153, 157, 170; 147, 148
Oxford music hall, 23–4, 37, 45, 120; 26

Pacra, 66, 70, 110, 128
Padilla, José, 185–6, 232
Paiva, 232
Palace music hall, London, 23, 193, 240
Palais Chinois, 69–70, 106
Palais de Glace, 152, 155
Palais-Royal, 110
Palast-Theater, Berlin, 74
Palmer, Gaston, 118
Palo, 207
pantomime, 43–5
Paragon music hall, 40
Paramount theater, Paris, 232

Pari-Kiri, 182, 197
Paris, M., 106
Paris Commune, 59
Paris Exposition, (1937), 236
Parisiana, 104, 161, 170, 178; *104*
Pastor, Tony, 34, 124
Paulus, 83, 106, 107, 128; *85*
Pavillon de Hanovre, 65
Pavillon d'Horloge, 65–6, 85
Pavlova, 171n., 208
Pepys, Samuel, 18
Perret brothers, 207–8
Peterloo, 45
Petit-Casino, 107
petit vaudeville, 137–8
Le Pétomane, 105, 116, 145
Philadelphia, 136, 216
Philharmonic Hall, 23
Piaf, Edith, 60, 127, 233
Picabia, Francis, 212
Picasso, Pablo, 171, 172, 229n., 240
Piccoli, 121
Pilcer, Harry, 127, 182–3, 208
Pilcer, Murray, 183
Plaisirs de Paris, 116
Plantation, 218
pleasure gardens, 19, 76
Plombin, Charles, 203
Podreca, 121
Poiret, Mme., 173
Poiret, Paul, 173–5, 177, 178, 198, 200, 204; *175, 213*
Polaire, 14, 107, 127, 152, 153, 177, 185, 239; *142, 240*; at the Eldorado, 110; at the Scala, 128, 140–1, 170; appearance, 143–5, 149–50; at the Olympia, 183
Polin, 14, 128, 140–2, 170, 227; *82*
Pollock, Channing, 234
Ponchon, Raoul, 110, 171
Ponti, Carlo, 11
Poole, J.J., 36
Poole, John, *Hamlet*, 31n.
Porter, Cole, 27, 205
Pougy, Liane de, 153, 156; *84*
Powers' Musical Elephants, 205
Pradier, Pierre, 209
Premice, Josephine, *237*
Prévert, Jacques, 60
Priestly, J.B., 235
Prince of Wales Theater, London, 122
Printemps, Yvonne, 114, 178, 183, 204
Privas, Xavier, 61
Prokofiev, Serge, 171
Proust, Marcel, 152, 155n.
Pujol, Joseph, *see* Le Pétomane
Purcell, Henry, 56

quadrille naturaliste, 90–1, 92, 95, 103, 116, 123
quadrille réaliste, 155

The Quaker Girl, 170
Queen, 137

Ragtime Band, 183
Raimu, 127, 141, 178, 204
Rainier, Prince of Monaco, 11
Raleigh, Sir Walter, 15
Randall, Carl, 201, 232
Ranson, 204, 207
Rasimi, Mme., 166, 176, 181, 205n.
Rastelli, Enrico, 118
Rayon d'Or, 92
Reggiani, Serge, 65n.
Régnier, Pierre de, 214–15
Reinhardt, Max, 228, 239; *Sumurum*, 175–6
Reiter, 145
Réjane, Mme., 92, 155, 156; *103*
Renaud, Line, 11, 12, 233
Renaud, Madeleine, 87n.
Renoir, Jean, 60; *Partie de Campagne*, 65n.
Renoir, Pierre Auguste, 59, 79; *58*; *Bal à Bougival*, 64; *Moulin de la Galette*, 65n.
Renouard, Paul, *73*
Rentz, Madame, 27, 28, 31, 74
Rentz, Thérèse, 74
Restaurant Julien, 155
Reuter, Otto, 74
Reutlinger studio, *148, 154, 174*
Revolg, 206
revue à grand spectacle, 112–16, 117, 219
Rhodes, William, 19, 45
Ribémont-Dessaignes, Georges, 60
Rice and Prevost, 130
Richepin, Jean, 61, 83n., 224n.
Rictus, Jehan, 64
Rimsky-Korsakov, Nikolai Andreievich, 171
Ring, Blanche, *129*
Rip, 158, 159, 177, 201; *161*
Risley, Professor, *22*
Rivel, Charles, 119
Robeson, Paul, 196, 216
Robey, George, 38, 41, 48; *47*
Robinson, Yvonne, 206
Robson, Frederick, 42n., 66
Rochefort, Henri, 92
Rodgers and Hart, *Pal Joey* 53
Rodrigues, Amalia, 184
Rogers, Will, 196
Romance, Viviane, 178, 204
Rome, 72
Rosalie, 196
Rossi, Tino, 138–9
Rostand, Edmond, *L'Aiglon*, 114
Rothschild, Baron de, 153
Rouault, Georges, 240
Rowan and Martin, 128
Royal Circus, 42
Royal Panopticon of Science and Art, *70*

Royal Standard, 24
Rozières, 27n.
Rubinstein, Ida, 180
Rudorff, Raymond, 61, 64, 88–9, 99
Ruez, 161
Ruhlmann, 204
Rujsin, Ivan, 76
Russell, Lord John, 45
Russell, Lillian, 135; *136*
Russia, 72, 75–7
Russian Imperial Ballet, 77
Ryss, 121

Sablon, Jean, 139
Sadler's Wells, 43, 45
Sahl, Mort, 128
St. George's Hall, London, 121
St. George's Tavern, 21–2
Saint-Granier, 209, 223
St. Louis, 54
St. Louis Exposition, (1904), 135
St. Petersburg, 75
Salabert, Francis, 223
Salici Puppets, 121
Salis, Rudolphe, 60–2, 63, 111
Salon des Indépendants, (1911), 172
Salone Margherita, 75
saloon theaters, 20–1
Sandow, Eugene, 192
Sandrini, Pierre, 225, 235; *231*
Sandurova, Elizaveta, 76
Sans Souci theater, 43, 45; *20*
Santley, Mabel, 31; *30*
Saratoga, 191
Sargent's Great Vaudeville Co., 27n.
Sari, 77, 78
Satie, Erik, 171
The Saturday Review, 46
Saturnalia, 43
La Sauterelle, 92
Scala, Paris, 70, 78, 107, 113, 140–6, 170, 176, 201
Scheffer, Serverus, 108
Schier, Rudolf, 74
Schubert, 196
Scotto, Vincent, 227
Seeley, Blossom, 189
Seltenhammer, Paul, 206
Sem, 152
Serpolette, 92
Sevastopol, 45
Seven Volants, 120
Shakespeare, William, 16; *17*
Shanks, Alec, 210n.
Shanley's, 191
Shaw, Bernard, 46, 98; *Man and Superman*, 15
Sheridan, R.B., *The Critic*, 31n.
Show Boat, 196
Show of 1928, 226
"sight acts," 130–2
Signoret, Simone, 65n.
Silverman, Sime, 230n.
Simenon, Georges, 10

Simon, Michel, 10
Sinatra, Frank 190, 239
Sinoël, 139
Sissle, Noble, 217, 218
Sitwell, Sacheverell, 77
Les Six, 171
Skelton, Red, 128
Smith, Jack, 138-9
Smolinska, 221
Société Mutuelle des Artistes
  Lyriques, 66
Sorel, Cecile, 114, 236-7; *236*
SPCA, 191
Spencer, Eva, 217
Spezialitätentheater, 74
Steens, 121
Steinlen, 97, 240
Stern, Ernst, 175
Sternberg, 229
Stoll, Sir Oswald, 171
store shows, 34
Story, Wilbur, F., *53*
Stravinsky, Igor, 171
striptease, 110, 157, 190
Stuttgart, 72
Sulbac, 128, 141, 146, 170
surrealism, 219
Surrey Music Hall, 42n.
Surrey Zoological Gardens, 19,
  45
Sylvain, 98
Symons, Arthur, 94, 108

Taine, Hippolyte, *Notes on
  England,* 19
Tanguay, Eva, 187-8; *186*
Tarlton, Richard, 45
Tati, Jacques, 51, 128
tavern concerts, 20-1
Tcherina, Ludmilla, 123
Teatro d'Attrazione, 75
Tender, Alice de, 141
Tera-Guinoh, 220-1
Texas, 33
Thackeray, William Makepeace,
  The Newcomes, 20; *21*
Theater Royal, Haymarket, 17n.
Théâtre de la Renaissance, 175
Théâtre de Vaudeville, 27n.
Théâtre des Capucines, 161
Théâtre des Nouveautés, 95
Théâtres des Variétés, 134, 150n.,
  239
Théâtre Réjane, 176
Théo, 70
Thérèsa, 14, 66, 69, 82
Thibaud, Anna, 127, 141, 143,
  170
Thomas, Dylan, 105
Thompson, Lydia, 27, 28, 71,
  72; *29, 53*
Tichborne, Roger, 46n.

tights plays, 27-31
Tiller Girls, 217
Tilley Vesta, 40; *38*
The Times, 22
Tinney, Frank, 128
Tirmont, 221
Tivoli gardens, Paris, 65
La Tortoyada, 146
Toulouse-Lautrec, Henri de,
  78-82, 87, 91, 92, 94, 95, 99n.,
  124, 172; *62, 79, 80-2, 86, 90,
  93, 97*
Trenet, Charles, 10, 138-9
Trianon, 75
trick cyclists, 120-1
Tucker, Sophie, 51, 189, 196,
  205, 239
Turin, 72

Umberto's, 75
United Booking Office (UBO),
  124, 126, 188
Universal Exposition, Paris,
  (1889), 83; *101*; (1900), 124
Urban, Josef, 194-5

Valente, Maria, 225
Valentin le Désossé, 81, 94-5,
  108n.; *79*
Valentino, Rudolph, 198
Valhalla, 74
Van der Clyde, *see* Barbette
Van Dongen, 82
Vance, the Great, 36, 37; *37, 57*
Variety, 54, 230
variety shows, 117
Varna, Henri, 118n., 158, 160,
  176, 197, 204, 226, 227, 232n.,
  233; *214*
Vauxhall Gardens, 19
Velez, Lupe, 51
ventriloquists, 121
Vere, Elise de, 141
Vergeron, 70
Verlaine, Paul, 94, 108
Verne, Jules, 83
Victoria, Queen of England,
  47-8
Victoria, Vesta, 38, 40, 100; *48*
Victoria Palace, 24
Victoria Theater, New York,
  125
Vilbert, 128, 141, 170
Villon, François, 61, 64
Vogue, 207n.
Volterra, Léon, 158, 160, 182,
  183, 197, 200, 202-3, 205n.
Voyons Voir, Oh Venus!, 108
Vuillard, Jean Edouard, 208

wagon shows, 34
Wall Street crash, 230

Wallace, Nellie, 38
Washington, Freddie, 216
Washington, George, 31n.
Waters, Ethel, 51, 218, 239
Wazzan Troupe, 120
Weber, Louise, *see* La Goulue
Weber and Fields, 189
Webster, *The Tavern Bilkers,*
  43-4
Webster, John, 16
Weisiger's Hall, 27n.
Welch, Elizabeth, 219
Weldy, Max, 229n.
Wences, Senor, 234-5
West, Mae, 196
West Side Story, 240
Western Vaudeville Managers'
  Association, 124
Weston's Music Hall, *24*
Wheeler, Jimmy, 41
White, George, 124, 198, 219
White, Pearl, 199, 202, 239n.
Wilde, Oscar, 153n.; *84*
Willemetz, 201
Willette, 61, 87-8, 98
Williams, Herb, 128, 130
Williams, Spencer, 226
Willy, Louise, 157
Wilson, Garland, 219
Winchell, Walter, 228
Winchester Hall, 21, 22, 42n.
Winstone, Captain, 205
Wintergarten Theater, Berlin,
  74
Wisdom, Norman, 128
Wise, Ernie, 51, 128
Wittop, Freddy, 204
Woods' Museum and
  Menagerie, 28
World War I, 72, 180-1
World War II, 10, 224n.
Worth, 173

Xanrof, Léon, 96, 101

Yako, Sado, 157
Yarborough, Katharine, 216
The Yellow Book, 94, 99, 102
Yvain, Maurice, 200

Zamora, José de, 204, 206, 226
Zelaska, 88, 116
Zidler, 66, 85-90, 92, 94, 95,
  97-8, 105, 106, 108, 116, 158;
  90
Ziegfeld, Florenz, 80, 124, 141n.,
  188, 191-8, 219, 223; *151*
Ziegfeld Follies, 189, 191,
  194-6, 198, 228
Zig, 206
Zinoviev, 207
Zola, Émile, 60, 61, 96, 98, 100